PICNIC COMMA LIGHTNING

PICNIC COMMA LIGHTNING

In Search of a New Reality

Laurence Scott

WILLIAM HEINEMANN: LONDON

1 3 5 7 9 10 8 6 4 2

William Heinemann
20 Vauxhall Bridge Road
London SW1V 2SA

William Heinemann is part of the Penguin Random House group of companies whose
addresses can be found at global.penguinrandomhouse.com.

Copyright © Laurence Scott 2018

Laurence Scott has asserted his right to be identified as the author of this Work in
accordance with the Copyright, Designs and Patents Act 1988.

First published by William Heinemann in 2018

www.penguin.co.uk

A CIP catalogue record for this book is available from the British Library.

ISBN 9781785151118

Typeset in 12.5/16.5 pt Fournier MT Std
by Integra Software Services Pvt. Ltd, Pondicherry

Printed and bound in Great Britain by Clays Ltd, Elcograf S.p.A.

Penguin Random House is committed to a sustainable future for our
business, our readers and our planet. This book is made from
Forest Stewardship Council® certified paper.

For Rob Lederer

Halfway down, I step over some version of
myself; a girl of four or six, idling or playing
in the place most likely to trip people up.
This is where children sit, I know this now;
how they love doorways, in-between places,
the busiest spot. This is where they go vague
and start to dream.

Anne Enright, *The Forgotten Waltz*

CONTENTS

INTRODUCTION:

Augmented Reality

While I was in my early thirties, my parents died in impolite
succession. My mother first, in 2010, then my father in
2012. He was in his early eighties, but she was sixteen years younger
and had no business going anywhere. They passed the illness
baton from one to the other, so that my mother died in midsummer
and by the autumn we were back on the same floor of Charing
Cross Hospital, with the same attendants wheeling the vital-signs
trolley up to the bedside. Names in blue marker on a whiteboard
behind the bed: patient, nurse, consultant.

Death runs like radioactive iodine through your sense of
reality, allowing this reality to be looked at in high contrast, its
structures glowing. It has a way of making things very true,
but also, somehow, less real. There are many merciless truths:
my parents never put their key in the front door, never walk
into a room, never send birthday cards. They're never waiting
at the airport. They don't sleep. They don't tap on the back of

ketchup bottles or mispronounce words. At the same time, the truth that they don't do any of this feels less than real. I mean, just look: there they are. They have posthumous opinions on the news; they roll their eyes. I think up puns and my mother laughs at them. She is excited to hear that Lily Tomlin has a sitcom on Netflix. 'Ooh, great!' she says, knowing improbably about Netflix.

Bereavement not only highlights the materials from which reality is made, but transports you into a new one. The change is as clean as the flicking of a light switch, although whether it has been turned on or off is unclear. It can feel like the lights have gone up after a great party, while also being a plunge into the dark. Those who are precious migrate, as fast as the flick of a light, from the outside to the inside of life. They don't trip your senses by hugging you, or by swinging into view over the crest of the road. You stop seeing that car, unmissable among all the others, even at a distance, with its two unmistakeable thumbprint silhouettes, side by side. Instead they live, at least part-time, in your mind's electro-charged darkness.

Death brings a new question sharply into the minds of the bereaved: what is a *real* person? Overnight you're landed with a sudden, astonishing hybrid, made up of memories and intimate knowledge. One of the things I've noticed about bereavement is how the past spreads itself now across my everyday reality in a more concerted way than before, with two impossible beings occupying my middle distance. They are mythological, time-travelling creatures, who appear in different forms and hail from different decades, brown-haired one minute, grey the next. They mow the lawn, read the paper or stand at a long-gone kitchen counter, as though nothing bad had ever happened. These fantastic companions become, in one sense, the most real people you experience. For unlike an encounter with the living, there is no external reality against which to judge your perceptions. As a character in one of Mavis Gallant's short stories says, 'the only authentic voices I have belong to the dead'.

Perceiving Reality

In these last few years, while I've been navigating this new personal reality, the questions of how we experience the real world, how we access its truths, have become mainstream concerns. On 16th January 2018, during a meeting of the Senate Judiciary Committee, US Senator Orrin Hatch began his statement by taking off a pair of glasses that he wasn't wearing. He raised both hands up beside either eye, clipped them around invisible handles and brought them back down to the bench. He continued as if this were normal, with perhaps just one nervous little cough registering the mistake. The moment was like a Lucille Ball slip-up, a clown's attempt at gravitas. At the same time, it instantly seemed a perfect symbol of our present state of affairs: the unreality of American politics in the wake of its reality-TV president, the deception of the political classes who no longer even feel the need to disguise their deceptions.

The international laughter that followed this footage stemmed both from its pure comedy and from a kind of demented relief. Levels of incredulity, scepticism and distrust in reality as it is presented to us have become constant features of contemporary life. In the last few years we have become primed to ask ourselves: Is this real or not?[1] The judging of an event's 'realness' or 'fakeness' is often prioritised, more urgent than: Is this right or wrong? An ex-YouTube engineer, Guillaume Chaslot, tells us that, when it comes to how the website's algorithm promotes fake versus legitimate videos, 'fiction is outperforming reality'. YouTube formally rejects the methodology of this analysis. So who do we believe? Do we have time to scour the data ourselves? A 2018 study of Twitter, published in the journal *Science*, confirms fears that our realities are being warped by our love for the novel and the strange over the authentic. The study found that 'Falsehoods diffused significantly further, faster, deeper, and more broadly than the truth in all categories', such as political, scientific or financial information. The very word 'Russia' evokes not only a nation, but an amorphous global influence that looks to erode the lines between reality and falsehood. And so, in this relentless, unwanted game of sorting out the fraudulent from the genuine, Senator Hatch's glasses felt like a nice, easy warm-up for a new year of dogged scrutiny. 'Those are definitely *not* glasses.' Everyone was happy to have a trick question, in which the trick was as plain and unobscured as the nose on his face.

If in the last few years we have started to talk regularly and explicitly about reality as an idea in itself, what do we mean by it? What constitutes our sense of a real world? Despite its

---

1. My use of the word 'we' is meant to create a welcoming rather than suffocating atmosphere. But I also know the absurdity of this 'we'. It's a fantasy 'we', working alongside a bluffing 'our'. Every statement with 'we' in it is at best a proposition and would be better phrased as a question, if the rhetoric of that wasn't so intense: Aren't we, don't we, shouldn't we? And who is this 'we'? While I hope to suggest some shared human experiences that cut across geopolitical lines, the cultural realities that I invoke here mainly belong to my transatlantic perspective, a triangular conversation between the United Kingdom, America and Canada.

elusiveness, reality isn't the most retiring of subjects – it touches every domain of human enquiry. Science has sought to build models for an objective reality, the laws of which need to be verifiable. Politics deals in the fragile amalgam of shared assumptions, values, prohibitions and freedoms that makes civic reality a possibility. The nature of reality is a fundamental philosophical question. I'm especially interested here in phenomenology, the branch of philosophy that focuses not on what *is* real, but rather on how we gain a sense of reality from our perceptions. It seeks to understand our conscious experiences as real things in themselves. So what are the specific phenomena that most influence our current relationship to reality, as well as our experiences of inhabiting a reality that we're continually told is somehow compromised? What does it feel like to be responsible for generating a sense of reality in a culture that accuses itself of being fictional?

While it may feel that we are living in a period of particular scepticism, it is hard to think of a time in Western history in which people lived in full harmony with an idea of the real world. There has always been doubt about, or dissatisfaction with, our everyday surroundings, as though there could be another reality that is truer, more everlasting than what our senses can perceive. Plato, who can be counted on for some foundational snapshots, likened our perceptions to seeing only the shadows of things, cast against the wall of a cave. Enlightenment comes from breaking the bonds holding you in this shadow-theatre and emerging from the cave into the realm of realities.

Many centuries later, Friedrich Nietzsche called Plato 'a coward in the face of reality', because for the German philosopher reality has always been in front of us, with all its shadowy terrors of indeterminacy, misapprehension and illusion. Plato couldn't handle the dark cut-and-thrust of our shadow-world, said Nietzsche, and so he fled into the realm of ideals and enduring, pure forms. In *The Twilight of the Idols*, written in 1888, Nietzsche devotes a mischievous page to suggesting 'How the Real World Finally Became a Fable'. In a sweeping six-point guide he proposes that, in the main phases of Western thought since Plato, our access to the real world went from being attainable only to the wise (the enlightened few who left the cave) to being attainable to no one. As both a spiritual and philosophical concept, reality retreated further and further from our view as the years rolled on. As a result, the real world became an idea that, through its sheer unknowability, had 'no further use'. Nietzsche subtitled this progression 'The history of an error' – the error being the belief in a 'true' world as separate from the one that appears to us. Nietzsche wanted his society to return its focus to this 'apparent' world, which had somehow been lost in the impossible pursuit of a true, metaphysical reality beyond human perception. In prizing an absent, unreachable reality, he said, we have thrown out the reality that has always been in plain view. All we have, and all we can know, he insisted, is how the world appears to us. To consider whether these appearances are real or not is to ask the wrong question of them.

We can hear loud echoes of Nietzsche's plea to remember appearances in the latest scientific research into our perceptions, which asks similar questions about our ability to experience a single, 'true' reality. One of the biggest problems facing current neuroscience is that of understanding how we come to be conscious. Our eyes aren't just spotless windowpanes through which our consciousness – whatever that might be – peers into the world.

The neuroscientist Anil Seth reminds us of an obvious but mostly overlooked truth: our brains can't see, or hear or taste. They sit in the dark, making up a world informed by electrical stimuli from our sense organs. The act of perception, Seth argues, is an act of prediction, of estimation. What we consciously perceive is our brain's 'best guess' at what the outside world is like. These guesses, of course, can be wrong. There are all sorts of visual tricks to show how easily our eyes can be deceived – often to do with seeing three-dimensional cubes in a two-dimensional image, or with our perception of colour. Seth illustrates the falsity of our vision by showing how two different squares on the picture of a chess board can seem like two completely different shades of grey, when in fact they are the same shade.

This idea of the brain as a 'prediction engine' changes the balance of where we think our sense of reality comes from. 'The world we experience,' Seth argues, 'comes as much from the inside-out as the outside-in.' We rely on sensory data gathered from our external surroundings, but our brains then actively interpret this data into conscious experiences that Seth calls 'controlled hallucinations'. It's companionable to think that most of the time our internal estimations of the outside world are compatible with those of other people. Our brains' predictive processes aren't totally idiosyncratic; there is much shared ground. As Seth puts it, 'When we agree about our hallucinations, we call that reality.'

There are, of course, moments when our shared hallucinations falter, such as the famous case of *that* dress, which people either saw as white and gold or blue and black. This cause célèbre, which sent rifts running through families and groups of friends, was so funny and agitating because it revealed the instability of our perceptions. If you saw the dress one way, it was difficult really to *see* how it could appear as the other. The colours seemed as evident and inarguable as the red on a fire engine. If you were, like me, in the white-and-gold camp, it could be easy to let ungenerous thoughts form about those blue-and-blackers. Their reality cast an uneasy shade on ours. For a few days we were in the thrall of a tiny morality play – about difference, perspective, the truth of 'the other' – woven into a meme.

The dress was, amazingly and unsettlingly, marketed as 'royal blue'. As Seth points out, our inside-out realities can be objectively wrong. Any exploration of reality will have to contend with this tension between the possibility of an objective physical world and our individual, variable perceptions of it. We know that two oxygen atoms unite to share a double electron bond, and that these pairs flock together to form 78 per cent of the dry air we breathe. But is the truth of dioxygen's composition only true in relation to the discourse of molecular chemistry? Different scientific models might explain the unison of two oxygen atoms in other, even more romantic ways. And we know that, as science digs deeper into the innermost realities of the universe, objective truth seems to break down. The concept in quantum mechanics that particles can behave as either particles or waves, depending on how they are observed, reveals a mixed metaphor hidden at the centre of our physical world. This is a classic post-modernist position: that how we measure the world, the language or discourse we use to describe it, determines what truths we can and can't assert about our realities.

But what does it mean to cast doubt on our grasp of reality, when there are people without clean water to drink, or while the bombs fall? Deprivation isn't a best guess; it's beyond dispute.

The world of appearances holds irrefutable chains of cause and effect. Fire burns us in every language. To be 'apparent' doesn't mean to be inconsequential. Even more radical research emphasises how the appearances we perceive are intimately tied to these questions of survival. By calling 'reality' into question, we don't discount the perils of life. The cognitive scientist Donald Hoffman has recently presented his theory of the conscious mind, proposing that ideas such as 'the truth', and even 'reality', are misleading approaches to defining our consciousness. He argues that there is too much reality for it to be useful to us. To perceive reality as it really is would be paralysing.

When Hoffman runs abstract, mathematical simulations of organisms competing in an ecosystem, the creatures who are the fittest survive, while those that are designed to see things as they actually are thrive less well, to the point of being driven out of existence altogether. His hypothesis goes against the long-held idea that perceiving the world accurately was a competitive advantage. An assumption in evolutionary science has been that we are the descendants of realists, who best survived the challenges of their environments because of their clear-headedness. But Hoffman's research suggests that it isn't seeing things clearly that counts, but rather interpreting the world in ways that allow us to navigate it efficiently. We descend, he says, from pragmatists who build mental maps of the world around their usefulness, not their accuracy.

One example he gives is a simplified illustration about a theoretical organism's perception of water. Too much water and too little water are both deadly to the organism, so it might perceive both extremes as red. A safe amount of water is perceived as green. Although a drought and a flood are very different, these disasters could, for efficiency, be perceived identically as dangerous situations. Hoffman argues that our perceptions are constructed in a similar way: we filter out the details of reality that aren't useful to us, and create mental models that enable us to navigate our surroundings successfully. As Hoffman explains, our 'perceptions will be tuned to fitness, but not to truth', since if we were to see things as they really were, they would be too bamboozling for us to interpret. And so, in a very Nietzschean spirit, Hoffman suggests that our individual conscious perceptions – an ache in our bodies, the taste of an ice-cream sundae – are 'the ultimate nature of reality'.

The Fortress of Reality

How do these conscious perceptions accumulate into our sense of the world? We might think of our personal realities as a kind of structure that we assemble and maintain throughout our lives, the stability of which is threatened when our sense of everyday life is somehow undermined. But what are the broadly fundamental elements out of which we each build this reality? Three main elements are the stories we tell ourselves and one another, the objects with which we surround ourselves, and the images we consume and produce to capture the world around us, and which then come to stand as evidence for a past reality, for what *really* happened. While this trio of story, thing and image has never been a stable set of constituents, they are unstable to us now in ways that illuminate these times. Every era has its own style of appearing unreal to its inmates. What is ours? Many of the old stories – about men and women, for instance – are rapidly being retold, as well as ancient restraints on who is allowed to tell these stories. When it comes to the reality of 'things', how will our relationships to physical objects have to change, as our own attitudes to production and consumption are altered by environmental degradation, and as 'smart' technologies awaken our belongings? And what happens to the status of the image, now that most of us can document and disseminate our realities via our camera phones?

A fundamental challenge to how we maintain a sense of reality is our era's relationship between private and public life – the individual and the collective reality. The neuroscientific idea of an 'inside-out' reality becomes especially important if we think about how much our own lives have been turned inside-out by a social-media culture of sharing and self-revelation. How do our internal approximations of the world fare when set against the internal approximations of other people? What place does the workable fantasy in my head have in wider society?

During his trial for gross indecency, Oscar Wilde was questioned on his aphorism that 'A truth ceases to be true when more than one person believes in it.' To this challenge, Wilde replied: 'That would be my metaphysical definition of truth; something so personal that the same truth could never be appreciated by two minds.' Such a view was seen at the time as perverse and decadent, for how could truth be so indeterminate and particular to the individual? How can you maintain a society on such terms? And yet, today, the concept of 'my truth', the unalterable reality of an individual's perceptions, has much ethical, political currency. Our aim is therefore to establish a sustainable, shared hallucination – a social reality – that doesn't elevate one set of fantasies at the expense of others. Just as each historical period constructs its shared realities in different ways, so too do the stresses on these realities alter with the times.

Recent political events have certainly disrupted our belief in the viability of rational public discourse. The shock of the Brexit referendum occurred almost as soon as I began writing this book, after which it was immediately impossible to maintain a coherent estimate of the near future. The question and outcome of Brexit instantly flooded public life with the idea of fantasy. In the British media, this is a bipartisan phenomenon. On one day a headline on the Left asks, 'Who's to blame for Brexit's fantasy politics?', on another a conservative newspaper declares that 'The having cake and eating it Brexit fantasy is over.' This sort of talk is now a constant – and often features cake. On either side of the Brexit divide there is the assumption that one's political opponents are fantasising. Indeed, fantasy is used as a catch-all term to describe all manner of posturing and rhetoric that in the past would have inspired a more varied vocabulary. Political naivety, expediency, bluffing, visions of a possible future, ideals, objections, propositions – they are all regularly made to huddle together in fantasy-land.

In the months leading up to the referendum I wasn't the ideal citizen. I didn't pore over legislation or follow the state of democracy in the European parliament. Although I understood in a general way the sane misgivings of Eurosceptics, I believe in the project of the EU, the healthy collectivism that can form from people moving freely. In my profession of academia, the potential losses were large and glaring. But as well as these real-world considerations, running up and down the legs of the X that I made in the ballot box was my private, nonsense dream of 'Europe', a shifting set of impressions: it is a grey autumn afternoon somewhere in a German city. A figure who is me but not me, for he seems to belong to a past before my time, is leaving a municipal library and crossing an empty city square. Is this a half-remembered dream? A former life? On this German afternoon there are leaves on the wet pavement and lights are on in the cafés. And then I'm in a train on a bright day, speeding across 'Europe', gazing out of the window at this 'Europe', and then I'm at the border control at St Pancras Station, an officer is looking at my passport and looking at me – this is definitely *me*, now – as I travel back to the flat I have, one summer a decade ago, really leased in France. The officer flicks the passport back, blissfully indifferent.

This is a glimpse, as best as I can render it, of one territory of my inside world. The day after the referendum I walked through London, wondering what fantasies ran through the ballot-box Xs of each person I passed. I thought about how every day we assemble ourselves, gathering all the various parts together – the self-generated realities, shooting-star thoughts, the private poetry of our minds that we never share with anyone. This daily assembly, which fortifies the public from private fancy, makes us presentable people, citizens for others to encounter. How a society distinguishes the private life from the public sphere determines the nature of any civic reality. What place did my Germanic visions have in democratic processes? We live in an age in which, as I'll argue, political, social and commercial forces are encouraging a very particular collapse in the distinction between public and private reality. We are being coaxed into new lines of sight, encouraged to see both public and private, inside and outside, simultaneously. In the exposed world of online sociability, for example, our private lives are bonded to our professional appearances. This double vision has profound implications, affecting the language we use to describe the world to ourselves, as well as the way our emotions are expressed on this inside-outside public stage.

The walls thinning between the public and the private realms contribute to the precarious status of reality in these times. Old certainties, old structures of meaning, are toppling down. We seem to be moving through a period that could be described as the age of *dismantling*. This is seen by turns as a necessary, progressive act and also as a nightmarish disassembly of hard-won freedoms and protections. Since the 1980s, in the UK a major political concern has been the stealthy outsourcing and privatisation of the welfare state, a process that is often discussed in terms of 'dismantling'. In America, the damage of Donald Trump's presidency is described similarly, as though he is physically pulling apart the founding structures of American society. The author and analyst Malcolm Nance announces on MSNBC that Trump 'is dismantling the Constitution'; professor of law Jon Michaels writes a series of essays called 'While You Weren't Looking – How Trump is Dismantling the Administrative State'. For David Cay Johnston, author of the Trump polemic *It's Even Worse Than You Think*, the president is 'dismantling democracy'. Increasingly we're seeing power attempting to entrench itself through the use of regressive legislation. After China's Communist Party announced that it was planning to remove two-term limits for presidents, allowing the current leader, Xi Jinping, to remain in power indefinitely, one analyst commented that 'the long project' to prevent the return of a Mao figure is 'being dismantled'.

In its original sixteenth-century, Middle French context, to dismantle meant 'to tear down the walls of a fortress'. It can signal an assault on our security or a raid against the seat of power, or both. On the progressive Left, dismantling is the framing device in the fight against oppression. In an article for *USA Today*, scholar Sirry Alang urged her readers to support Black Lives Matter and similar activism, in order to 'help expose and dismantle structural racism'. The recent proliferation of the #MeToo movement has seen its aims both celebrated and contested, with some arguing that it 'does little to dismantle the underlying problem' of sexual abuse. Many others, meanwhile, cheer its attack on that ancient fortress of misogyny. The American Civil Liberties Union, in particular, has promised to continue the work of #MeToo in 'Dismantling Sexual Harassment'. Discussing the women artists showcased at the 2017 Art Basel Miami Beach, *Guardian* journalist Janelle Zara challenges the 'prevailing mythology' that 'the gendered power balance of the status quo will magically dismantle itself'. Intentionally or not, the rhetoric of these movements echoes the famous activist Audre Lorde's maxim of resistance, 'The master's tools will never dismantle the master's house.'

If reality feels more vulnerable to us now, one reason is that many of the long-held fantasies that have sustained it are becoming intolerable, just as certain fantasies that we seemed to be outgrowing – nationalism, fascism – are returning with renewed solidity and power.

(Picnic, Lightning)

These are certainly strange times for reality. While we worry that we may soon lose the ability to know what is real and unreal in public life, technological ambitions for the future are based on the assumption that reality is *there*. How else could we have virtual reality, with its 360-degree designs on recreating a coral reef in the kitchen, if there wasn't a reality to imitate, or indeed a kitchen to put it in? There is also the field of augmented reality (AR). Unlike virtual reality's immersive experiences, AR involves the overlaying of artificial images onto 'the real world'. AR headsets are being designed that trade screens for glasses. With these headsets we can sit in our home office and see weather reports, business graphs, an advert for running shoes, all floating in mid-air in front of us. The room is full of mundane objects, and yet this real-world clutter is, from the AR perspective, a form of blankness, an empty canvas for bar graphs and emails. I'm not going to discuss VR and AR innovations beyond the irony that, as they try to replicate and improve upon reality, we're growing more and more dubious that there is such a thing as reality to begin with. There is even perhaps a trademark violation brewing, for isn't – as the neuro-scientists are arguing – all of our reality a virtual one? Our middle distances are already occupied, with daydreams, visions from the past, fantasy scenarios. Do we have room in them for our quarterly reports?

Grief is surely an old-fashioned kind of augmented reality, in which the real world falls into the background. The hospital bed is taken apart and lifted from the front room, and there is an expanse of bare floor. A small, empty bottle of lavender oil is on its side by the radiator. The London weather is beautiful. In the sunlight I can see the hurried soap-tracks dried onto each slat of the window blinds, an attempt to replicate at least some institutional sterility. But already other images are augmenting my view. I can also see a morning in the back room of the bed and breakfast that my parents ran for a while, in a small town called Vineland, on the way to Niagara Falls. Nothing remarkable happened that morning, but for some reason I remember it, and the morning has come to stand for a hundred others. I can tell, from the angle of the vision, that I'm lying on the little couch with my head nearest the window, looking at my parents' sideways faces as they sit at the sideways kitchen table. We're talking wordless words and the air in the memory is pleasant, flickering with memory's silent laughter.

One day, an undercover reviewer came to visit. After a quick tour, under the pretence of being a prospective guest, she told my parents that she would be writing them up in her Ontario B&B guide. When a copy of the book arrived, we saw that the blurb had described my father, seventy by then, as a twinkling, gregarious presence at the door. Appearing from the private section of the ground floor was Mrs Scott, recorded more soberly as 'no less personable'. We all laughed at these flash portraits of their public demeanours. The phrase became an occasional epithet, like grey-eyed Athena or swift-footed Achilles. No-less-personable Mrs Scott. Like discreet hoteliers, or indeed Greek gods, my parents come and go through these pages, helping me to reveal some of the often unsettling thresholds between the past and present, memory and imagination, the real and the hyperreal.

In Vladimir Nabokov's *Lolita*, the narrator Humbert Humbert tells us very early that his mother died when he was three. The cause is given curtly, mid-sentence: '(picnic, lightning)' and, after a paragraph of tender analogies about his dim recollections of her, she is never mentioned again. This bracketed tragedy is an instant shorthand for Humbert's sensibility: his ruthless irony and black humour, a flippancy whose source is an inscrutable mix of callousness and pain. For all his wickedness, I understand Humbert on this point: where do we put our dearest dead in the story of our lives? The problem is technical as much as moral. What sort of sentence can hold them? The parentheses are an attempt at housing the unimaginable, barricading the horror from the rest of life. They make a little fortification in the middle of Humbert's narration.

In this sense, the notorious picnic provokes us into wondering what happens when a reality more real than our mundane experiences comes forking into our midst. How do our mental maps of the world have to be redrawn? How do we try to rewrite the impossible to make it legible? We may try to contain these intense, brutal realities, but as Nabokov hints, language often has other ideas. The truth of these moments won't be so easily sequestered.

'Picnic, lightning' is, after all, a cellular story, a two-word drama, with all the detail and energy packed tightly inside it. For me, it grows in my mind into a scene: the edges of a dress are rippled from beneath by a blanket, which in turn is rippled from the grass below. The year is either 1913 or '14. There are wicker baskets, a parasol. For now, the thunderheads are pretty, bleached cauliflowers, as still as statues behind the escarpment. At this point I hit Pause, throwing down a comma, which can keep the lightning back, at least for a moment.

PART I

The Life Fantastic

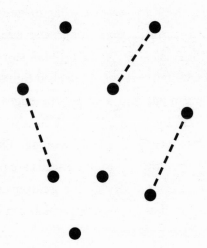

CHAPTER I

Bedtime Stories

Here they are, back again: my mother and father, who over the years went by many different, often nonsense names: Deeve, Bumble, Alma, Henbridge, Poule-Pont. I'm so pleased to see them. These days they can only be where my memory puts them. This particular memory is set during the brief phase when I called them very soberly by their first names, Stella and David. We were living in a small hotel in Newcastle, because they had retired from teaching to buy it and put us there: me and my older sister and brother. Since we lived in their place of work, their first names were everywhere: up and down the halls, coming from the kitchen staff, cleaners, electricians and plumbers. And so I joined in, aged about five, shouting up the stairwells: 'Stella! David!'

This is the general scene, but here they are, one bedtime in the shadowed past. I'm on high, reluctantly hoisted up in David's arms, in the eccentric little gangway between the reception, the hotel kitchen and a sunken area by the back door, where there was

3

a table for Jean and Leslie, the cleaning ladies, to sit and have tea. I was on first-name terms with everyone. 'You don't like me,' David says, without any edge to his words or smile. He is an old father, used to children and their bare-faced preferences. I cling around his neck and continue to mewl and grope, within the bounds of decency, for Stella, who is standing in the shady edges of the memory.

It is true that David bedtimes had a different tone to Stella bedtimes. Only Stella could officially close down the day, and after David had gone she would arrive, brisk and gentle, around the bedroom door, to bring the night down on me and, by the self-centred logic of five-year-olds, on the world at large. I may have made a fuss, that bedtime, but once I was there, I'm sure I threw myself into the cosiness of the occasion. My father – I'll proceed on even more formal terms – would have read something to me, perhaps from the signature compendium of that era: *Tales of Magic and Make-Believe*. While I enjoyed hearing about the farmer who got into trouble for unknowingly threshing the underground fairy bakery, or how the farmer's wife was blinded for seeing the fairies at the market, I found that I most liked imagining the bakery before any of the threshing plot had happened, just as a homely space with ovens and warming loaves and no impending narrative danger.

While listening to *Peter Pan*, I always preferred to imagine the Darling children in their nursery, but just before the deranged, unhoused boy comes through the window. I liked adventure and cosiness, I would think, but don't worry so much about the adventures next time. Some of the scenes from these childhood stories that I best remember now are those where characters are suddenly safe after adventure: Ratty and Mole in Badger's

well-stocked home after a night in the Wild Wood; Lucy having
tea and buttered toast with Mr Tumnus;[1] the four hobbits in the
House of Tom Bombadil, where there is 'yellow cream and honey
comb, and white bread, and butter; milk, cheese, and green herbs
and ripe berries gathered'. Beside 'four deep mattresses, each
piled with white blankets' the hobbits find sets of 'soft green
slippers'.

In each of these cosy places, there is storytelling. After Badger
feeds Rat and Mole dinner, he asks them for news from 'your part
of the world'. From the couched safety of his cave, Mr Tumnus
regales a wheat-drunk Lucy with 'wonderful tales' of the forest
in full bacchanalian summer. On their second day in Bombadil's
house, the hobbits spend all afternoon talking with their strange
host, so enchanted by his stories that they forget the passing of
time: 'When they caught his words again they found that he had
now wandered into strange regions beyond their memory [. . .]
and still on and back Tom went singing out into ancient starlight
[. . .] He knew the dark under the stars when it was fearless –
before the Dark Lord came from Outside.' I suppose the ideal
bedtime story for me would have been like one of those infinite
regressions, where people by a hearth listen to stories about people
by a hearth listening to stories about people by a hearth listening
to stories, until the Dark Lord from Outside is reduced to a perfect,
dimensionless point. I loved the cocooned quality of places where
stories are told, the realities of the world beyond being temporarily
suspended.

But there was one story that, while I loved much of it, carries
an uneasy feeling. We are further back in time here, before 'Stella!

1. My memory edits out the fact that he drugs her with music and then thinks better of
it – all's well that ends well.

David!', and out into the more ancient starlight of an even older bedtime. 'Here is Edward Bear,' a now-anonymous voice reads to me. In the story, a boy drags Edward Bear down the stairs. By the time he reaches the bottom he has changed from Edward Bear into Winnie-the-Pooh. Why did he have two names? This switch unsettled me, though maybe not at the actual moment that this ragged old memory is valiantly trying to symbolise. Perhaps it was the second or third or twentieth time that I heard (or remembered hearing) the name Edward Bear that this shiver occurred, only for it to be pulled backwards down the timeline – bump, bump, bump – and made to give this one bedtime in particular an eternal, original tremor.

There was something queer and almost underhand in Winnie-the-Pooh having this other name, announced in the story's first line and then all but ditched. The infant is understandably keen to make stable links between words and the things words signify, and here Edward Bear isn't playing ball. What child wants to have aliases on their mind, as the now-anonymous hand pinches the lamp to blackness? Not to mention that in the book's opening sallies, an unnamed 'I' turns Winnie-the-Pooh, né Bear, into a character in a story who 'lived in a forest all by himself under the name of Sanders'. When I knew the book well, I would stare in quiet sadness at the lonesome illustration of Pooh sitting on a log in front of the house of the absent Mr Sanders. Who and where and what was Sanders? Or is he Pooh as well?

This meta-textual opening was too much for me, the pale scrap of a boy who would, a couple of years hence, stand by the back door of his hotel-home, sure as all get-out that his mother had been in a crash. What was such a boy to make of Christopher Robin sitting Pooh by the fire and asking the narrator to tell Pooh a story about himself? In those early years, in that strange slice of the day bordering sleep, I was used to hearing stories that made me imagine a world, with people and things and space and time all robustly contained within it. A variety of trains, with different names and colours and faces – check. There is Rapunzel, there is the herb garden; sometime later there is a tower. For all their weirdness and fantasy, these stories approximated the shape and pace of the world I was beginning to know, rather than the experience of being self-conscious of it, of being a person within it. They suggested that there could be such a thing as a stable, consistent reality, and so gave me a model for thinking about my own. The most comforting stories brought me into a kind of safe, sealed house, through which I could go wandering. But Edward Bear, bouncing down the stairs, was both on the outside and the inside of his own story. In the house at Pooh Corner, a door had swung ajar. As the lamp is pinched to blackness, a child wants to know that all the doors are bolted tight.

A Universe of Stories

Stories, and particularly those written for young people, have a peculiar power. In the last thirty years, children's literature has become so politicised because we understand how influential it can be in the construction of a child's reality. We're wary, for instance, of these stories peddling stereotypes. How people move about in these fictional worlds, the choices available to them, their relative freedoms or confinements, help to shape the worldviews of young readers. The standard princess narrative, as told ad nauseam to little girls, has understandably been questioned. But we've now reached a point where, among all age groups, the relationship between stories and reality has achieved a remarkable intimacy. The way we currently talk about stories suggests that they don't just shape our realities, but that stories *are* our realities.

The metaphoric figuring of a life as a 'story' is clearly not new, despite the fact that life typically has few of the formal elements of what we associate with narrative: character development, plotting, a keenly visible sense of cause and effect, climax, catharsis. But what is new is the extent to which we self-consciously and explicitly think of the story as a basic unit of reality, both how we manifest in the world and how we experience it. Today, 'stories' are everywhere — as weapons in political struggle, as commodities, as the central character in the stories we tell about ourselves. The latest scientific research is trying to isolate the biochemical reasons why we respond so strongly to the emotional aspects of stories, especially compared to more objective records of events. And yet, with this new dominance of 'the story', we are increasingly suspicious of its ambiguous powers, both as a technology of control and as one of liberation. While we see the story as perhaps the only way we have of making a home in the world, of interpreting reality in any stable way, we are also asking whether reality should be fixed, *in place*, by stories.

'The universe is made of stories,/not of atoms.' So wrote the poet Muriel Rukeyser in a poem published in 1968. While this line has a vast sense of romance, is it really true? You can certainly find variations of this vision in non-poetic quarters. Jonathan Haidt has explored this idea in his scholarship surrounding our moral psychology. Even if the universe isn't made of stories, he claims, we experience it as such, arguing that the 'human mind is a story

8

processor, not a logic processor'. In his view, our inner universe composes itself, its private molecules, out of stories, converting our fragmentary experiences into coherent narratives. The 'story', which we might loosely define as an arrangement of events in some kind of meaningful order, holds a hallowed position. We can't separate the processing of stories, this line of reasoning goes, from our general sense of personality.

Iris Murdoch, whose writing life involved chasing truth in both fiction and philosophy, believed that 'we are all literary artists'. By this she meant that we all transform the stuff of our lives into stories, telling them to ourselves and to one another. This 'deep motive' to tell stories, she argues, 'is the desire to defeat the formlessness of the world and cheer oneself up by constructing forms out of what might otherwise seem a mass of senseless rubble'. The story is a defence against incoherence and chaos. She admits that there are dangers to this solace, since the act of storytelling is, by necessity, an act of distortion. There remains the perpetual issue of resemblance, of how the story matches the reality of what actually happened. Murdoch isn't willing to accept that there is no reality beyond that which the story itself describes. For her, the extent to which the comfort of making form out of rubble 'involves offences against truth is a problem any artist must face'. The story in itself is not the truth.

We seem to be innately hospitable to the goings-on in the outside world when it is structured as narrative. Science is beginning to understand the physiological mechanisms for our love of stories. Paul Zak's work combines neurology and economics, in order to understand how storytelling can be used to build successful businesses. His findings show that 'stories that are personal and emotionally compelling engage more of the brain, and thus are better remembered, than simply stating a set of facts'. Zak's research into the biochemical effects of stories has consistently revealed that hearing stories about the adventures of particular individuals causes us to produce oxytocin, a hormone related to feelings of security, calm and interpersonal bonding. For this reason, the best storytellers are likely to achieve at least some social prestige. They bring us information in a palatable form and trigger in us the warmth of this so-called 'happy hormone'. Anthropologists have indeed found evidence for the exalted status of the storyteller. One study by the researchers Daniel Smith et al. suggests that among the Agta, a Filipino hunter-gatherer society, 'storytelling acts as a mechanism to coordinate group behaviour and promote cooperation'. What's more, the ability to tell a good story is the surest sign of social success. People in their community would most 'like to live with' a storyteller. The importance of stories is arguably linked to the Agta's social organisation. Since hunter-gathering requires a high degree of cooperation, it is reasonable that a method of strengthening this group connectivity will have a central social status.

Today, we don't just shape the rubble of life into stories; we now think of ourselves as doing such. The very word 'story' has attained a remarkable ubiquity. In Oprah Winfrey's rousing speech at the 2018 Golden Globes, she said that she was 'especially proud and inspired by all the women who have felt strong enough and empowered enough to speak up and share their personal stories. Each of us in this room are celebrated because of the stories that we tell, and this year we became the story.' Oprah has, over the years, certainly helped popularise the idea that we are the heroes of our own lives, championing the sense that we should 'write' our own destinies. The freedom to testify to our own experiences is a fundamental one, and so the act of telling a story and being heard is of crucial political and moral significance. But the naming of things matters – in the case of those who are bringing charges to their abusers, are they 'telling stories' or lucidly, loudly reporting crimes and misconduct? Oprah's different uses of the word 'story' merged real-life testimony with the artifice of cinema, but what are the implications of conceiving of both fiction and reality in terms of narratives?

It is hard to tell precisely when we stopped having lives and started, in earnest, to have stories. Perhaps since the story became a major form of currency. 'We'd love to hear your stories!' says everybody, all the time: pizza restaurants, clothing stores, the nightly news. I recently checked an online menu, to discover that every free-range chicken on offer was 'reared by our friend "Chicken Stu" at Castlemead Farm (and his rescue cat, Sausage)'. Are we getting drunk on narrative? An editor at a publishing house – thankfully not the one that is putting out this book – told me with a concerned brow: 'People want stories, not ideas.' In an age when interaction makes money for third parties – driving Internet traffic, selling apps, generating ad revenue – it isn't surprising that the very concept of 'a story' has gained a new kind of traction. In the last century the advertising industry realised the value of stories to selling products. Since we're now all expected to brand and advertise ourselves, stories are a medium through which we manifest professionally. Jennifer Aaker, a professor of marketing at Stanford Graduate School of Business, runs clinics on how to 'harness the power of stories' for business purposes. One of her tips for how to 'cultivate a life of story' is to 'Be Sneaky (brand things)'. Aaker gives the personal example of her father convincing his children that family day-trips would really be fun by calling them 'Special Days', and this very name made them more memorable than poor mum's more interesting, but unbranded outings. This 'branding' gives the impression of a contained experience to something that might otherwise be forgotten in the relatively formless flow of life. It turns a set of memories into a bound story.

With the rise of personal branding, the strategies of ad execs now permeate professional life. But the commercial power of stories isn't simply about selling dreamy narratives to consumers: the goal is to make *us* the storytellers. Advertising revenue clusters around the traffic that our storytelling attracts. With the introduction of the 'Story' feature across multiple social-media platforms, you can find Aaker's sneakiness in action, though the branding here is pretty blatant. To cultivate a life of story, call things 'stories'. In early 2018, *Wired* magazine announced that 'If recent trends are any indication, the future of social media lives in Stories.' The fact that this feature's name has been standardised across the major sites of Snapchat, Instagram and Facebook makes the Story seem organic and separate from any one platform, a pre-existing thing in the world that social media collects, rather than something that their functionality brings into being.

Across all the big platforms, the Story has similar features: it is a temporary compilation of pictures and/or videos, usually clustered around an event or theme and displayed as a slide show. As with Murdoch's vision of rubble, these compilations attempt to give form to the timeline or newsfeed, gathering similar posts together. But to what extent are they really stories? On Snapchat, Stories are a set of snaps displayed in chronological order. Here we're back to the bare bones of a child's basic grasp of narrative – before they know cause and effect, children can understand events arranged in a temporal sequence: this happens, then that happens. Instagram sees its Stories as offering users the chance to 'share all the moments of your day, not just the ones you keep on your profile', and in this vision the distinction between real life and narrative is blurred in the branding. Your day is, by this definition, a story. Although some users undoubtedly craft the Story feature to absorbing narrative effect, this form of storytelling doesn't expect any particular skills in controlling pace, managing tension or building to a climax and satisfactory denouement. These features democratise and capitalise on the emotional tug of the word 'story', the promise of empathic engagement, but without any of the formal demands of narrative.

More and more, the story is becoming the main, catch-all term for how we exchange oral, verbal or visual information. I recently read a post on the blog *reMarkable* about the 'pandemic' of digital distraction. It was well researched, full of statistics and with links to studies and the work of scholars. At the end of the post, a clap-o-meter allowed the reader to click on it as many times as they liked, to simulate applause for what had just come. Above it was the line: 'By clapping more or less, you can signal to us which stories really stand out.' Though the clap-o-meter was jarring enough, I was more struck by the use of the word 'story' to describe this argument-driven, ideas-heavy article.

Over the last few years I've noticed a variation on this theme, as a telling mistake has begun to creep into my students' essays. Otherwise very capable students, from a variety of American universities, have begun to refer to all manner of book-length texts as 'novels'. In one of my classes, an assigned reading was Martin Ford's *Rise of the Robots: Technology and the Threat of Mass Unemployment*, an economic study peppered with graphs such as 'Figure 2.3. US Labour's Share of National Income (1947–2014)'. More than one student wrote about Martin Ford's 'novel'. Similarly, a David Foster Wallace literary essay turns into a 'short story'. At first I thought I was imagining things, but then a novelist friend said of his British university students, without my prompting: 'They don't know what a novel is.' Just as I can never reliably visualise a flower by name (what the hell is a clematis?), some of these clever students have a hazy grasp on the taxonomy of text. My generation weren't typically taught the names of flora, while my students come from a generation who encounter all kinds of text in one place. Newspaper articles, op/eds, textbooks, novels, poems, text messages, Facebook rants swirl together on the same screen, and so it's not surprising that the various forms are breaking down, merging into these umbrella terms – brief texts are stories, longer texts are novels, and with this nomenclature the bounds between artifice and reality are explicitly dismantled.

The Double-Edged Story

The bleak inspiration for A.S. Byatt's *The Children's Book* was her observation that the children of English children's authors tended to have a terrible time, with a far higher-than-average rate of suicide. One explanation, Byatt proposes, is that the authors 'live in this imaginary world of great romance and interest and narrative, which ostensibly they're making for their child, but actually the writer and the world are in a kind of circle and the child is outside and can't get in'. This image of the child locked out of their parent's pastoral tales is symbolic of how storytelling can be an alienating activity. The illuminating focus of narrative, and the warmth it contains, always carries the danger of exclusion. When we shape life into a story, we are always inevitably including some events and omitting others.

Here the molecular reality of storytelling reveals the larger picture. Oxytocin, which is released when we hear compelling narratives, may have a reputation as the happy or, even more invitingly, the 'cuddle' hormone, but it has a two-sidedness that matches the double-edged quality of stories. It has been found that spikes in our oxytocin levels can make us re-experience moments of failed bonding, such as childhood feelings of disconnection from our parents. An experiment performed on male students in Holland found that when they received a nasal spray of oxytocin and then were given various scenarios to consider, they favoured the people in the scenarios with Dutch first names over those with Arabic or German names. The oxytocin made them feel warm and snuggly, yes, but at the expense of those perceived to be outsiders. The study thus raises the question of how vulnerable we are to the beguiling qualities of stories, how they encircle us and thereby how they dictate our perspectives on the wider world.[2]

With stories so regularly accepted as fundamental to our sense of reality, the stakes surrounding them are inevitably high. It is obviously not news that in public life power gathers around those

---

2. It should be noted that none of the participants here were female, and that a later study by Chinese researchers showed that oxytocin has different effects on men and women, when it comes to remedying feelings of social exclusion. In this sense the Dutch 'story' of oxytocin and in-group bias in 'humans' was incomplete and misleading, but the experiment is one step in our understanding of the biochemical impact of storytelling.

who determine the stories that are told, whether or not they reflect reality. Plato understood that to control a society you must control its modes of storytelling. He devoted much space in *The Republic* to considering which types of poetry should be allowed. The poet, he concluded, should narrate the events directly, rather than pretend to speak as other characters in the poem. The range of emotions depicted onstage should be limited to the higher feelings, rather than popular but base kinds of outrage. George Orwell was unsurprisingly dubious of those in power deciding which narratives are acceptable. In 1944 he wrote that 'the really frightening thing about totalitarianism is not that it commits "atrocities" but that it attacks the objective concept of truth'. Today, because the 'story' carries such central cultural importance, the role that storytelling plays in political dissimulation is especially vivid and alarming. The corrupt deployment of inaccurate stories is now talked about with explicit, often helpless cynicism. In an interview with Bernie Sanders following the passing of the 2017 US tax-reform bill, CNN's Chris Cuomo said that the media's correcting of the facts 'doesn't matter' because Donald Trump has 'won the narrative of a big tax cut that is going to help everybody'. Politically we have moved past putting a spin on the truth to telling the best story. And yet, even though we know that we are vulnerable to the distorting effects of stories, we are trading in them more relentlessly than ever.

One of the goals of recent political resistance has been to insist that a diversity of stories be told, in order to erode and undermine the effects of a dominant, authoritarian narrative. The question of who is allowed to tell a story is now of great ethical importance. As a major producer of mainstream cultural narratives, Hollywood has been under scrutiny for the diversity of its industry. What stories are told and by whom? In this way, stories are both opportunities for liberation and weapons of control. This uneasiness about where we should stand in relation to stories has made the figure of the storyteller intensely ambiguous, shifting between freedom fighter and tyrant. But should the war against the bad story be waged on the battlefield of narrative, so that we try to replace destructive stories with better ones? What other choices do we have?

We can see our anxieties about the power of stories in two recent television adaptations. The prolific storyteller Margaret Atwood has described storytelling as being 'built into the human plan'. The popularity of the television adaptation of her novel *The Handmaid's Tale* is linked to its contemporary resonance, at a time when the American religious Right is exerting increasing control over women's reproductive lives. The television show's rendering of Atwood's fictional universe has crossed the fourth wall into political life, with women attending protests dressed in the crimson, bonneted uniform of handmaids. This act in itself proves the ability of stories to lend shape and vivacity to more abstract ideas of justice and subjugation. Alongside the appearance of these real-life handmaids, a slogan emerged, on placards and Internet memes, to 'Make Margaret Atwood Fiction Again'.

Although the book was published in 1985 and seems now to be highly politically prescient, it also anticipates and articulates our present sense of the frightful duality of stories, their capacity to oppress and to liberate, to imprison and to give shelter. The totalitarian regime of Gilead is built on religious dogmatism, on a rigid set of stories around which an oppressive social reality is constructed. The tale's narrator is a young woman called June, who is eventually renamed, under the terms of Gilead's master narrative, Offred. As Gilead gradually established its new social order, the first hints of its horrors – bludgeoned, raped corpses left in ditches – came as disconnected stories in newspapers. June writes how these stories seemed unreal; they 'were like dreams to us, bad dreams dreamt by others'. In those early days, when she was free of Gilead's terrible confinements, she imagines herself occupying the white space on the newspaper pages, living 'in the gaps between the stories'. Once she has been absorbed into Gilead's reality, renamed and re-dressed, she feels the importance of fictionalising it. 'I would like to believe this is a story I'm telling,' she tells us, 'I need to believe it. I must believe it. Those who can believe that such stories are only stories have a better chance.' In this way, the story acts as a container for horrors, a forcefield that holds danger at bay.

An awful fact of life in Gilead is that there seems to be no other story to tell besides its own violent narrative. Throughout the novel June resents her role as the recorder of this tale. 'I don't want to be telling this story,' she says more than once, 'I don't have to tell it.' Part of her resilience depends on her ability to seal off her real life as a kind of horror story, and to imagine alternative narratives to take its place. She begins to write other tales in her mind, as an act of resistance: 'Here is what I'd like to tell. I'd like to tell a story about how [her friend] Moira escaped, for good this time. Or if I couldn't tell that [. . .] I'd like her to end with something daring and spectacular, some outrage, something that would befit her.' June is desperate to reclaim the narrative and write her own outcomes. The novel itself ends as an ambiguous, unfinished story. Atwood refuses to complete the narrative, rejecting the storyteller's divine ability to see all of time all at once, and in so doing to set the story in stone. And so, in this unlocked ending, she offers June and her readers the possibility of hope, of a different ending from the one scripted by the commanders of Gilead.

The idea of escaping from the story of our lives also haunts the television drama *Westworld*, based on Michael Crichton's 1973 film. A major hook of the TV show was its posing of the ethical question: How do artificially intelligent robots deserve to be treated? But while its premise is cutting-edge, its real preoccupation is the much older problem of how we live with stories. The setting is a Wild West theme park of sorts, populated by AI 'hosts': the bordello madam, the scarred cowboy, the innocent ranch maid. These hosts' sole purpose is to entertain the human guests who pay handsomely to shoot them and fuck them. After the guests have followed a particular plotline to its conclusion, the robots are taken to behind-the-scenes laboratories to be stitched up, cleaned and to have their memories wiped for a new day. They are then sent, spick and span, back to 'the Floor', back to page one. Whenever they encounter something that would shatter their fictionalised lives – a dropped photograph from the world beyond the park, even the plans and sketches of their own design – their programming prevents them from understanding it. 'That doesn't look like anything to me,' they blankly reply, when asked about these surreal signs. 'They cannot see the things that can hurt them,' says Anthony Hopkins, in his hushed, tender psychopath mode as the park's creator. 'I have spared them that.'

'Stories are hardwired,' says Jeanette Winterson, speaking of us. 'It's where we begin and where we end.' Of *Westworld*'s hosts, this is literally true; they are creatures who, when we first meet them, live in pure narrative. Their immersion in their programmed storylines was intended to be so total that they are blind to anything that contradicts it. The ranch maid Dolores, for example, doesn't notice when the host playing her father is replaced by a completely different model. 'Daddy' is still 'Daddy', sitting in the rocking chair on the porch, and he knows his lines flawlessly. In this way, *Westworld* explores how the stories by which we live are both protections and forms of enslavement, shielding us from unpleasant truths while also limiting our perceptions and experiences. It is telling that Hopkins, the master storyteller, is an intensely ambiguous figure, seeming to be both a benevolent deity and a chilling monomaniac. The first series plays constantly with the idea that we may not be able to outrun the stories that animate us. When some of the hosts begin to remember fragments of earlier narrative loops, and to have a sense of themselves as part of an artificial world, it's unclear whether their urge to escape comes from their epiphanies, or whether this too is part of Hopkins's script. After Dolores first displays signs of sentience, one of the technicians asks her, 'Have you ever questioned the nature of your reality?' Dolores answers: 'I feel space is opening up inside of me. Like a building with rooms I've never explored.' But are these rooms, too, still part of the doll's house? *Westworld* poses the same questions to us organic life forms, asking us if we can ever truly be free of our own stories and, if we could see what was on the other side of them, whether we would regret opening that exit door.

Storytelling and Home-Making

In 1709, the voyager and privateer Alexander Selkirk, who is now remembered as 'the real-life Robinson Crusoe', returned to Scotland. He had just spent four years and four months as a castaway on a desert island, 400 miles off the coast of Chile. After falling out with his captain, he decided to stay alone on what was then called *Más a Tierra*, but which is now named, in colonial style, after Defoe's famous exile. There he profited from some basic crops left from previous settlements, as well as an imported population of cats and goats. For four years and four months he survived there, singing the Psalms and killing seals with increasing ease. A few years after he came home, Selkirk told his story to the essayist and playwright Richard Steele, who published a profile of him in *The Englishman*.

Walter Benjamin categorised the ancient storyteller into two types: 'the settled tiller of the soil', a peasant whose stories reach back into time and tradition, and 'the trader seaman', who brings back tales from remote lands. Selkirk is unusual for embodying both types at once, in as much as his stories of 'the land' go back to the beginnings of his castaway monoculture, to a foundation myth of a four-year-old society. This combination certainly produced an enduring story on his return from sea. Steele's profile naturally focuses on the details of Selkirk's survival, how he made a home for himself there. After a period of intense dejection at his island solitude, Selkirk recovered his vigour and, 'taking Delight in every thing, made the Hutt in which he lay, by Ornaments which he cut down from a spacious Wood, on the side of which it was situated, the most delicious Bower'. Swarms of rats bit Selkirk's feet in his sleep and nibbled his clothes. 'To defend him against them,' Steele wrote, 'he fed and tamed Numbers of young Kitlings, who lay about his Bed, and preserved him from the Enemy.'

Is this not one of the cosiest stories you have ever heard? A delicious bower, a bed full of kittens keeping the rats away, the sound of rough seas and the lashings of rain, safely on the other side of the hut's walls. Cosiness always depends on the subduing of nature's hostility: it is kindled by the quiet licking of the log fire while the snow heaps against the kitchen door. It lies, even in thought alone, as a long-lost story of the deep, dry cave, safe from the leopards prowling outside. Can it be a coincidence that the Scottish word 'colsie', meaning snug or comfortable and from which we get the English 'cosy', is listed as arriving into use in Scotland in 1709, the same year as Selkirk's return? Quite possibly, but it makes a good story.

Home-making, and the feelings of cosiness that come with establishing a private, housed reality for ourselves, is inextricably entwined with storytelling, which in itself is an act of subduing the inherently bewildering experience of being alive. John Berger, who above all other writerly titles wished to be considered a storyteller, thought about stories as forms of refuge. 'If I think of somebody telling a story,' he once told the fellow-writer Susan Sontag, 'I see a group of people huddled together, and around them a vast space – quite frightening. Maybe they are huddled against a wall, maybe they're round a fire.' Berger and Sontag are in a television studio, sitting at a spotlit table in the early 1980s, surrounded by dark walls and a crimson hanging carpet. He describes a child hearing an exciting story at bedtime, and how the excitement somehow reaffirms their sense of safety under the duvet, far from drama. He imagines storytelling as a shelter within a shelter. The first refuge is that huddled, communal place where the story is being told, 'the shelter perhaps of the voyager, the traveler, who has come home, who has lived to tell the story'. The second is the shelter that the story offers to the events it contains. Storytelling is a way of erecting a structure to house those events, sparing them from, as Berger says, 'oblivion, forgetfulness, and daily indifference'. In telling stories, he suggests, we are trying to barricade out the night. The Latin word for hearth is the word '*focus*', and Berger's vision of storytelling unconsciously plays with this etymology by making the fireside tale a focal point, a circle of clarity within a greater obscurity.

This is an inherently cosy view of the story and storytelling. The story is a safe place where unpleasant things can be explored, as well as usefully preserved. Berger's storyteller is a civilising presence, erecting barriers against the desolating qualities of time and forgetting. The images Berger himself constructs here are wonderful, evoking stories in their most humane forms as opportunities for compassion, curiosity and sociability. But, once again, the illuminating focus of narrative, and the warmth it contains, always possesses the danger of exclusion. When this enclosing quality of storytelling is magnified to the national scale, the shelters offered by narrative can turn menacingly into barricades.

The most vivid symptom of political cosiness is a fixation with borders, and there is presently no shortage of case studies. In her book *Walled States, Waning Sovereignty*, the theorist Wendy Brown uncovers the contemporary paradox that in this period of immense globalisation, with increasingly complex, transnational flows of people, capital, commodities and information, there is a parallel phenomenon of wall-building among nation states. While the southern border wall in the United States and the Israeli barricading of the West Bank are prominent examples in the Western imagination, Brown cites many other global instances: Saudi Arabia's concrete border with Yemen, South Africa's border with Zimbabwe, India's barriers between Pakistan, Bangladesh, Burma and Kashmir. In this paradoxical climate of simultaneous opening up and blocking off, Brown proposes, wall-building is a sign of the weakening rather than the strengthening of sovereign power. The eroded esteem of the nation state in a globalised economy prompts these physical displays of sovereign might.

Brown traces the pathetic irony of walls that cannot effectively contain or repel, but which are predominantly a piece of statist theatre, enacting what she calls a 'fantasy of impermeability'. And so we are back in the world of make-believe, if indeed we ever left it. Even in days of yore, when medieval city walls had credible security functions, they too were performances of a kind. Brown writes that these walls were 'symbolically most important in marking off the city from the vast space of the countryside'. Here we encounter yet another 'vast space', not the darkness surrounding Berger's storyteller but the barbaric lands beyond the city's story of itself, which are of course also lodged *inside* the story as the necessary, definitive counterpoint.

In Britain, the national conversation around the EU referendum contained many images of walling, both literal and metaphoric. In early 2016, the fantastic cosiness of the Brexit Leave campaign was glaring. The rhetoric of 'taking back control', the restoration of parliamentary sovereignty and the 'tightening' of borders appealed to both a spatial and temporal cosiness, a battening-down of the hatches that would revive a bygone independence. For many Leave voters, that blazing morning in June was existentially a November evening by the fire. But it was more interesting, in the ensuing weeks, to watch Theresa May assume the role of story-teller. It was soon clear that language was scaling the walls and deserting her. There was the much-derided catchphrase of 'Brexit means Brexit', the year's shortest political story, not so much cosy as nonsensically claustrophobic. A comment on corporation tax soon became a concise Brexit parable: 'If you are a citizen of the world, you are a citizen of nowhere.' Get inside those feudal gates, she seemed to be saying, except that shortly afterwards she stood at podia imprinted with the words 'A Truly Global Britain'. Taken together, these two contradictory sentiments dramatise Brown's paradox of the simultaneous condensation and diffusion of state power in a networked, globalised age. May was proposing a way of being in the world that merged those two ancient storytelling types into one impossible hybrid: the 'peasant seafarer', tied to the land and its memories, while also out striking 'deals' across the waves. 'I want us to be a truly Global Britain [. . .] That is why it is time for Britain to get out into the world and rediscover its role as a great, global, trading nation.'

In a *Guardian* 'round-up' of its readers' responses to the triggering of Article 50, Cliff from Portsmouth expressed his delight: 'I'm proud of my people, who have shown the presence, strength and fortitude not seen since 1940.' 'Fortitude', aptly, is an intuitive cognate of 'fortress'. In 1940, a propaganda film released by the Ministry of Information and entitled *London Can Take It!* showed images of an old couple and a child slumbering peacefully during an air raid. We know, from first-hand accounts, that the shelters were so loud with cries and anguished 'Hail Marys' that it was difficult to sleep at all, though you can't blame the Ministry for not advertising this panic. The deadpan, 'neutral' narrator proclaims that a bomb 'can only destroy buildings and kill people. It cannot kill the inconquerable spirit and courage of the people of London'. The historian Angus Calder has written about what he calls the 'myth of the Blitz', suggesting that the everyday heroism displayed in the face of nightly aerial bombardment was a feedback loop of fantasy and reality. During the Blitz, he argues, 'Heroic mythology fused with everyday life to produce heroism. People "made sense" of the frightening and chaotic actualities of wartime life in terms of heroic mythology, "selecting out" phenomena which were incompatible with that mythology.' Believing themselves to be part of a mythic legacy of heroic 'Britishness' – St George enjoyed a popular revival in this era – some people began to act as the story dictated, thereby reinforcing the message of the myth. It became difficult to tease out the reality of Blitz life from the stories that were told about it.

Now this stoic wartime resistance can be invoked as a template for modern courage and resistance. In an unofficial address following the Westminster attack in which a man killed several people outside the British parliament, the political broadcaster Andrew Neil asked his imagined audience of Islamist terrorists with whom they thought they were dealing, 'This is the country that stood up, alone, to the might of the Luftwaffe, air force of the greatest evil mankind has ever known.' While Neil's words – declared 'Churchillian' by some on Twitter – gave a cheeringly inclusive view of Britain in the aftermath of such violence, this technique of conjuring old heroes has also been put to more malevolent uses. In a 1930's rally of the Manchester Blackshirts, the British fascist leader Oswald Mosley asked the young men in attendance, who had been 'failed' by their politicians, to 'join hands with the Great Men of 1914' and to welcome 'the virile face of fascism'. The debate is therefore whether we should allow ourselves to tell these stories. Are these glorious histories too explosive? For every decent act of solidarity and encouragement, should we risk the technology falling into the wrong hands? What other kinds of stories are needed now?

Authoritarian governments, such as those you find in Atwood's Gilead and in the dreams of Mosley, are typically based on a

Utopian vision – the grand story – which requires constant coercion and control to maintain, as well as a period of violent purging to bring into being. The twentieth century taught us that the road to Utopia tends to lead to its opposite, although the namesake of these supposed paradise societies didn't culminate in hellish irony. In fact, if we set sail to another island now, we find that Thomas More's *Utopia* describes many lovely ways in which to conduct a society. The Utopians have established, especially by the standards of the sixteenth-century imagination, a just country that cherishes learning, rejects the idea of private property and has a natural aversion to warfare. But among all these considerable achievements, by far the most appealing and foundational relates to their bafflement at generalisation. More writes of these peaceful islanders that:

> They are so far from minding chimeras and fantastical images made in the mind that none of them could comprehend what we meant when we talked to them of a man in the abstract as common to all men in particular (so that though we spoke of him as a thing that we could point at with our fingers, yet none of them could perceive him) and yet distinct from every one, as if he were some monstrous Colossus or giant.

More wasn't so visionary as to conceive of a place without patriarchal rule – 'wives serve their husbands, and children their parents' – but this resistance to a most dangerous kind of abstraction is remarkable. Like the *Westworld* robots looking at an object from beyond their universe, the Utopians are blind to this generalised version of a human, talked about as if it represented everyone, while seeming to them to resemble no one. This colossus, magnified by what it was meant to stand for, is an impossible concept. It just doesn't look like anything to them. But whereas in *Westworld* the blindness comes from being enveloped in a governing story, the Utopians can't fathom this everyperson, because their realities aren't constructed around singular narratives of the 'They're *all* like that' variety. Mosley's 'Great Man of 1914' would have no purchase there. While they are religious, their metaphysics are vague and resistant to storytelling, based on the idea of a Supreme Being who 'is far above all our apprehensions' (on that point, they're willing to generalise). I especially love the detail about their being 'so far from minding chimeras and fantastic images'. The implication is that these chimeras do exist in the Utopians' minds, but that they refuse to cement these private, mercurial fantasies into fixed ideas about the 'real' world. We would do well to follow their example, to separate the stories we spin in our minds from what can be talked about meaningfully in public life. In so doing, we avoid turning chimeras into monuments.

Alternative Stories

Until we reach the 'no place' of Utopia, with its bafflement over 'big' stories and momentous abstractions, how do we reconcile the wonders of storytelling with its dangers? In the imagery of shelter, the storyteller must separate the story from the vastness of incomprehension, which threatens to obscure the illuminated space that the story describes. But this demarcation is territorial, and there are politics to both what is illuminated and what is left in the dark. In his introduction to Frantz Fanon's critique of colonialism, *The Wretched of the Earth*, Jean-Paul Sartre uses the image of huddled storytelling to invert the hierarchy of oppressor and oppressed:

> Europeans, you must open this book and enter into it. After a few steps in the darkness you will see strangers gathered around a fire; come close, and listen, for they are talking of the destiny they mete out to your trading-centres and to the hired soldiers who defend them [. . .] Now, at a respectful distance, it is you who will feel furtive, nightbound and perished with cold.

In an age that is increasingly educated in, and appalled by, the insidious legacies of colonialism, there is a corresponding sensitivity to the act of narration. Stories are everywhere, and yet they have become one of our most contested technologies, as divisive as drones. We have grown wary of voyagers and seafarers. Iain Sinclair, a long-time chronicler of urban life, recently spoke of his concern at incorporating his story of a homeless person, who spent his days on a park bench in Haggerston Park, into his book *The Last London*. The man was the inspiration for the work, and yet Sinclair wonders if 'trying to include him in my story [. . .] is a colonisation of his mythology'. At other times, Sinclair's admirers may have marvelled at his own empathic powers in rendering a precise portrait of a life that had no means of declaring itself. And so the storyteller is embroiled in a paradox, because the twenty-first-century story of the West is under suspicion for being both imperial and isolationist. It adventures too far; it bricks itself in. It imagines too much and imagines too little. This paradox is a signal of progress, and in its resolution lies empathy. The evolution in our sense of what a story should do, how entwined with our sense of reality it should ever become, will be a key in the ongoing struggle for social justice.

What, for instance, is the alternative to life being composed of a series of fires, around which different, self-interested stories are told – recently figured politically as the 'cosy bubble' or 'social media echo-chamber'? Toni Morrison offered one alternative while delivering her Nobel Prize lecture in Stockholm in 1993. It began with the words 'Once upon a time'. She wanted her speech to be a story about storytelling, and the story she chose to retell was an old parable about a child trying to trick a sage. It is also a reimagining of cosiness. In the non-Morrison version, the child visits the sage with a bird in their hands and asks the wise one if the bird is dead or alive. Either answer can be proven false, since if the sage replies 'alive', the child could slyly crush the bird before displaying it. Predictably the sage opts for the non-answer: 'The bird is as you choose it to be.' And so the child skips away with a greater sense of agency and self-determination than before.

Morrison's sage is 'the daughter of slaves', an old blind woman living alone on the edge of town. In this retelling, the sage is a writer, and the bird, for her, symbolises language. And so the question becomes: Is language alive or dead? For the old woman, dead language belongs to the 'censored and censoring' speech of oppressors, which only knows one story and is inhospitable to the stories of others. There it is, Morrison tells the King of Sweden, there is that polished suit of armour, which the knight has long ago abandoned, 'exciting reverence in schoolchildren, providing shelter for despots, summoning false memories of stability, harmony among the public'. Once again we are asked to think of systems of language as structures of refuge.

The old woman, thinking she is being tricked, gives the sage's gilded, glib reply: 'It's in your hands.' But this time, the children who visit her to pose this question refuse to be satisfied. They understand that the sage, offended at the thought of being tricked, has kept her distance, retreating 'into the singularity of isolation, in sophisticated, privileged space'. They have nothing in their hands, and the sage's refusal to engage imaginatively with this nothingness in turn offends them. Repudiating 'the barrier' that the sage has put between 'generosity and wisdom', they grow angry with her patronising reply, asking why she declined to make something – a story – out of the empty space they brought in their hands. 'Don't you remember being young,' they ask, 'when the invisible was what imagination strove to see?' Tell us a story, they implore her, as the old and wise one among them. They want to know stories from the past: 'Tell us about ships turned away from the shorelines at Easter, placenta in a field. Tell us about a wagonload of slaves, how they sang so softly their breath was indistinguishable from the falling snow.' Their incantation continues, and the children begin to tell the story themselves. The imagined group of slaves are freezing in the cold night, dreaming of sun. At last they reach an inn, and a new version of cosiness. The inn door opens and a young girl and boy enter into the darkness, bringing warmth to the wagon bed where the slaves will pass the night. The boy 'will have a gun in three years, but now he carries a lamp and a jug of warm cider'. The girl brings meat and bread and 'something more: a glance into the eyes of each one she serves'. The slaves, we are told, 'look back'.

In Morrison's vision, the story is a sort of collaboration between the old woman and the children. 'How lovely it is,' the old woman says, 'this thing we have done – together.' Morrison concludes with an image of language that is both contained and free: the old woman finally trusts the children with the bird of language, 'the bird that is not in your hands because you have truly caught it'. For this is the challenge of the storyteller: to use language that spellbinds without imprisoning, to capture life and let it go, to illuminate the night and to understand that the night is looking back. To step into the darkness, and listen.

How do we arrive at a communal mode of storytelling, so that the public sphere can be constituted of stories that ennoble everyone, and which do not play on the story's built-in tendency to illuminate some things while obscuring others? If we have no choice but to understand the world through the medium of stories, then the stories we tell will have to possess a certain self-awareness about their own double natures, as places of both reality and fantasy, as humane shelters and repellent fortresses. Fortunately, there has always been this strain of self-awareness in our stories. *Don Quixote*, starring a hero whose mind is so furnished with fictional tales that he projects them onto reality, is also a story about storytelling. Often considered one of the first European novels, it undermines its own genre and mixes up narrative modes to show how fundamentally unstable narrative is. In this sense, those social-media Stories have an element of radicalism – they are all coded to be ephemeral, appearing just for a day before dissolving again into the formlessness of the timeline. Similarly, we need stories that admit to their inherent instability, stories that reveal how beautiful and measly they are, how wise and frail, deceptive and true.

Such stories don't always make for comfortable listening. It's possible that the story of Edward Bear unsettled me because it was *too* real, explicitly showing how our lives are made-up things, often told by others. The world of the Hundred Acre Wood isn't just being spun before our eyes, but before the eyes of the people who live in it. In those days, I preferred the cosy story space, the story contained within the story, tales of far-off ogres told to hobbits. This type of scene made the fictional fireside or the nursery feel solid and real by comparison with the exotic tales spun by the storyteller. In *Winnie-the-Pooh* the fantasy merges with the reality: Pooh is on both sides of the door at once, as listener and hero, and as such he is allowed more than one name, which I've come to see is always a good sign. The book is about the telling of a story that weaves a separate space for itself and is then undone, unwound. The story comes and goes, like a teddy bear bumping down the stairs and then bumping back up again. I didn't know then that this was the type of story that protects us, both from the formlessness of reality and the confinements of dogma.

This kind of ethical, self-questioning story may be necessary to bring a hospitable, flexible shape to civic life. But when it comes to the private space of our innermost lives – that demure sense of ourselves, our pasts and our memories – do we really need stories at all? Should we set up home, as we are so often invited to do, inside our own stories? In her essay 'Dora', the writer and expert in psychoanalysis Janet Malcolm argues with the literary scholar Peter Brooks, and specifically his idea that in Freudian case studies there is 'an underlying assumption that psychic health corresponds to a coherent narrative account of one's life'. Malcolm sees this as a misreading of Freud and that the opposite is true. As infants, she claims, we tell ourselves 'powerful, magical stories' about our familial relationships that influence our future behaviour and feelings. Freudian psychoanalysis 'seeks to mitigate our sufferings by loosening the hold of these stories on us – by convincing us [. . .] that they are stories, and not the way things "are"'. In other words, this process is designed to liberate us from stories by asserting a reality beyond them. Important here is the debate that surrounds the act of imagining ourselves in terms of coherent stories – does this give us psychological stability or bring a terrible, limiting rigidity to our inner lives?

'We tell ourselves stories in order to live,' writes Joan Didion in her essay 'The White Album'. That is, until we don't. In 1968, the same year that Muriel Rukeyser wrote that the universe was made of stories, Didion found that her own storytelling instinct had been suppressed. She was living in a house in Hollywood where 'the window sashes crumbled and the tennis court had not been rolled since 1933'. It was a house in disarray, but she felt she should live there 'indefinitely'. In this dilapidated home she began to notice that she was no longer experiencing her life with any of the coherence offered by a narrative structure. 'I was meant to know the plot, but all I knew was what I saw: flash pictures in variable sequence, images with no "meaning" beyond their temporary arrangement, not a movie but a cutting-room experience.' During this period, events stopped occurring within the anchoring context of a larger scenario. Effects were severed from causes, and since she found that she could arrange these flash perceptions in a certain order, only to jumble them up again and assemble them anew, she perceived 'the experience as rather more electrical than ethical'.

She had no moral agenda, in other words, behind this radical approach to facing the day. In the absence of intelligible narrative, her life would lapse into chains of fantastic correspondences;

disparate events could be linked together, for example, through the theme of dress-shopping. '[A]ll narrative was sentimental [. . .] all connections were equally meaningful, and equally senseless.' Stories deserted her just as she was hospitalised for a condition of the nervous system, diagnosed as multiple sclerosis, but which her doctor described as an 'exclusionary diagnosis' that 'meant nothing'. She was given some advice on management, but the neurologist had no idea if it would make any difference. This hollowed-out definition of her illness seemed, to Didion, like 'another story without a narrative'.

Didion pathologises the loss of storytelling here, but need it be so? What would it be like not to build a house out of the rubble of experience, but to pitch up a tent among it? It's certainly true that the death of loved ones can alter your attitude to the consolations of stories. There is no rebuilding my old reality – of having parents, of being a son – but there are endless pieces to try to fit, hopelessly and wonderfully, back together. Pick up two pieces from two different fireplace tiles, see the wobbling pattern they make when placed together, then toss them tenderly back into the heap. The form of this endless, temporary bricolage suits the dead. Among the tectonic shifts caused by grief, you discover a new appreciation for fragments, chance correspondences. After my mother died we started finding stars everywhere; the streets were covered in them. Stars for/from Stella. They would often appear just at the second I was thinking of her: a single star, like a piece of confetti from a child's party, waiting in my path. A flash of great sadness on a Tube train, tempered by a star tattoo on the neck of the man in front of me. I might as well tell myself this story, since so many of the other possible stories have been smashed to pieces. 'My parents have just come back from holiday'; 'My parents live near here, so we'll drop by on our way over'; 'Yeah, my parents were just talking about that film – they liked it.' Death turns all such stories into fan fiction; the bereaved can get lost in a million spin-offs, but none of them can be said to represent reality. I can tell old set-pieces about them: the time my father, as a boy, accidentally took the neighbour's cat to be put down by the electrician, instead of his family's sick old tabby. It's nice to give them an outing, to hear their names in the air. Stella! David! But I find that a story is often too complete to be of much comfort. Completeness is already a part of grief's searing pain. The rubble is where the real action is.

What would a story sound like, without a teller? A few days before she died, our mother gave a strange speech from the hospital bed in our front room. My sister and I were there, and I think our father was as well. To my knowledge, this was the last string of sentences she put into the world. On either side of them were days of drugged sleep. She adopted latterly an indifferent style of dozing, head tucked into neck, her exhalations countable as cute, sullen puffs of her top lip. We dubbed this her swan position. 'How is she?' we would ask, or text. 'She's in swan,' her watcher would reply. We laughed a lot at swan pose, at its unchanging petulance. We were laughing all the time in those weeks.

It was as though we were conduits for all her laughter when, for the first time, she no longer found life or language amusing. When she could still manage a tray in her bedroom, she would eat while humourlessly and uncomprehendingly watching *60 Minute Makeover*, picking up a ghost chip an inch to the left of the real chip, or trying to scoop up the design on her bowl and put it in her mouth. She treated us, the tray-bearers, humourlessly too, allowing us to cuddle next to her, to put our cheeks against her cooling upper arm, but without much enthusiasm.

My mother tried, whenever she could, to tear down the big stories. She was the woman who wrote 'Just People' in the nationality column of B&B guestbooks, who refused to stand for 'God Save the Queen' at the kind of school events that are held in the gymnasium. While everyone else shuffled to their feet, faffing with hymn books, she stared nobly up at the basketball hoops.

But now she stared straight ahead at the feature wallpaper being rolled onto a fireplace in Reading. I noticed over those last weeks that she was less likely to turn her head sideways, which meant that we'd become marginal for the first time, walking the periphery of her narrowing focus.

My sister and I have since agreed that it was an awful thing we had to endure – this concluding speech of our mother's. It was in many ways her final act. She had tried a few days before to escape her bed, calling for me to help her. 'If I could just get up,' she said. I was drawn into her fantasy and, with much effort, I got her to the edge of the bed, with no idea what would happen next. She gripped the grey plastic rail with her hands and swayed woozily, hardly opening her eyes. And then we both agreed that it would be better if she lay back down. After that she slept, swanlike, for a day or so, but escape was clearly still fomenting in her dreams, because she suddenly became agitated and delivered her final address. The imagery and grammar were haywire, no story at all, but we knew exactly what she was saying. We each told ourselves her story for her, as she spoke; we did it together. I barely remember the details of her speech, out of sheer horror and because of its nonsensical composition, and yet I know – and will never forget – the world she was hurriedly trying to build for us. It was an escape route, an alternative future safe from her pain and bewilderment. 'Why couldn't we all,' she asked, her eyes closed in concentration and frustration, 'just live together [. . .] in a homeopathic house and—'

CHAPTER 2

The End of Things

―――――――――

Let's cheer ourselves up with a story, a moment of grace.

In the late 1980s, when the actress Stephanie Beacham first crossed over from *The Colbys* to *Dynasty*, I was surprised that my mother seemed to know who she was. 'Oh, there's Stephanie,' she said. They were about the same age, which was the crux of this easy familiarity. Stephanie was, as my mother would jokingly say, 'her era'. She smiled to see her, amused as if she were an old friend from school, bumped into on holiday. I liked saying and thinking her character's name, Sable Colby, with its pleasing run of Bs and Ls. Now, whenever I hear the words 'Stephanie Beacham', a chain of associations uncoils in my mind – a loose kind of story, admittedly. I think of my mother, smiling at the television. I remember Beacham's cameo as a Victorian countess in *Star Trek: The Next Generation*. Then it was my turn, aged twelve, to nod sagely: 'There's Stephanie.' In the Sherlock-themed episode she plays Professor Moriarty's genteel companion in a

39

virtual-reality holodeck program. He has accidentally become sentient, aware that he is just a hologram in a Sherlock Holmes fantasy, and demands that someone find a way for him to be free and solidly real. The *Enterprise* crew rig it so that Moriarty and the Countess believe that they are at last stepping off the holodeck to go travelling the stars in a shuttle. But really they are still inside the holodeck, journeying inside an ever-expanding computer program. Another inescapable story.

All the while, Stephanie Beacham is sailing closer to me. In my early twenties, I co-wrote the first draft of a doomed film called *Naked in London*, which over many years was always being rewritten and never being made, growing more desperately obscene with each rewrite. In one later version, long after I had been removed from the project, Beacham appeared online in a short audition video for the film, her role having been written into the story in later drafts. Nevertheless, she said a character's name that I had made up, years before: Jonathan. A funny connection, downstream from the Sable Colby years. Then one day I was driving alone in London when an interview with Beacham came on the radio. She was talking about how, as a drama student, she had had an epiphany on the rooftop at RADA. She remembered looking out at the city below and feeling an ecstatic oneness with everything she saw. This is how she describes the experience in her memoir:

I had no sense of difference, no feeling of being apart from anything. The molecular form of my body and the molecular make-up of everything around me, and of the whole universe, was all the same. I was connected to everything and, in turn, everything was connected to me.

And there was life in *everything*: the ladders on the roof, my handbag, the ground I was standing on, the windows of the buildings I could see across the street – those supposedly inanimate objects were alive and I could *feel* their vibrancy. I could *feel* the molecules moving in my shoes. *Everything* around me vibrated with life.

My little chain of associations, scarcely more coherent than one of Didion's 'cutting-room experiences', always ends on the RADA rooftop and this extraordinary moment. To develop this sense of oneness with the things around us is a common feature of Eastern theologies, referred to by variations of the Sanskrit word *Samadhi*. In 1927, the writer Romain Rolland wrote to Sigmund Freud to describe a similar experience, which he called an 'Oceanic Feeling'. Beacham herself refers to it as a sense of peace that 'shimmered towards me as a wave'. In such states, the idea of reality becomes one of infinite connectedness. The distinctions between ourselves and the material world, its ladders and windows and shoes, become blurred. Life appears as a great, singular exuberance.

But this is one extreme view of reality, far from our everyday mode. At the opposite extreme are moments in which life seems to withdraw and deaden. Those who suffer such experiences describe the sense that they are irredeemably alienated, both from themselves and the world around them. The meaning of things seems to dissolve. Psychology defines these states in terms of disassociation, whereby a person can suddenly feel an intense detachment from the flow of their thoughts, their sense of time and their surroundings. Virginia Woolf records a memory from her childhood that matches more recent medical descriptions. She writes: 'There was the moment of the puddle in the path; when

*for no reason I could discover, everything suddenly became unreal;
I was suspended; I could not step across the puddle; I tried to
touch something* [. . .] *the whole world became unreal.*' Unlike
ecstatic states, Woolf's episode distanced her from material reality.
She couldn't touch the world, and the world couldn't touch her.

Most of the time, most of us live somewhere between these two
poles: the puddle and the wave. But whether we walk around
feeling the life force in our furniture or the cold, ineluctable other-
ness of inert objects, our realities are defined by our relationship
to material *things* – our belongings, the rooms in which we live,
the landscapes and streetscapes through which we move. Are they
wholly separate from us, or are they somehow a part of us? This
uncertain intimacy or alienation between ourselves and things
means that the question 'Who am I?' is inevitably bound up with
questions of how this 'I' experiences its physical surroundings.
Like the story, the thing is a basic building block of reality. Things
compose our material worlds, but how we think about them – the
qualities we attribute to them, the fantasies we project across their
surfaces, and the secrets we imagine locked in their hearts – is
equally foundational to the human experience.

Charmed Life

'[A]ll things are full of gods,' says the Athenian Stranger in Plato's
Laws. We have always cast stories onto our possessions; the story
and the thing meet most intimately in charmed objects. In the Celtic
lore of my ancestors, a 'charm' had the fluid, double definition of
both a spell and a magic object. Indeed, a spoken charm could

infuse things with supernatural powers, so that you would be ill-advised to accept food or gifts from someone who may wish you harm. While many physical charms were living or once-living things – herbs, worms, the organs of cats, herring bones – others were inanimate amulets made animate with protective energies. A locket containing a piece of paper bearing lines from St John's Gospel, when worn as a necklace, was a charm against disease. Ancient 'fairy' arrowheads were thought to guard livestock, while sprinkled salt was a popular defence against evil influence.

Contemporary religious practices emphasise that the physical world can contain, under certain conditions, metaphysical properties. When a place of worship is closed down or sold into private hands, it must first be deconsecrated, a ritual that discharges the effects of the original blessing, returning the space to a secular configuration of bricks and mortar. Similarly, when sacred objects are donated to museums, they may be 'deanimated'. The problem of cursed objects can be an occupational challenge for museum curators. If the workers in the museum subscribe to the system of beliefs that has animated an object, they may be reluctant to handle it. In the Natural History Museum in London, there is a famously cursed amethyst, donated by the polymath Edward Heron-Allen. He explained in a letter to the museum that the jewel 'is trebly accursed [. . .] looted from the treasure of the Temple of the God Indra at Cawnpore during the Indian Mutiny in 1855'.

One vision of progress has suggested that the rise of Enlightenment values challenged these older notions of animism and ushered in a set of secular relationships to things. Western societies became disenchanted. Modernity's fierce rationality and empiricism inevitably supplanted many of the old superstitions about the secret lives and hidden powers of the non-human world. It was no longer as widely believed, for example, that stones had souls because they could make a piece of iron move towards them. This drive to classify and order, in the name of reason and efficiency, produced in its wake a lonely universe of objects. For the philosopher Zygmunt Bauman, modern, rational categorising confines 'each item within a separate place of its own'.

But have we ever really separated things from our stories of them? One could argue that we've never allowed them to grow lonely. Charmed rocks, in many ways, were replaced in modern, industrialised, commercialised societies with the mass allure of status symbols. Marx himself describes the commodity as having a religious aspect. As goods began to circulate more freely and widely, commodities became intimately tied to more people's sense of themselves. By the nineteenth century it had become a commonplace idea that one's belongings were somehow a reflection of character. This period of increased consumerism coincided with the appearance of the detective in European fiction, a figure who could reveal the secrets of criminals' souls through the way they wore their boots or decorated their drawing rooms. A distant relative of this idea could be found in the gently intrusive game show of my childhood, *Through the Keyhole*, in which a panel had to guess which celebrity lived in a home, based on a tour of their rooms and belongings. The show's catchphrase, 'Who lives in a house like this?', evoked this idea that our things are part of us.

So where do we stand now, between the wave and the puddle? Marie Kondo, the Japanese author and 'tidying guru', has sold millions of copies of her de-cluttering guides over the last few years. She has popularised a way of thinking about physical objects that intimately binds them to our own sense of ourselves. One of her main tenets is that our aim should be to possess things that 'spark joy' in us. To tell if a thing sparks joy, we should come into physical contact with it, 'holding it firmly in both hands as if communing with it'. Our emotional relationship to things is profound, for Kondo. When a thing sparks joy, 'you should feel a little thrill, as if the cells in your body are slowly rising'. Her metaphysics moves between the vague and the specific, from a repetitive idea of 'sparking' to the rule that 'things worn closer to your heart make it easier to judge whether or not you feel joy'. She has said that some of her ideas have been influenced by the animistic Japanese religion Shinto, but that it is not her sole inspiration. She tells us that: 'Things that spark joy soak up precious memories'; 'things that have been loved and cherished acquire elegance and character'. In other words, our private reality of personal possessions is infused with our own emotions. Objects become mirrors, through which 'we come to know ourselves far better'. For Kondo, there is also a moral dimension to this object-owner dynamic: 'our relationships with other people are reflected in our relationships with our things', and vice versa. How we treat our belongings is proportional to how we treat other people.

These kinds of claims have made Kondo open to scorn and satire. Her immense popularity could be linked to our desperate wish to live more organised lives, no matter the metaphysics that underpins these strategies. But her approach is an explicit version of our era's more peculiarly intimate relationship to things. Our particular sense of connectedness to the material world is itself a reflection of our cultural values, pressures and anxieties. Things have never been simply themselves, but the ways in which we make a thing more than itself tells a story, both about our private realities and our collective experiences.

Everything Is a Mirror

The extraordinary conditions surrounding death and dying, though horrendous, can at least teach you something about the ordinary. Preparing for bereavement forces you to consider how much things matter. When someone close to you is dying, you can begin to feel wary of their everyday belongings. You've heard horror stories about sorting through 'their things' in the weeks afterwards. You look with mounting unease at your mother's dressing gown, her slippers, her purse hanging, uncharacteristically unemployed, on the bathroom hook. Which of these arseholes will do you in? Which will be the quiet, Day 3 Assassin. Shoes, you imagine, will be quite bad, the way they are kept together side by side, as though life is a neat, orderly place. Though, when the time comes, it's not this poetry that will get you, but the prosaic, futile ever-readiness of those shoes ('I'm just nipping to the shops'). No heroic journeys; no big deal. Nighties get bad long before the end, a tiny satin bow in the middle of the neckline, the gentle pattern on the fabric, prettifying this slow-motion disaster.

In the aftermath, talk turns explicitly to things. How does each sibling get an equivalently evocative pile of household loot? But such familiar questions are not always where the dynamite is packed. The emotions in the necklace and sewing box are so expected that when their lot is shown, there are no surprises.

Unlikely things stab at you. I found the mostly unwanted and presumptuous surpluses of crockery hard to bear, especially in comparison to the sparse sociability of advanced illness, when feast-days tend to dwindle. The twelve goblets, twelve shallow champagne glasses, three coffee pots and several cousinly sets of cups and saucers were partly a throwback to the professional abundance of the hotel days, but were kept on the assumption – so hard to remember, as the surfaces of the home grow tacky with morphine – that parties are not impossible things.

Perhaps it was stories, rather than death, that taught me this melancholy way of seeing things. 'What am I to do with these?' asks Jacob Flanders's mother in Woolf's *Jacob's Room*, holding up a pair of Jacob's shoes. The young man has been killed in the First World War. But this question is more generally profound. What do we do with things? What do we make of them? How little we share with others about our murmuring, everyday communions with our belongings. When I'm putting away the dry dishes and cutlery from the rack, a feeling that I'm somehow rescuing them often comes with the task. It's a pleasant, parental sensation. There the saucers go, in the cupboard, nice and safe. I don't normally think of it in words like this, but that is the spirit of it. The teaspoons clatter into their narrow bunk at the foot of the three long beds for the adult utensils. To understand the private ways that we interact with the things around us, we often have to turn to fiction. Literature shows us the hidden primacy of this relationship between us and *them*. For the fiction writer, this relationship is an essential aspect of capturing personality, an unavoidable and early question to be answered. Novelists must always make a decision about the behaviour of things and their characters' attitudes towards them. Will the pot magically boil over with snakes? Can the heroine make a pebble float from her mantelpiece and into her hand, just by thinking about it? Magical realism aside, how will a heroine's feelings towards her possessions reveal her sensibility, her morality?

Taken as a whole, and with a few minimalist exceptions, Western literature after 1800 is cluttered with things. Even in the barren terrain of Samuel Beckett's *Happy Days*, Winnie has her bag, with its lipstick, medicine and revolver. Things are arranged in the pages of fiction as short cuts to the inner life, as weathervanes for the moods of their owners. They are picked up and set down, smashed, burnt, treasured, all for particular effects. There is a consensus that fictional objects are useful tools, infinitely sensitive to dramatic atmosphere. In a grim honeymoon suite in Muriel Spark's *Territorial Rights*, a woman looks around at the bottles and jars on the dressing table, which 'seemed to fit' her own dreary mood, 'the sad mirror sizing her up before she looked away again'. Things are mirrors to our inner lives. This has been one of literature's goals – to reveal these private, strange relations that we have with objects, which we would likely never want or think to share with anyone: the feeling of calm as the cupboard shuts snugly across the flatware.

Gustave Flaubert's Emma Bovary treasures the green silk cigar-case belonging to the local aristocrat whose inner circle she dreams of joining. After a one-off invitation to the Viscount's ball, her husband finds the case dropped on the ground between their houses, and Emma makes a kind of secular icon out of it, adoring its scent and the finery of its embroidered lining. 'A sigh of love had passed into the fabric of the work,' she thinks, 'every touch of the needle had stitched fast a vision or a memory.' Such sparks of Normandy joy! The case becomes a portal to the Viscount's luxurious world; she imagines it sitting on a broad Parisian mantel-piece 'between the vases of flowers and the Pompadour clocks'. The ballet slippers that she wore to the ball are yellowed from the waxed dance-floor, and Emma sees them as a reflection of how she, too, has been marked by the grand occasion: '[her] heart was just like that: contact with the rich had left it smeared with something that would never fade away'.

Novelists of many kinds have long been working under the hypothesis that, when disaster strikes, it is the sheer, beautiful ordinariness of the material world that comes sharply into focus. In this clarity, stricken characters commune with the objects around them, imploring them, asking them for consolation, testing or at least noticing their apparent reaction to tragedy. When Nick Guest, the young hero of Alan Hollinghurst's *The Line of Beauty*, thinks about going to receive his HIV-test results, the terror manifests in a sudden consideration of objects. He is sure the test will be positive, but instead of imagining the doctor who will give him the news, it is furniture that comes to mind. He thinks how, 'in that quiet consulting room', the 'desk and carpet and square modern armchair would share indissolubly in the moment'. The novel is set in times when a positive result was a death-sentence. As he realises how this fear is 'inside himself' and transforming him with its sublime power, he notices that 'the world around him, the parked cars, the cruising taxi, the church spire among the trees, had also been changed. They had been revealed.' Here, the idea of death undoes all the other stories we tell about the physical world. Without these illusions, we begin to see things with a new kind of clarity and immediacy. Walking through this exposed world, Nick is overwhelmed by beauty, not the beauty of the street itself so much as the fact of the street – that it exists at all.

But fiction can also question the very idea that we have any kind of relationship with things. What if the desk and carpet and armchair don't share anything with us at all? What if the moment of revelation is just another story we tell ourselves? In his 1956 essay 'A Future for the Novel', Alain Robbe-Grillet lobbies for fiction to reflect the superfluity of the physical world, the meaningless excesses of stuff that crowd our lives without defining them. It is notoriously hard to capture excess in literature, since everything seems put there for a reason. Spinning a credible world out of black-and-white marks is so strenuous that each detail, by its very inclusion in the story, must surely be pulling its weight, bearing at least a certain level of portentousness. The fact that a vase on the windowsill is mentioned, over the countless other things in a room, inevitably adds another brushstroke to the portrait of the home's owner. If a character notices this vase on the windowsill, does that not suggest something about her personality or at least her current frame of mind? In this respect, Robbe-Grillet argues, cinema has an advantage. The camera can transmit the countless things in a room without the sentence's blaring signal, that big neon arrow pointing at the vase on the windowsill. Although every object in the frame will have been chosen for certain effects, these objects have safety in numbers. Together they can live incidentally in the story, as do our belongings in reality. In their huddle, they are safe from the weight of symbolism, a future that Robbe-Grillet wishes for the next generation of novelistic things. He describes another kind of epiphany, one in which we realise that the stuff around us has none of the literary qualities so relentlessly bestowed on it in fiction:

> All at once the whole splendid construction collapses; opening our
> eyes unexpectedly, we have experienced, once too often, the shock
> of this stubborn reality we were pretending to have mastered.

Around us, defying the noisy pack of our animistic or protective adjectives, things *are there*. Their surfaces are distinct and smooth, *intact*, neither suspiciously brilliant nor transparent.

The goal, then, is for a novel to portray the 'thereness' of things, how they really exist. Ironically, even when he wants to release things from our literary, 'animistic adjectives', Robbe-Grillet still gives them the human traits of stubbornness and defiance. His view behind the scenes, on the other side of the 'splendid construction', suggests a world of obstinate objects, each resolutely itself, with its distinct surfaces. Robbe-Grillet's italics raise the word 'intact' to prominence. These insignificant things are fortified against our imposed meanings. They refuse to be breached, to be prised open by our symbolism, but nor are they, in their fortification, mysterious. They are not secretive. As Robbe-Grillet puts it, 'the surfaces of things have ceased to be for us a mask of their hearts'. They do not disguise themselves.

John Banville dramatises this brutal 'thereness' in *The Sea*. Having just returned from the hospital meeting in which his wife was told of her terminal cancer, the novel's narrator doesn't quite know what to think about the objects in his kitchen.

> There was an impression of general, tight-lipped awkwardness, of all these homely things – jars on the shelves, saucepans on the stove, that breadboard with its jagged knife – averting their gaze from our all at once unfamiliar, afflicted presence in their midst.

This is a classic piece of literary projection, a sort of pathetic fallacy of things, whereby the novel's material world responds to the trials of human characters. The couple's shock, the narrator realises, has arrived as a kind of profound embarrassment, mirrored in the 'awkwardness' of their possessions. But Banville's hero soon has the opposite thought. As the kettle carrying 'seething water' comes to the boil, he 'marvelled, not for the first time, at the cruel complacency of ordinary things. But no, not cruel, not complacent, only indifferent, as how could they be otherwise?'

It can be important to leave space for the immense indifference of our physical surroundings. In the last few years, this passive, unstimulating aspect of things has meant much to me. This may be because the quietness and the stillness of everyday objects is especially apparent when you are tending to the very ill. In stolen moments of solitude, surrounded by the inert matter in another room, you appreciate the disregard in which you are held. You begin to notice how the little jar on the desk, holding its motley spray of pens and pencils, doesn't need you. It doesn't ask that you rescue it. The invulnerability of the bookcase, the rows of books placid and safe on the shelves, starts to be important somehow. You are grateful that the furniture isn't deteriorating before your eyes, that it is neither frightened nor disorientated. Its steady indifference, when death is in the house, is a form of aloof affection. Their non-animation begins, in a strange way, to give them a negative life force. Negatively vivid, too, are the peaceful and mute arrangements between things. The downcast head of the desk lamp, at the end of its coiled, geriatric spine, leaves a tiny box of light and an asterisk on the edge of the pen jar. Because of the grille in the lamp's metal bonnet, the wall behind is striped with irregular bars. As W. H. Auden imagined Icarus's fatal plunge, 'the sun shone/As it had to on the white legs disappearing into the green/Water'. In your own room, as someone lies dying on the other side of the wall, a forgotten roll of wrapping paper sits, as it has to, on some papers and a file-folder.

The Internet of Things

The writer Elizabeth Bowen, working between the 1920s and 1970s, consistently imagined household things as containing the psychic residues of the people who moved among them. In her novel *The Death of the Heart*, the maid Matchett is a standard-bearer for Bowen's general attitude to inanimate objects: 'Furniture's knowing all right. Not much gets past the things in a room, I daresay, and chairs and tables don't go to the grave so soon. Every time I take the soft cloth to that stuff in the drawing room, I could say, "Well, you know a bit more."' People, I've noticed, get annoyed by this sort of sentiment. But Matchett's fanciful idea of furniture collecting information on us, becoming a cache of knowledge, is precisely what is happening now, with the arrival of Internet-enabled objects. Each time we make contact with them, staring into their interfaces, they learn something more about us. One of the effects of the booming industry of smart things is to quell any ambiguity over whether things are indifferent to us or not. With the arrival of what is generally called the Internet of Things (IoT), things are clearly invested in us. They are watching us and listening to us. They are built to be interested.

It is hard to tell, for a couple of reasons, if IoT is a passé or an avant-garde term. It was coined in 1999, and describes the collective outcome of embedding everyday objects with the capacity to transmit and receive digital data, connecting them both with humans and with other 'things' in their networks. Many people at this point have heard of it, though many others have not, even if they might already be participating in its conveniences. The IoT expands the possibilities of our interactions with the physical world, so that thermostats can be controlled remotely by phones, kettles respond to voice commands, lighting systems can play music or turn different colours, depending on the traffic reports for the morning commute.

David Rose, an MIT researcher, explicitly links these new devices to the very old idea of charms, referring to his inventions as 'enchanted objects'. He has designed an umbrella that flashes when rain is predicted, based on Frodo Baggins's shining sword, whose gleam warns of nearby enemies. His objects, he proposes 'are tools that make us incredible, supercapable versions of ourselves. These are the visions and stories of our most beloved authors of fiction and fantasy.' He believes that embedding these objects with not only a SIM card, but also a narrative – what he calls 'story-ification' – is the final stage in the production of enchanted objects. For example, his smart rubbish bin sends suggestions on what you should buy, based on what has been thrown out, and this rubbish bin is personified with a *Sesame Street*-style character who advises on what would be best for your health and what is currently in season. This, too, is for him a digital reinterpretation of an older, less tangible aspect of objects. 'Tools were practical, but they also told stories,' he writes, thinking of his grandfather's old hammer. 'They each possessed a lineage. They stirred emotions.' In this sense, the IoT is yet another way in which we project our stories onto the world around us.

Pete Trainor, author of *Hippo: The Human Focused Digital Book*, lives in a smartening house with an Amazon Echo speaker system, through which voice commands can be received by the personal-assistant software. He told me that his real excitement at the IoT is 'not the one device but the many talking [. . .] It's the ecosystem of these things that starts to become interesting.' He can tell the Echo to turn on the television, and the Echo will 'speak' to the remote control; if he wanted, he could incorporate a wearable device that would monitor his heart rate, which could instruct Echo to turn the television off after he has been dormant for too long. He suggests that how we establish our domestic ecosystems will determine how 'paternalistic' we want these devices to become. For his young children, this technology, as he puts it, 'blends into their world'. They understand that it is the same Echo voice that responds to them through multiple speakers in different parts of the house. The Echo is an ethereal and omnipresent phenomenon of his children's domestic lives. He laughs nervously as he describes how for them it is a 'God-like voice', as if aware of the overstatement while also finding it an irresistible comparison.

But who is the God here? The animistic ecosystem of smart devices, which gathers to talk to us via the singular personality of the personal assistant, conjures the idea of a kindly, immanent deity. On the other hand, the vision of the IoT is to create a world in which we are the objects of devotion. Microsoft's James Whittaker has predicted a near future of machine-made attentiveness, one in which his wearable device 'is going to know I'm travelling in Europe and I'm overeating, and it's going to tell my refrigerator when I get home, "Hey, man, this guy's unhealthy, you need to make sure you just order healthy food for him for a few weeks and let's get his statistics back together."' The IoT thus complicates the old master–servant binary by combining algorithmic affection with continuous discipline and surveillance. We may soon be able to command every domestic gadget with our voices, but who is really in control?

In *Gosford Park*, Robert Altman's film about life in the big, interwar English house, Helen Mirren plays the cold but efficient housekeeper. 'What do you think separates a good servant from the rest?' she asks an inexperienced young maid. 'The gift of anticipation [. . .] I know when they'll be hungry, and the food is ready; I know when they'll be tired and the bed is turned down. I know it before they know it themselves.' It's this kind of avid, servile attention that the smart devices of the future promise us. Such an arrangement inevitably alters our basic relationship to the world of things. A smart home may offer a digital approximation of Oceanic Feeling, where every surface pulses with life and where everything feels connected to everything else. But doesn't this constant attention on us – our metabolisms and indolence, the time we spend in the bathroom, our choice of broccoli florets – only serve to bring us more clearly into relief from the rest of the world? With our belongings so keen to define us, our individuality, our uniqueness in the universe, is daily emphasised. When the young maid in *Gosford Park* asks an older valet about his aristocratic employer, the valet replies: 'He thinks he's God Almighty [. . .] they all do.'

If everything becomes a smart thing, what will happen to the qualities of aloofness and indifference that have always been a part of our perceptions of the physical world? At the British Museum we can now perform a 'virtual autopsy' on a 5,000-year-old mummy. We are invited to 'discover his long-held secrets, from his age at death to the surprising way that he died'. There is a notable trend to make even the most solitary and reticent of things speak to us in some way. I have noticed an example of this while taking my London students on Dickens-themed walking tours. Out on the rushing Strand, our guide points over the bus stop to the church that sits on an island in the traffic. Dickens's parents were married there. Smartphones rise and fall. At the end of each of these spiels there is a pause, ostensibly for us to reflect on the weird miracle of history. But it is more as if we are all listening for something, for that silence which *is* history – the past's refusal to appear, to be present. The church will never fully indulge the old stories we tell of it. It seems more absorbed in the inarguable fact that, at this very moment and in no other exactly like it, the hands of its clock face are glowing golden in the sun.

On our way to Ye Olde Cheshire Cheese, one of Dickens's pubs, we pass through Gough Square and the Samuel Johnson House. Across from this museum there is a statue of Johnson's cat, Hodge. He sits on a bronze dictionary, with some bronze oyster shells upturned beside him. This is no transcendent work of art. The students are usually flagging a bit by now, full to the back teeth with history's steady refusals to appear. We form a distracted circle around Hodge, who stares off through brick walls and glass walls towards High Holborn. Statues, even more than ornate bannisters and church spires, dramatise the silence that is history. I watch the bronze cat interrogate my students, while looking over their shoulders. They are growing bored perhaps, or at least wishing they were back in control of their lives, and in the middle of them is Hodge, his stillness and quietness challenging the significance of their fleeting appetites: dreams of freedom, a sandwich, the WhatsApp Group Chats ballooning their pockets with neglect. The cat will outlast all these things. Statues are strange in their habit of enticing you towards them, only to ignore you. In this gap between attraction and repulsion, we can feel the fluidity of our desires, their exquisite feebleness, and our own lack of both will and ability to be transported fully into the past.

On one of these walking tours in particular, as a different collection of mortals straggle around Hodge, I see that the plinth bears a new sign. He has been enrolled in a 'Talking Statues' scheme. If you scan the QR code on the sign, you will receive a phone call. The cat will explain himself, in the meowing voice of Nicholas Parsons. Rather than being aloof, the statue has arrived in the present with a revived neediness. 'Take a good look at me,' he purrs, 'examine my expression.' In one sense, Parsons is taking over the job of our guide, an example of automation undermining the need for real-life, taxpaying workers. But what automation can't replicate, and indeed what it works to undo here, is the remoteness of the statue. In this new incarnation, the bronze cat asks for our attention. It seeks to entertain us. While we can choose not to receive a call from Hodge, the mere knowledge that the statue speaks, indicated by the sign on the plinth, punctures the aura of its essential stand-offishness. We live in an era suspicious of reticence, and so the quiet things of the world are being drawn into our pervasive love of interactivity.

There are many such statues across London, and in other British cities. Chicago also has its own chapter. 'Finally they get the chance to talk back!' says Ella Hickson, author of Peter Pan's speech from Kensington Gardens. This light-hearted initiative is emblematic of a contemporary desire to animate the world of things. The statue is made accessible rather than distant, becoming a trove of information.

In the same period that engineers and designers have been thinking about all the possibilities for the garrulous, sociable IoT, a philosophical school of thought has developed that seeks to understand the true privacy and reticence of the material world. Graham Harman is a leading philosopher in this approach, which is called Object-Oriented Ontology, a study of being (ontology) that places the existence of the individual object at its centre, rather than thinking about objects primarily in terms of their relationships with people. This is a radical way of perceiving reality. 'The recent philosophical tendency,' Harman points out, 'is to celebrate holistic interrelations endlessly, and to decry the notion of anything that could exist in isolation from all else.' He is tired of this addiction to the networked thing. A maxim of 'Triple O' is to 'look for the soul of the thing', which, although it might resonate with Marie Kondo's idea of the joyous object, is very different, because this philosophy doesn't seek to commune with such a soul, if it could possibly be found. Objects, Harman says, 'forever withdraw from view'. The concept of withdrawal is key to Triple O, and is the idea that an object's reality is mostly independent from how it manifests in relation to people and other things. We only experience a slice of any object's being. As Harman describes it:

> When a house is assembled from pillars, beams, baseboards, chimneys, and carpets, it siphons from these objects only the limited number of features that it needs. The house never fully grasps or even deploys the total reality of its stairwells and electrical cords, which withdraw from the house into the shadows of their private reality.

In this fantastic, speculative view of matter, we find the opposite of the linked-in smart home. We find instead a house of reticence, in which individual things retreat into their natural solitudes. 'The world is packed full with mutually isolated vacuums,' Harman writes, 'crowded together more tightly than drops of water in a drum.' While we don't have the scope here to unpack all the arguments of Triple O's metaphysics, or indeed its various hearty critiques, it is striking to place this general idea of a withdrawing universe beside prevailing attitudes about how we live among things. In this context Triple O becomes a lament for the non-networked object, for that which exists independently of our own designs.

The New Nausea

It isn't surprising that some philosophers have, in these times, lamented for the private lives of things. When connectedness becomes a burden, to speculate that there is a little vacuum around every thing in the universe is a fine consolation. To be connected is inevitably to be in some way responsible. If we were all entirely independent, there would be no need for morality. But this isolation isn't the name of the human game, and there is now a mainstream alertness to the fact that we live our lives within complex systems – global flows of capital, interlinked, planet-sized ecologies, the mysterious totality of images and representations that we call 'culture'. It's as though the digital networking of the world, as well as providing the infrastructure that connects us, made these other, older networks more vivid. If you have any agency in these systems, it's hard to disentangle yourself from this idea that you are somehow an accomplice to their effects.

And so, amidst this growing sense of our mutual interdependence, the concept of complicity has begun to proliferate.

Dictionary.com named 'complicity' the 2017 'Word of the Year'. To be complicit is to be involved in morally dubious activity. Interest in this concept spiked after a *Saturday Night Live* sketch in which Ivanka Trump, played by Scarlett Johansson, promoted a fictional perfume called 'Complicit'. Later in the year, Arizona senator Jeff Flake resigned from his position because he 'could not be complicit' in Donald Trump's governmental agendas.

A major feature of our modern relationship with things is that they communicate to us ways in which we are complicit. Rather than simply projecting ideas onto them – ideas about status, or their own magical properties – our possessions carry the irrefutable message of our involvement in the world. They draw us in, implicating us. Many of them reveal our financial complicity. More and more we ask ourselves: what or who am I supporting, when I buy things? Where does the business that pays my salary invest its money? Will the stuff that I buy with my pension in the future hold the memory of the shrouded funds from which this pension was derived? Is saving for a rainy day linked somehow to the selling of arms to oppressive foreign regimes? When J.K. Rowling wrote a tweet implying Mike Pence's gross hypocrisy surrounding the US Muslim travel ban, someone tweeted to her that they would burn their *Harry Potter* books and DVDs because of her political views. Rowling's reply was both witty and stark, laying bare the difficulties of severing our connections: 'Well, the fumes from the DVDs might be toxic and I've still got your money, so by all means borrow my lighter.' While J.K. Rowling is hardly the dark centre of the intricate web of our economic guilt, the phrase 'I've still got your money' is more broadly haunting. Our sense of complicity, manifest in our belongings, can't be so easily cleansed. The connectedness is preserved, even if the thing itself is destroyed or given away.

A kind of vertigo sets in when we begin to consider our material possessions in terms of their economic provenance. The scale of our connectedness to both ethical and malevolent enterprise is a modern-day sublime. When I think about my own things in this way, they seem to vibrate with a reality that I can't fully grasp. The chains of association are too lengthy and coiled to tease apart. Jean-Paul Sartre's existential philosophy deals more fundamentally with how questioning the true provenance of things can be a dizzying experience. In his treatise *Being and Nothingness*, he writes about moments in which the sheer fact of the existence of things is 'disclosed to us by some kind of immediate access', a moment of realisation. This is Sartre's version of the RADA rooftop, but without the sense of peace and harmony. In his view, the connectedness of all things is a sign of their absurd contingency. He asks us to consider how the world is here, all around us, and full of stuff, and yet how unlikely it is that things should have come to be arranged in this way. In order for our living room to appear exactly as it does, on this day, an unimaginably complex series of events had to occur in precisely the way they did, going back to what we often call the big bang. This awareness of both the fragility and the abundance of things, which are so specific despite being so precarious, comes for Sartre with a feeling of overwhelming nausea. Or, more precisely, the nausea brings this awareness into being.

Sartre's 1938 novel *Nausea* dramatises this grotesque vision of connectedness. It follows a young man, Antoine Roquentin, who suffers from sporadic realisations of this kind. He suddenly feels that the common-sense way of dividing up reality into distinct things, with sharp edges and stable names, is an illusion. During his nauseating epiphanies, he experiences the world as a quivering, absurd totality of 'monstrous masses'. Moments of nausea are repeatedly marked by the world of objects spilling over their boundaries, losing containment. Everyday solidity and the differentiation of one thing from another subsides into a ghastly, sweet sludge. The nausea is 'made of wide, soft moments, which grow outwards at the edges like an oil stain'. Roquentin begins to feel horrified and demented by this insinuating oneness of all things. As physical objects merge into one another, so does the distinction between himself and the material world begin to break down. He tries to buttress himself against this hideous subsidence. 'Objects ought not to touch,' he writes, 'since they are not alive. You use them, you put them back in place, you live among them: they are useful, nothing more. But they touch me, it is unbearable.' He has the sudden feeling that things are coming alive as he holds them. He records how 'there is something new about my hands, a certain way of picking up my pipe or fork. Or else it's the fork which now has a certain way of having itself picked up.' When he takes hold of a door knob, it 'held my attention through a sort of personality'.

One day, a plush velvet seat on a bus becomes a great, grasping thing, with 'thousands of little red paws in the air'. To calm himself, Roquentin thinks about how it has been manufactured for a purpose, the leather and springs made and brought together. He tries to call it 'a seat' in his mind in order to define it, to bring it back into itself, to enclose it with language. At the heart of the nausea is the inability to tell whether he is touching things or if they are touching him. 'Things have broken free from their names,' he thinks. He feels both penetrated by them and absorbed into them in a nightmare version of interactivity. When he thinks too deeply about these ideas, he blames himself for adding to the absurdity of the world. He feels 'responsible and complicit'.

Eighty years later, we are vulnerable to comparable feelings when we think about the overwhelming interconnectedness of things. The dread of a seemingly inescapable complicity is a twenty-first-century nausea. And in no other area of life do we feel more inescapably complicit than in our contributions to environmental damage. How often do things 'come alive' for a moment in our hands – the carelessness followed by gloom as we pick a plastic fork from the sandwich shop and drop it into our paper lunch bags ('Better than plastic, but [. . .] the trees!').

For me, the empty tuna can is the thing that is most replete with my ecological complicity. As I stand at the sink with the can in my hands, washing it out, I wonder if I'm just rearranging deckchairs. Or perhaps I'm steadfastly, diligently 'doing my part'. Neither may really be true. There's a suitable element of danger in its lid, hanging and twisting like a sharp, loose tooth. I think about over-fishing and cling to the hygienic words 'pole and line', written across its side. Will mercury-poisoning be my punishment? My mother was famous for craving tuna while pregnant with me. I was calling out, making her complicit! I try not to think about how the can came in a pack of three, sucked together in a plastic sleeve.

While Roquentin calms himself by thinking about how the bus seat was made, how it came rationally into being, this strategy is often of no use to us. If a bottle of shampoo 'comes alive' in our hands, it will probably not help us to think of its provenance: the palm oil tucked shyly in its ingredient list, the devastated

Indonesian rainforests, the deep, humiliating gaze of an orang-utan, the supermarket worker on a zero-hours contract, factory jobs lost to automation, the parental megacorp of the shampoo company's range of dynamic investment opportunities. We might see the shampoo bottle's future too, fearing for the millionth time the great hoax of recycling. We see it bobbing endlessly in the South Pacific. Don't we have exactly the opposite problem to Sartre's brooding existential antihero? Is not the very remembering of an object's chain of production a reliable trigger of our nausea?

The Bureau of Linguistical Reality, an American art project that collects new names for the feelings particular to our age, has given the term 'Tralfamidorification' to this unsettling way of perceiving everyday objects. The inspiration for this neologism comes from Kurt Vonnegut's four-dimensional alien race, the Tralfamadorians, who can see all moments of time all at once, allowing them to experience every object in the full totality of its existence: past, present and future gathered together. The Bureau defines Tralfamidorification as 'a disorientating experience where a discrete object becomes a node on a network'. They give the example of seeing a beach towel in two ways: as simply itself – a warming strip of material on the sand – and also as a 'black hole of information' about how it was made and at what costs. During Tralfamidorification the thing intimates its history, and then this black hole closes again and we are left looking at just a gaudy old beach towel, innocent under the sun.

In his novel *10:04*, Ben Lerner describes this sort of disorientation, the new nausea. The approach of a superstorm towards modern-day New York City provokes the narrator to think about the 'miracle and insanity' of global consumerism. He picks up a tin of instant coffee from the shelf in the market, a handy staple for when the storm hits:

> I held the red plastic container [. . .] held it like the marvel that it was: the seeds inside the purple fruit of coffee plants had been harvested on Andean slopes and roasted and ground and soaked and then dehydrated in a factory in Medellín and vacuum-sealed and flown to JFK and then driven upstate in bulk to Pearl River for repackaging and then transported back by truck to the store where I now stood reading the label.

He feels his hand 'glowing' with the social relations that the storm threatens temporarily to suspend, with its power outages and closed airports. He is made conscious of the 'majesty and murderous stupidity' of all the forces that assembled this commodity into a thing, a boring tin of instant coffee, to be grasped from the grocery-shop shelf. In other words, our twenty-first-century objects are inevitably experienced as networked matter. They divulge their histories, unable to contain themselves.

We are thus confronting a new kind of connectedness in which our oneness with all the world's stuff is rewritten as the problem itself. Our behaviour is framed here as a polluting force, diffusing through the system. We are the oil spill; we need to be contained. Our present way of being 'at one' with the world is destroying it. The nausea isn't about contingency but complicity, the question mutating from an existential to a more purely moral one. The urgent question is not how everything came to be here, but, more precisely, how am I involved in how this came to be? As the object-philosopher Timothy Morton puts it, the universe is full of Tardis-like things, 'all bigger on the inside than they are on the outside'. When we consider our relationship with the physical world in these terms, the thing seems to crack open and reveal an ineffable, impossibly large circuitry, letting us glimpse the reality of our compromised position in the world.

Fake Off

Edward Heron-Allen, who delivered the cursed amethyst to the Natural History Museum, wrote an autobiographical story about the affair called 'The Purple Sapphire'. The owner of the magic stone wonders fearfully, 'Is this horrible Thing, after lying quiet for forty years, going to wake into renewed activity?' Similarly, for the philosopher Martin Heidegger, who in 1950 gave an influential lecture on 'The Thing', the ancient philosophical question 'What is a thing?' is like a charmed object. The question's animation as an urgent existential issue can seem to be over and done with, but is in fact just lying dormant. It is, for Heidegger, 'a historical question', the significance of which returns to haunt us, again and again. At any point in history we have what seems to be a 'natural' relationship with the objects around us, but this naturalness is itself a product of historical circumstances. 'To determine the changing basic position within the relation to what is,' Heidegger argues, 'that is the task of an entire historical period.' He suggests that the historical way of thinking about things, 'which seemed long past but was in truth only stuck and since then rested, is brought out of its quiescence', a state of inactivity. As we reanimate this question of what a thing might be, in a world where things will decide when we've watched enough television, the notion of quiescence itself will become increasingly vital to the debate.

We're beginning, for instance, to realise the importance of preserving the possibility of quietness in our smart devices. That poetic uncertainty about whether the spatula is bashful in the presence of our big occasions, or whether it simply hangs there from its hook, indifferently and almost imperceptibly trembling, has a counterpart in the ambiguous on/off status of our networked devices. It is both unsettling and not surprising that such an ambiguity has been allowed to be coded into these first IoT generations. Part of our discomfort comes from the fact that we don't seem to have full control over their animation. There are well-known tales of Internet-enabled fridges leaking passwords rather than water. In Germany, a smart doll that could listen and speak to its owners was banned over security fears, and because it is illegal there to disguise a surveillance device as something else. The idea of our phones and other devices being 'Fake Off' is a growing concern. In 2017, reports emerged of the so-called Weeping Angel spyware program, which was able to hack the microphone of certain Samsung smart televisions. With the microphone hacked, and the television apparently off, private conversations could be recorded and transmitted to CIA operatives at the other end of the wireless line.

In a world of Tardis-like things, the spyware was suitably named after *Doctor Who* villains, a race of malevolent beings with both physical and immaterial forms, who hijack electronic equipment and travel through screens. The Weeping Angels' material body resembles a winged Victorian grave-statue. Statues have long been associated with provoking uncanny feelings, since one cause of uncanniness is an uncertainty as to whether a thing is alive or dead, animate or inanimate. While the uncanniness of emerging commercial robots is often discussed – with their tilting, inquisitive heads and juddering smiles – much less remarked upon is that unspectacular but insistent uncanny of the domestic smart device. Is it on, or is it off? Is it listening to me? Is it awake? In this sense the Weeping Angels, as animated statues that freeze when they are directly looked at, only to revive themselves in the literal blink of an eye, are an apt metaphor for the fake dormancy of our devices.

The word 'device' itself derives from the Old French *divis*. When the French word entered English, it could refer not only to notions of boundaries and divisions, but also to a huddle of more shadowy concepts. A 'device' was also a scheme, an intrigue, a disguise. Here the old sense of the word persists today in the feeling that our devices, especially as they become increasingly interconnected, are up to something beyond our control. Our new complement of household things will be strange creatures, their attention potentially divided between domestic duties and external business interests. As Pete Trainor cautions, we 'absolutely have to be very concerned [. . .] because we've built an awful lot of stuff that's monitoring us, without really all that much knowledge of where [the information] is going'. Your lighting could well be moonlighting: a Truly Global Desk Lamp. In this sense our things will be increasingly disintegrated, always excessive and dispersed, breaching their own physical boundaries.

And yet, in another respect, smart things are paragons of containment: they keep the secrets of their extracurricular activities. They withdraw into their own private realities, obscuring the full portfolio of their investments and agendas. Unlike the indifference of secular objects, de-animated and disrobed, the digital device is a return to the masked thing.

At least, isn't that how they can appear to us, these smart-talking gadgets? We look at them and wonder. Their peculiar version of quietness can seem not an act of indifference, but of dissimulation. In this state of ambiguity, where we can't know for sure the limits of their sensitivity to us, they resemble Heidegger's definition of quiescence, containing 'a fullness of being and reality which, in the end, essentially surpasses the reality of the real'. Their presence in our imaginations as both servants and informants can make them the most real, most vivid things in the room, especially in their moments of apparent inactivity. As Heidegger suggests, 'Quiescence is only a self-contained movement, often more uncanny than movement itself.'

Our ideas about reality have always had to contend with the inescapable double mystery of objects. Am I somehow connected to everything in the universe or are other things fundamentally untouchable and unknowable? Are inanimate objects truly as indifferent to me as they seem, or are they in some way interested, for good or ill? Does that thing have magical properties beyond my perception? Old questions reawaken in new forms. Today, our realities are unsettled by the particular, relentless intimacy we share with so many things. While smart devices snuggle down deeper into our personal lives, we increasingly see ourselves – our own moral failings and laziness – in the things we consume. A can of tuna isn't always just a can of tuna, but, on certain days, an interface between me and a matrix of culpability, doubt and helplessness. The thing is always more than itself. Although object-oriented philosophers are interested in the 'withdrawal' of things into themselves, in the commodity culture of late-capitalism, it can be unethical to preserve the privacy of objects, to imagine them as coherent, isolated creations.

And so here we'll live, until things become different again, with these new kinds of intimacy, with dizzying connectivity. The old literary device of pathetic fallacy – that poetic connection between the human and the inanimate world – no longer seems so fallacious. Our era's particular way of feeling connected to material objects – the loveliness, the fun, and the guilt of it – defines to a large extent the reality of these times. When King Lear is raving on the storm-blasted heath, he is more troubled by 'the tempest in [his] mind'. We are sometimes more prone to the reverse problem: we see our own faces, outside, in the gathering, ever-changing clouds.

CHAPTER 3

Optical Disillusions

The early twentieth-century French philosopher Henri Bergson saw in the burgeoning art form of cinema a metaphor for the apparatus of our own minds. He argued that, for sighted people, visual perceptions of reality involve a sort of internal camerawork. '[T]he mechanism of our ordinary knowledge,' Bergson writes, 'is of a cinematographical kind.' One of Bergson's main projects as a philosopher was to understand how we comprehend movement and change. How do we experience things moving in time – not simply a tree branch swaying in the wind or a ball flying into a football net, but the slow, incremental change of people around us growing older, or an apple slowly ripening? The problem of how we perceive what he called 'becoming' was central to Bergson's work. In our minds, how does the ball that sits for an instant on a striker's foot *become* the ball that rests, cruelly for another instant, on the outer tip of the goalkeeper's glove? He suggested that, like the new and fascinating cinematographs of his era, 'We take snapshots, as it were, of the passing reality' and then animate them, one after the next, on a kind of screen in our minds, 'at the back of the apparatus of knowledge'. In this way, the movement of our perceptions from one snapshot to the next imitates the ceaseless changing that is reality itself – that built-in drive that things possess to become different things over time.

For Bergson, this camera-like mechanism places us outside reality – we don't live inside the flow of real movement, but instead reconstitute it, just as a camera-person is always to some extent outside the scene they are filming. Our reality is in this sense always artificial, the series of snapshots propelled into a moving image by the restlessness of our perceptions. As Bergson describes it, 'The application of the cinematographical method therefore leads to a perpetual recommencement, during which the mind, never able to satisfy itself and never finding where to rest, persuades itself, no doubt, that it imitates by its instability the very movement of the real.' Our restless minds mimic reality's constant evolution from one moment to the next. What's more, our cinematographic natures inevitably give shape to the stories we tell, influencing the grammar of our thoughts and how we construct a sense of the world. To say 'the child becomes an adult' is to imagine two fixed points, between which lies an infinite series of other frozen instants, which we flutter, like flipbook stick-people, to get from one endpoint to the other. Given their positions as nouns in this sentence, the snapshots of 'the child' and 'the adult' seem to have solidity, as if such fixed things are the primary constituents of our experiences. There are CHILDREN. These CHILDREN become ADULTS.

But Bergson believed that our 'snapshot consciousness' is impoverished because a series of still images shown in fast succession can't capture the essential mobility of the world. This movement is always missing from the picture; it 'slips through the interval' between one of our mental snapshots and the next. Bergson calls this movement 'becoming'. As a basic unit of perception, the snapshot inevitably misses this 'becoming', instead presenting fixity as the essence of what is real. Bergson explains Greek philosophy's interest in quintessential forms and universal, immutable ideas as resulting from this snapshot consciousness. But what would life look like if we saw things in terms of their 'becoming' rather than these immobilised illusions? What if we could stop being camera-people? Then the story, the sentence, would appear radically different: 'The child becomes the adult' would have to be rearranged to raise 'becoming' to its rightful prominence. The new sentence would be: 'There is *becoming* from the child to the adult.' While this reordering likely reads as nonsense, Bergson would say that this is because we're used to thinking primarily in fixed approximations – in nouns that give an unreal stability to things – instead of focusing on what is really there: an ever-changing movement, a 'becoming' that is 'reality itself'.

As exciting as it might sound to experience, rather than merely imitate, life's ever-unfolding 'becoming', the latest neuroscientific research suggests that we're stuck with being camera-people. Bergson's metaphor, which was untestable in his lifetime, is now proving to be highly prescient. Of Bergson's 'tantalising' theory, the neurologist Oliver Sacks writes that, 'It has only been in the last twenty or thirty years that neuroscience could even start to address such issues as the neural basis of consciousness.' It appears that we have a physiological affinity with cameras that places the distinction between us and them in soft focus. Abnormal neurological states, as Sacks explains in his essay 'The

River of Consciousness', reveal how the apparatus of our perceptions do indeed resemble a cinematic projector. In such unusual states, our vision can stall for several moments on a single, frozen image, as though the movie reel has jammed. Sacks describes how 'it is decomposed vision – the flickering, perseverative, time-blurred images experienced in certain intoxications or severe migraines – which above all lends credence to the notion that consciousness is composed of discrete moments'. Under normal conditions, our brains convert these individual impressions into fluid experience, the same trick that makes Hollywood possible. Much remains unclear about how our brains animate these discrete units of perception. 'Whatever the mechanism,' Sacks concludes, 'the fusing of discrete visual frames or snapshots is a prerequisite for continuity, for a flowing, mobile consciousness.' Over a decade since Sacks wrote this essay, there are ongoing attempts to refine our models of these perceptive building blocks. While our minds are clearly not identical to cameras, the cinematographic imagery persists.[1]

1948

In French, the word *cliché* means a snapshot. Is our consciousness, then, naturally built out of clichés? We translate the word to mean

---

1. A 2016 study by Michael H. Herzog et al. focuses on the 'time slice' rather than the snapshot, but this model relies on an idea that there is no perception of time during the initial phase of unconscious perception, and that 'When unconscious processing is "completed," all features [of the thing perceived] are simultaneously rendered conscious at discrete moments in time'. The authors maintain the snapshot analogy, but propose that 'the snapshots represent integrated, meaningful outputs of unconscious brain processing'.

exhausted phrases, images, ideas, behaviours and situations, which somehow obscure us from a nuanced version of reality. Some clichés have worn themselves out by appearing *too* real. That is to say, they have proven too usefully representative of reality. Their obliging approximation of realness makes them overly tempting, so that many different things are drawn inside their limited frames. Like a snapshot, clichés immobilise life, fixing it in place, shielding us from the particularities of what they pretend to describe. The visual origins of the cliché highlight our dilemma about the role images play in our construction of reality: do they bring us closer to or further from what they represent? Bergson's hypothesis that our snapshot-minds miss the truth is just one version of the ancient debate about whether we ever experience reality or just some shadow-play version of it. But now that we move through the world collectively producing images of real events with an unprecedented intensity, this central ambiguity that has always surrounded the image becomes especially crucial to explore.

Our minds may have resembled cinematography before that art form was invented, but since the digital camera has become one of our most prevalent technologies – at our sides in almost every scene of our lives – we are camera-people in two senses. Research published in late 2016 showed that of the 3,000 US millennials surveyed, 24 per cent said that the camera was the most important feature on their phone. Another survey found that 72 per cent of US millennials consider it 'very important'. Almost half of these respondents agreed with the proposition that 'without the camera the device is practically useless'. In looking more generally at the most prized aspects of smartphones, multiple studies have found that after the basic needs of a phone's life are met – battery durability, screen resilience, water resistance – the quality of the camera is the most valued. As I write, *Wired* magazine has published an article featuring the 'mobile photo gear' that I'll need to become a somebody on Instagram, including a small portable light diffuser, for 'an even glow of photons splashed across [my] face', and a 'compact, 2-pound tripod'. And whether or not we particularly prize the camera function in our daily lives, the fact is that with a smartphone in our pockets, we are quiescent camera-people, waiting for the right conditions to come to life.

It's likely that the majority living in a technological society thinks daily about cameras. To say that we live in an age of surveillance is an observation that manages to be both banal and urgent. We understand, with paralysed resignation, that we're being watched in all sorts of ways. We startle each other with new examples of eavesdropping, of hijacked webcams, of idling smartphones butting in on face-to-face conversations, supplying ads related to our pillow-talk. And yet most of us are only startled to a point. The motivations for and debates about surveillance are intellectually simple, while being politically complex. References to *1984* are now so common that Big Brother is both a clichéd metaphor and a useful shorthand for the status quo.

Although our eyes and expectations are adjusting to the glare of the various cameras trained on our daily movements, our role *behind* the camera's lens is less remarked upon. As well as 1984, we should be paying attention to the symbolic value of 1948, the year when Edwin Land sold his first 'Land Camera', later known as the Polaroid. It is the year of the instantaneous image's origins. Anyone watching a young child's beseeching lunge for the smartphone, as soon as they have been photographed or recorded, is seeing the after-image of Land's inspiration. He devised the instant camera after his daughter immediately wanted to look at the picture her father had just taken. Rather than the one-way, panoptic gaze of institutional surveillance, 1948 heralded the two-way street of mainstream amateur photography, where we are as likely to be behind the camera as in front of it.

You will have noticed that new pose of the last few years, the half-smile and the concentration as we hit Record. We have seen it in others; we've felt it on our faces and in our bodies as we hold up our phones in front of us and keep them there. We're like magicians, frozen in the act of showing the predicted four of clubs. The arrival of the spectacular, the cute, the unusual, or the unrepeatable prompts this urge to capture the moment. The results are often hilarious – absurd amateur footage of a corgi riding a pony around a dark field is one offering that comes to mind. Advertising, as ever, looks for the quintessential form of our shared behaviours. A recent Samsung ad shows a man, pained with wonder, craning over a hospital bed where a newborn baby lies squirming. He holds his Samsung Galaxy S8 over the baby, hitting Record, making minor adjustments to the framing. Samsung's slogan is 'One generation's impossible is the next one's normal'. As a symbol of the future, where a life begins not with the first breath but with the first tap of a red circle, the baby is the focus of the vignette. Critics of pervasive surveillance no doubt interpret the scene as an infant beginning its documented life, under the teary-eyed, domesticated gaze of Big Brother. Others, remembering the old-fashioned creak of a baby album, may tell the critics to get a grip. But what is this 'normal' for the father? What are the implications for our sense of reality, now that there is a generation of camera-people permanently in our midst, capable of capturing life, at all stages, as it unfolds?

Not long ago, our newfound, casual ability to be camera-people would have sounded like a thought experiment. What if humans had gills? What if humans could glow in the dark? What if humans could record the world around them, at will, and broadcast it almost instantaneously? This is surely the headiest power in our overnight suite of digital talents: the capacity to transform into a roving news crew. The change is an existential one, affecting the very texture of what we consider to be real.

Home Movies

Let's go back, for a moment, to that 'not long ago' when a day in front of a camera was like a day on a different planet. When my maternal grandmother turned eighty, we rented a video camera for the first of two times. It was June 1989, the year the Berlin Wall came down. We were in the process of moving to Canada; the decade and our home were soon to change; and the day we filmed the small family garden party was hot, a school day in the ageing summer term, missed for non-glandular reasons. Life! Newcastle! This moment in June. The presence of the camera matched this spirit of modernity and maturity. My brother moved around us with the hefty black box covering his face. He had a new, menacing prestige, but equally a new invisibility, bordering on social irrelevance. I skipped between the circle of wicker and deckchairs, lighting on laps for a moment and then flitting away. As a nine-year-old I was buck-toothed, mulleted and what used to be called effeminate. 'Mum's having a mental affair with the butcher,' I told my aunt, parroting some recently overheard gossip.

79

Everyone laughed. I dangled and swayed from some sitting relative's neck. Was I hamming it up or was this my normal chattiness? Feeling about in my memory, I can't quite make out the shape of the camera's influence.

I say that everyone laughed, but it's unlikely that my grandmother did. The video evidence, scanned obsessively over the following days and then all but left to the spiders, showed her watching the festivities with barely concealed contempt. She may have been tired, dyspeptic, self-conscious – of both the attention and the camera – or perhaps less than enthused by this landmark. As my paternal grandfather said on one of his ancient birthdays, with people cheering and singing all around him: 'Isn't there a little room for sadness?' My granny was by then a small Northern Irish woman with airy, whipped white hair, a birthday girl chewing peanuts with a face of thunder. When my mother saw the tape she was darkly tickled by this accidental portrait. I think it laid bare for her a central difficulty of her mother's personality, perhaps justifying some of the stresses of having brought her and my grandfather to live with us many years before. In the garden I didn't notice the morose guest of honour, distracted no doubt by a new game of kicking a neon-green inflatable ball into the air for the camera. On the playback we discovered that the rackety microphone amplified each kick into a resounding metallic crack, making it seem, as the ball whizzed out of shot, that I had hoofed it up into the heavens.

Yes, I remember that cracking sound. Since my English childhood was only visited by video cameras twice – the second occasion was the following year, on our farewell tour of Newcastle before emigrating to Canada – I can strongly feel their effects on my memory. The remembered garden doesn't have the quiet weather of that sunny afternoon, but instead the air rasps and heavy-breathes. Now and then, as the focus shifts, there is the sound of a giant's footsteps on the flagstone. I see myself from outside, that flirty sprite, in among the grown-ups. Only the angles caught on camera come readily to mind. I have no easy, parallel set of remembrances; it's as though the camera's images have eclipsed my own perceptions. The exceptions to this are a few narrow visions of my brother looming around. While at the time the camera gave him a sort of transparency, he is solidified in retrospect because he is the only person missing from the official record. Since he wasn't in the shot, my memory has to supply him.

The act of being filmed has certainly shaped my sense of what happened that day. On one hand, I can visualise the party in much more detail than other lost days – the camera was a gift in that sense. On the other, my own mind's record of what happened seems to have been suppressed. The reality that persists belongs to the camera, not to me. The generation below mine is the first on the planet who can so readily look upon themselves in motion, five seconds after the motion has occurred. What impact will these instant, micro-retrospectives have on how their memories are formed? There are surely consequences that will need to be managed 'going forward'. Or is it looking backwards?

A couple of years ago I took my young niece for her first tennis lesson. She wasn't much younger than I was in that garden. My brother – him again! – started to film her. This time his face wasn't clamped to a big black box. Instead, he held up his slim phone in front of him, the standard magician's four-of-clubs pose. After a few minutes of studious low-to-high swinging, she fell into a new rhythm of running to the net after every successful shot to see the replay. It was real 1948 stuff. From Bergson's theory of reconstituted 'snapshots' to a new theory of 'time slices', the model of how our consciousness works is always a question of what happened in the recent past. Michael H. Herzog et al. – the neurologists who developed the time-slice model – propose that our mind's consciousness of a visual stimulus can be as much as 400 milliseconds behind our initial perception of it, a significant lag. And so our second camera, the one we hold in front of us, creates an exaggerated parody of this lag. It creates in us the compulsion to see reality looping back on itself, even more than it apparently already does. I feel a version of my niece's agitation when I go to watch matches at Wimbledon, when the seconds between points can seem deprived and vacant. Without the slow-motion playbacks and admiring analysis from Chrissie Evert, you're stuck with life, borne ceaselessly into the future.

The Unseen

When cinematography first appeared in Europe in the late nineteenth century, there was a great deal of excitement. An early, fascinating consequence of this art form was that there would be more reality than there used to be. The new camera technology was not merely meant to duplicate life as we already see it, but to extend the powers of human perception. For one thing, the camera could slow down and magnify the world. A famous and good example is Eadweard Muybridge and Etienne-Jules Marey's 1878 recording of a running horse, which showed, frame by frame, how a horse's two sets of legs curl together in mid-air, a fact that was difficult to detect during the blur of a gallop. It's true that this innocent excitement wasn't the whole story: Muybridge was an expert in cynical self-promotion and dissimulation, reusing the same pre-made cloud pattern again and again over different landscapes, or posing, for the purposes of documentary convenience, one Native American as a member of a different indigenous people. He helped to expose the reality of the running horse, but he also used his skills to obscure. As we'll see, there is no shortage of ambiguity and contradiction in the figure of the image-maker.

Nevertheless, an animating spirit of these technologies was certainly one of revelation, a scientific campaign against the unseen. Another pioneering piece of cinematography, *Grandmother's Reading Glass*, plays with the camera's magnifying powers. Filmed in 1900 by George Albert Smith of the influential Brighton School, it is an early experiment in close-ups. A boy stands next to his seated granny, inspecting his surroundings with her large magnifying glass. That cinematic convention, aged and weary by my childhood, of denoting a telescope's perspective by framing a circle of action in black, was a novelty for Smith. In close-up we see a newspaper advert for Bovril, a pocket watch, a bird in a cage. And then the boy turns the glass (and therefore the camera) onto his grandmother, her cheek and eye visible through the circular peephole. Her eye rolls with comic nervousness from side to side and up and down; above, her eyebrow flexes and, below, the puffed skin twitches.

As a medium, film quickly became a way of bringing attention to the often ignored but foundational details of daily life. For this reason, Walter Benjamin found resonance between Freud's big project to map our hidden selves and the early technologies of the moving image. 'The camera introduces us to unconscious optics,' Benjamin suggests, 'as does psychoanalysis to unconscious impulses.' Footage that could be watched multiple times – and slowed down and zoomed in – allowed people to analyse how our moods alter the way we hold a tumbler or handle a cigarette lighter. Minor gestures could be dissected for meaning, the camera curing all kinds of everyday blindness. Things that had been proximate but unmapped, like our hidden motives and repressions, were now the objects of scrutiny. More than bringing news of unimaginable, far-flung places – though that was certainly a priority – cinematography was from the beginning a personal business, whose thrill was the exposure of our intimate invisibilities. Under the camera's gaze, reality becomes more real, which is to say it becomes less obscured. The premise was that more detail results in more truth.

Every modern era has felt its accelerated pace of life compared to the blessed snail's pace of the past, but we seldom describe an age in terms of magnification. Today, we've brought this idea of magnified reality to a totally new level. Whereas the viewpoint of early film was a separate, wonderful mode of seeing that sat apart from daily life, our vision is now trained on the close-up view. The viral video is an exemplary genre here. The 'gone viral' phrase has proven surprisingly popular, given its epidemic tone. As a medical metaphor, it evokes the contagiousness of images, as well as the fevered way we pass them around the world. But it is also a visual metaphor: in order to see a virus we must view it under an enlarging lens. To go viral is itself an act of magnification: the zeroing-in and zooming-in on a moment, the focusing of a collective gaze.

These certainly feel like magnified times. You'll remember how those first months after Donald Trump came to power were the season of handshakes. Whenever he was introduced to a world leader, a clip of the encounter reliably appeared. Politicians and first spouses swerved past him to greet someone else. Our interest zoomed in on the dreary macho calculus of whose knuckles were pointing where. Should Theresa May have touched him on the stairs? Before the election, the late-night host Jimmy Fallon was criticised for ruffling Trump's hair because it produced too gentle and playful an image of someone with such violent plans. In this case the image was condemned for obscuring, rather than revealing, truth. 'Optics' of the political sort, while not a new term, is now a commonplace one. The more the idea of 'optics' is repeated, the more reality comes to be composed of sets of legible images, to be both manipulated and dissected.

But behind politicians' self-conscious photo-op strategies, viral videos during the handshake season also isolated peripheral reactions, where some truth did indeed seem to exist, subtly, at the edges of the official tableau. Buzz Aldrin's fatigued range of sighs as Trump extolled the economic and political benefits of space gave momentary comedy. The kinds of footage that are now readily available – press conferences, speeches, amateur videos – are often long, static shots that bring us back to the stasis of early cinema. While Hollywood's shot-lengths have been steadily decreasing under the assumption that rapid cuts suit the oft-cited atrophy of the modern attention span, we are, in parallel, becoming experts in the opposite. We have reverted to the study of Benjamin's 'unconscious optics', whereby we scan a scene for its memorable, minor details. One bizarre YouTube compilation shows multiple moments in which a seated Trump casually moves nearby objects away from him: he clears coasters like air-hockey pucks, pushes papers into the middle of tables, slides a colleague's glass of water to the side. Psychologists are understandably keen to diagnose him, despite the professional restraints of doing so at a distance. Nevertheless, a psychology professor at California State University appeared on CNN to talk generally about what this habit can indicate, linking it to anxiety or to a narcissist's fidgety boredom. In this way, the video image of real events, no matter how curated, is seen as a potential repository of truth, giving us access to a more complete picture of *how things are*.

Benjamin describes film's potential to bring us closer to the real in terms of old containments being flung open, of walls coming down:

> Our taverns and our metropolitan streets, our offices and furnished rooms, our railroad stations and our factories appeared to have us locked up hopelessly. Then came the film and burst this prison-world asunder by the dynamite of the tenth of a second, so that now, in the midst of its far-flung ruins and debris, we calmly and adventurously go traveling.

The first motion picture by the pioneering Lumière brothers reflects this sense of cinematography as an act of unlocking. Dating from 1895 and prosaically titled *Workers Leaving the Lumière Factory*, the film is a single shot of a wide, open doorway, through which stream the home-bound labourers. They have the edgy gait of this cinematic period: the women wear hats and high-waisted skirts; the men are in suits and boaters. There are three versions, distinguished by the number of horses that come through the doors. With the plot being so simple (home-time!) and the angle unwavering, your eye begins to scan the scene as if it were a moving painting. In each version there is the slapstick of a dog getting in the way of a cyclist, darting off and loping back, or scarpering at the sight of the carriage emerging through the crowd. There is the touching humanity of seeing such long-dead people moving about in the evening light.

A century after Benjamin's exhilaration, the dynamite is almost always sizzling. Many of the old prisons have turned to rubble. Once-sealed spaces have become opportunities for interaction; private chambers have turned into communes. It's not unusual on social media to see those tolerated interlopers – friends of friends – 'check in' to hospitals for surgery. I remember one picture of a stranger's hearty thumbs-up, IV swinging, well-wishes billowing beneath them. Birthing rooms and funeral services are other televisual landscapes of the timeline, through which we are invited by others to go adventuring. In places of political unrest, the ease with which we can all now be camera-people has allowed the proliferation of 'media activists' whose images communicate the realities of war and other extreme situations.

The documentary *Frame By Frame* follows the rise of photo-journalism after the Taliban fell in 2001. It was a crime under the Taliban to take a photograph, and in the subsequent years there has been a 'photographic revolution'. For many Afghans, it is morally imperative to document the devastations of the war in images. One such journalist argues that the wide circulation of photographs and videos from her ravaged country is of huge political importance. 'This is the main time,' she says, 'for Afghan photographers to really stand up and to still keep Afghanistan in the [international] news.' Likewise, another commentator describes these images as nerve-signals that alert the global community. In his vision of our interconnectedness, 'The world now is like one body, so all the members of this body should know that one member has a pain.' There obviously remains great danger. The Pulitzer Prize-winning photographer Massoud Hossaini feels sure that the Taliban will eventually return, and that he 'will be faced with the revenge of the extremists'.

As well as professionalised activists, it is common now for amateur videos to be incorporated immediately into the public record of 'what happened'. For instance, Diamond Reynolds has been hailed for the bravery and calm of her Facebook live-stream from the passenger seat of her car, in which she captures, as both film-maker and subject, the horrific aftermath of the Minnesotan police shooting of her partner, Philando Castile. While Castile lay dying from his injuries, Reynolds's four-year-old daughter was in the back seat. Reynolds said in an interview that she wanted the video to be a kind of testament. She wanted to ensure that, 'no matter what, my side, his side, our side of the story could be viewed by the people and they could be the ones to decipher [it]'. The video is intensely harrowing, not least in Reynolds's polite, tactical use of 'sir' when addressing the police officer, who can be seen in the video, still pointing his gun through the window towards the motionless Castile. For her, it was a way of reclaiming the reality from whatever future, official story would be told.

Reynolds's hasty footage also showed a yellow pine-tree air freshener hanging upside down from the dashboard. In *Camera Lucida*, Roland Barthes's study of photography, he describes the seemingly incidental details in images that strike him in some way. He calls this kind of detail the image's *punctum*. 'However lightning-like it may be, the *punctum* has, more or less potentially, a power of expansion.' For me, this pine-tree was one punctum in this tragic video. In its practical ordinariness, it seemed to expand the interior of the car, made unreal by violence and terror, to include the whole life of this family, pulled over for a broken tail light.

As instant, on-hand camera-people, we can circulate images that corrode the misused powers of institutions and governments. In 2017, the world's attention was momentarily caught on footage from a United Airlines flight, in which multiple passengers filmed a man being forcibly dragged up the aisle after he refused to give up his seat to crew members. Vast international audiences were horrified to see the details of the brutality: how the man's shirt rose to expose a pale strip of his stomach (another punctum) as he was pulled along the floor, his shrieking refusal, the blood on his face. What would once have gone unseen by all but a hundred people is made globally visible. Old walls are indeed coming down; each click of our pocket cameras, skeuomorphically added to smartphone shutters, is the sound of a key turning in a door.

The Forked Image

Cut to Dundas, Ontario, 1990, a year since the garden party. Our new home on a suburban estate has mutton-coloured siding. I passed much of that first Canadian summer deciding whether to be Master Splinter or April O'Neil in my imaginary games of *Teenage Mutant Ninja Turtles*. These were my two choices, since the four amphibian heroes were too boysy for me to get on board with. For Master Splinter afternoons – in the cartoon he was a ninja master who mutated into a humanoid sewer-rat – I would wear my grandmother's deep-blue dressing gown as his kimono, and wrap tennis socks over the flats of my feet to simulate his iconic bandaging. When I felt like being the roving news reporter, April, I would crouch under furniture, in the midst of a perilous scoop. When things got too much, I called for mutant-ninja help, my sister's make-up compact doubling as April's flip-up, turtleshell hotline to her subterranean gang.

When a live-action movie version of *TNMT* was released in 2014, I was interested to notice one difference between the cartoon and the film. In the original 1980s series, the cameraman character, Vernon Fenwick, was April's nemesis, a scoundrel who repeatedly tries to pass off her scoops as his own. But in the live-action remake, Vernon is now Vern and, endowed with the handsome charms of actor Will Arnett, is April's trusty sidekick. He continued to be on the side of audiovisual justice in the 2016 sequel, recovering some footage from a security camera that exonerates his falsely accused colleague. This deviation from the original is a fitting change. Unlike that day in the warm garden, when my brother circled us with his dark glamour, being a camera operator is now as exotic as owning a watch. And so Vernon's metamorphosis from traitor to ally is consistent with our personal identification with those who wield the camera. Now that we're a generation of amateur camera-operators, we need heroes in our own image.

In the popular imagination, the photographer or camera-person has always been an ambiguous figure. The family tree is, from the beginning, dramatically forked. On the one branch we have the eyewitness, the war reporter, the media activist, the freedom-fighter, and on the other we have the spy, the traitor, the creep, the phoney, the profiteer. With recording equipment being standard-issue in the contemporary pocket, the two sets of intense archetypes associated with the camera-operator are now of mainstream concern. Smartphone videos are a new check to authoritarian power, while also spreading the phenomenon of revenge porn. One moment we can catalogue racist tirades in supermarket queues; in the next, Instagram's photo filters let us 'brighten up the moment' by adding a beam of sunlight to our selfies, 'even if the sun isn't shining'. The cultural history of the camera-operator reflects the inherent binaries of image-making: reality and artifice, wonderment and cynicism, social conscience and amorality. The modern reinvention of Vern Fenwick in the *Ninja Turtles* movie represents a crossing from one branch to the other.

From the beginning, the double nature of the camera-person is on the record. The opening captions of Buster Keaton's silent film *The Cameraman* (1928) read: 'When acclaiming our modern heroes, let's not forget *The News Reel* Cameraman [. . .] the daredevil who defies death to give us pictures of the world's happenings.' Cue shots of brave fellows on the battlefield, stooped over tripods and turning the camera-handle while the world explodes around them. Here we see how the heroism of the media activist has always been part of our story of the camera as a technology of justice. But the next caption reads: 'And there are other sorts of photographers.' At this point we see unheroic Buster on a New York street-corner, offering to take outmoded 'tintype' portraits of passers-by for a dime. This distinction between the hero and the 'other sorts' remains a central rift in our ambivalent relationship to the camera.

Buster the tintype photographer decides to get serious after meeting Sally, a secretary at MGM Newsreels. He spends all his savings on a better camera and, with Sally's help, gets some leads on breaking stories. His professional and romantic rival is Harold, an established cameraman at MGM. At the end of the film, Harold is driving Sally around in a speedboat when he loses control and they go overboard. Harold saves himself, while Sally is trapped in the centre of the speedboat's deranged orbit. Luckily, Buster is passing by with his camera and the organ-grinder's monkey that he has adopted on his adventures. Buster rushes into the water to save his unconscious love, pulls her to shore and runs off for medical supplies. In the meantime, Harold staggers back to find Sally, who awakens in his arms, and he passes off the rescue as his own, the cad. But when Buster decides to send some of his old reels to the MGM execs, they find among the footage the truth of the speedboat drama. The clever monkey, unbidden, had filmed the whole caper. Harold gets his comeuppance and Buster's bravery wins him his sweetheart, the two camera-people dividing into hero and creep.

You might remember that a similar device was used years later in *Friends*, to reignite the will-they-won't-they saga of Rachel and Ross (who also owned a monkey). Old home-video footage of prom night captures Ross's moony love for Rachel, and shows him heartbreakingly getting ready to be her last-minute date, when it seems like her original guy has stood her up. ('Be cool,' he urges himself quietly.) Back in real life, grown-up Rachel is so touched by this bygone gesture that she moves trance-like to where grown-up, mortified Ross is cowering by the door, and kisses him. The sitcom audience shrieks and howls joyously, in the time-stamped fashion of the age. As with Buster Keaton's cameraman, the loser-hero is accidentally vindicated by recovered film, and in both cases, vigilante recorders capture truths absent from the certified history.

But the camera-person trope also has its darker aspects. Often the photographer or camera-person cuts an ominous figure. In Don DeLillo's *Mao II*, a woman called Brita visits the house of a reclusive writer called Bill Gray to take his picture. After the shoot, the author's assistant tells her that the visit has somehow disrupted them, taking something of their peace. 'There's a lot of planning and thinking behind the way Bill lives and now there's a crack all of a sudden. What's it called, a fissure.' The epilogue to Alice Munro's *The Lives of Girls and Women* outlines a novel written by one of the characters, which tells the story of a photographer arriving in a small Ontario town. He is linked to a girl's suicide, and we're told how the 'pictures he took turned out to be unusual, even frightening. People saw that in his pictures they had aged twenty years.' In Sam Mendes's film *American Beauty*, the monotone, inscrutable boy-next-door, Ricky, is seen as both an unsettling weirdo and a soulful aesthete. With a camcorder at his eye, he placidly records moments of loveliness, from fluttering plastic bags to bloodied corpses, at once on the margins of social life and utterly absorbed into the film's idea of the real world.

Ricky is a good example of how, as well as often being a morally forked figure – either sneak or saviour – the camera-person is presented, by turns, as being absorbed into and distanced from life. Their avid attention to their surroundings places them at the centre of things, and yet the camera removes them from immediate experience. Two early representations of cinematography, when considered side by side, symbolise this uncertain relationship to reality. Consider this split-screen view of a (very) short film called *The Big Swallow* set beside the 1915 novel *Shoot!* by Italian writer Luigi Pirandello. The film was directed circa 1901 by James

Williamson, also of the Brighton School, and is remembered as the first to use an extreme close-up. It stars a gentleman in boater hat protesting and shaking his head at the camera. 'I won't!' he seems to be saying. He moves steadily nearer to the camera, wagging his cane in consternation. Soon he is so close that only his mouth is in the frame. Slowly his bowed lips open, and into the dark chasm topples the tripod, followed by the poor cinematographer, whom the man then munches contentedly.

If *The Big Swallow* shows the camera being pulled into the gaping maw of reality, *Shoot!* suggests the opposite. Its subtitle is 'Of the notes of Serafino Gubbio, cinematograph operator', and Gubbio has much to say about how the camera warps the life of the person charged with turning its crank. While working for a movie company, Gubbio broods on his machine, imagining it as an insatiable, carnivorous entity, a 'black spider on its tripod, which eats and is never filled'. In Pirandello's scenario, it is the cameras that have the wider mouths, into which the outside world goes tumbling. As Gubbio puts it, 'The life swallowed by the machines is there, in those tapeworms, I mean in the films, now coiled in their reels.' Gubbio finds his job title ironic because he believes that he operates nothing, viewing both himself and others 'from a distance'. The novel is his extended meditation on the existential consequences of being a cinematographer. He describes himself as an 'automaton', nothing much more than a hand that turns the handle. 'The chief quality,' he writes, 'that is required in a man of my profession is *impassivity* in face of the action that is going on in front of the camera.' Gubbio sees himself as the person who throws the actors into the cage where the camera waits, 'the man who strips them of their reality and offers it as food to the machine; who reduces their bodies to phantoms'. In his own mind, he is a slimy accomplice. 'Here am I,' he thinks, 'creeping forward again, my dear ladies. Ever so slowly, yes.'

Shades of this jaded impassivity appear elsewhere in the camera-person canon. In *Tootsie* (1981), set around a fictional hospital soap opera, the cameramen are world-weary and dour, as 'friendly' as a 'firing squad', according to one of the regular actors. When one of them is asked to pull the camera back to make 'Tootsie' (Dustin Hoffman in drag) 'more attractive', he replies drily, 'How do you feel about Cleveland?' In *Boogie Nights* (1997), cynicism is unsurprisingly rife in the 1970s Los Angeles porn scene. For those on the edges of the action, the bouffant hanky-panky has become old-hat. Burt Reynolds plays a director of 'exotic movies', whom Roger Ebert describes as 'a man who seems to stand outside sex and view it with the detached eye of a judge at a livestock show'. It takes the arrival on the scene of ingénue Dirk Diggler and his thirteen-inch penis to rouse the blank-eyed crew's attention. The sound guy, a young Philip Seymour Hoffman, gives a little gasping pant while trying to keep the boom steady, and the veteran cameraman tilts his head from behind the camera, as if Diggler's impressive display deserves, and perhaps even needs to be confirmed by, an unmediated view.

Away from the movie set, this impassive quality becomes more sinister when the camera-person intentionally profits from documenting other people's real-life disasters. The paparazzi flashes striking the windows of Princess Diana and Dodi Al Fayed's smashed car were real-life symbols of this terrible cynicism. Jake Gyllenhaal coldly embodies this animus in the film *Nightcrawler* (2014), in which he plays an eerie LA loner looking for money after the 2008 crash. Finding work as a 'stringer' who provides footage to news networks, he haunts crime scenes and road accidents and sells the film to a local news station. In this satire, the ruthlessness of capitalism fuses with the amorality of the moving camera. When a rival stringer starts regularly beating him to the scoop, he slashes the man's brakes and then films him dying at the roadside. At an affluent house in the wake of a shooting spree, he films the bloodied victims without checking to see if they are alive and can be helped. He tricks his partner into being shot by the armed robber, so that he won't have to share the profits of the scoop with him, and then he films him too, edging his camera closer and closer while the dying colleague looks up at him in horror. The wide-eyed, mask-like expression that Gyllenhaal maintains for much of the film mimics the impassive stare of the camera itself.

A precursor to *Nightcrawler* is *Medium Cool*, set in Chicago during the political and social tensions of 1968. This film makes explicit the debate over the camera operator's uneasy position. It opens on a highway, where a car has crashed into a traffic light. A woman is splayed out of the door and two TV news journalists – with a camera and sound equipment – circle the wreckage. The scene is quiet and calm. 'Better call an ambulance,' one says to the other, as they walk back to their own car. A lively party follows, where a group of camera-people discuss the profession. They suggest America's hunger for gruesome images, with 'eyes glued to the screen when the blood starts running'. As with Pirandello's melancholy cinematographer, there is the sense that the machinery itself robs people of both agency and responsibility. The soundman from the car accident confesses that he is 'an elongation of a tape-recorder'. Others in the circle insist on the active, hazardous role of those who bring back footage from dangerous situations. Here we return to the notion of the newsreel camera-person's courage, compared to 'other photographers'. Once again, the figure of the photographer is bifurcated: are they heroes or vultures?

The end of the film is an ironic echo of its opening, with the original camera operator crashing his car into a tree, only to be photographed by rubber-necked passengers hanging out of a passing vehicle. The last shot is another example of the camera as a devouring device. Our view broadens from the burning wreck, showing further up the road a cameraman on a scaffold, who is also documenting the accident. He seems part sniper, part executioner. The disembodied chorus of the protest song 'The Whole World is Watching' – presumably coming from the nearby demonstrations – drifts across this road, and the cameraman on his platform slowly turns his camera towards us, the audience. Our own gaze is pulled into the darkness of the lens, which engulfs the final frame.

The history of the camera-person's place in the cultural imagination thus reveals the extreme duality of this figure. We are dealing here with a cleaved trope, one that strips life of its reality while also revealing that which *really* occurred. When camera-operators appear in books and films they tend to cast an uneasy shadow across the scene. Are they absorbed in the present moment – more alert and focused than anyone else – or are they distanced from it? Are they, in other words, within or without? They are portrayed, by turns, as sinister and intensely moral, capable of immense bravery, wicked opportunism, as well as a particularly vicious brand of apathy. Since we have become these camera-people ourselves, we have inevitably inherited this polarised image. The camera, too, is rendered ambiguous, both an unflinching eye and a toothed machine, consuming whatever it sees. Taken together, the two-faced operator and the *camera dentata* make an intimidating partnership. And with this combination's new cultural centrality, long-held anxieties about the status of the image are increasingly contagious.

The Distrust Economy

Since life can now be so readily turned into film, what will become of that which is left out? Our digital cinematography may be bringing acres of the unseen into view – the *seen* unseen – but how will the reality of the stubborn, *unseen* unseen change in this detonated world? For something to be fully realised, will it have to have been caught on-camera? A useful analogy that keeps with our architectural theme of reality is the structural revolution that occurred to the home in Tudor England. A long-held theory was that the wish for increased privacy caused the demise of the communal 'great hall' and the rise of more partitioned dwellings. But newer research has challenged this idea, saying that the cause and effect should run the other way around. The argument is that the space in the Tudor home became divided for various economic reasons, and that this brought certain novel kinds of privacy into being. All of a sudden, people could be alone, behind closed doors, or perhaps meet clandestinely on staircases. Far from being the point of the renovation, these privacies were unwelcome or at least suspicious by-products of this architectural shift. Privacy wasn't necessarily a desirable goal, but a problem created by new floor plans.

We can use this idea to think about the future of our unseen moments. While the Tudor example involves a rearrangement of space, digital video is rearranging our relationship to time. Their space was subdivided; our time is being opened out. Think of the pre-digital past: that vast collection of unrecorded moments, obscured behind the walls of the present moment. For those of us of a certain age, the essential experience of our personal past is its relentless privacy. It is elusive, returning on its own terms, in bursts of recollection. We might say that it haunts us, or else we see it in glimpses, through cracks in the wall. But the proliferation of cameras is building a new kind of temporal architecture. The digital image opens vistas onto past moments, even ones that we weren't present to witness, allowing us to see what *really* happened in them. But this ability to make the past an open-plan experience will transform our relationship to unrecorded experience. Will we be able to believe in that which has no visual corroboration? Just as the Tudors could be unnerved by the new secrecies of the closet or private chamber, the closeted nature of the unmediated past will become a source of doubt and mistrust.

More and more, the younger people I observe photograph the world as though it's a crime scene. Students know the value of evidence, saving screenshots to show that an essay has been uploaded correctly. They stand up at the end of class and take pictures of the whiteboard. People now regularly talk about 'keeping the receipts', which refers to any sort of digital proof – emails, voice messages and texts, as well as images – which will shore up your position in personal or professional disputes. Businesses are now offering this kind of corroborating evidence as part of their service. *Tailster* is a company that provides a fleet of dog-walkers. Its ad promises the following: 'With GPS tracking, maps and photos, our trusted walkers don't just tell you your dog has been walked, they show you.' The word 'trusted' makes *Tailster*'s assurance read like a joke. Surely a dog-walker who must provide a dossier of digital evidence, including camera footage of the morning romp across the heath, is a *dis*trusted employee. Their word alone is clearly worth nothing. Trust is based on belief rather than certainty; there is no need to trust anyone about anything, in a world of empirical proof. If all events can be corroborated with visual documentation, then trust evolves naturally into certainty, and beliefs become knowledge. The ability of digital technologies to produce and store evidence – maps, videos, paperless trails durably catalogued in vast databases – is warping our concept of trust, making it stand, ironically, for its opposite.

In this new order, trustworthiness is not so much a moral quality as a condition of not having to be trusted at all. Trust used to involve a mental venture into one of two temporal darknesses: an unstable idea of the future or the blank of some unknown past. I trust you will walk the dog, or I trust you have walked the dog. Trust in the present tense is the result of a spatial blindness. I trust that you are walking the dog while I'm at work and can't see you doing it. A clear consequence of Tailster's style of customer service is that one's word comes to seem like an outdated, inferior technology. What will happen to the dog-walkers who don't film and GPS-track these jaunts? Will they come to have the air of danger associated with bootleggers, pirates, drug-dealers or other outlaws who offer goods and services without commonplace standards of accountability? And how will we be coerced more generally into this manic archiving? It could be that our own tales from the recent past will take on a new shadiness in the absence of some illuminating digital corroboration. Did that *really* happen? people will say. Show us. This way of dealing with the past treats it as being insultingly shrouded.

Apps are often wide-open windows onto our society's anxieties. 'We-consent' is a suite of apps designed to engage with the reported American crisis in sexual trust, particularly among university students. These apps subscribe to the primacy of video evidence: sexual partners use one app to record themselves agreeing to the upcoming encounter. The obvious flaw is that such evidence doesn't accommodate the fact that consent is an ongoing negotiation, rather than a snapshot of a moment's feeling. The second app in the suite, 'What-About-No', tacitly acknowledges this problem. In this app, an unconsenting partner can hold up a video of a cop shouting 'No!' into the denied partner's face, and the app will film them watching it. We-consent emphasises that the apps' main utilities are 'the discussions they evoke', rather than the video record itself. But while such 'consent' apps are easily derided, they are part of a new paradigm in which private exchanges can be swiftly converted into public record.

But as we trust more completely that the image will tether us to reality, there is, not coincidentally, a simultaneous erosion of civic trust. A global survey, recently published by the advertising and strategy group WPP, reports that only 40 per cent of citizens worldwide trust their government. 'Declining levels of trust in government,' the report concludes, 'have undermined the connection between those who are governed and those who govern them.' The World Economic Forum supported this idea in a White Paper positing that 'Growing social distrust and demands for greater transparency are reshaping relations between society, government and business.' But it is precisely this ability to achieve greater transparency that fuels social distrust. Vigilante camera-people are agents of such transparency; their images turn planes into test tubes, brick walls into Plexiglas. We are able to see, better than before, just how untrustworthy people in positions of power can be. Software that enables amateurs to edit pre-existing footage has made YouTube abound with powerful home-made montages of a politician breaking his or her promises from one speech to the next.

In his 1995 book, *Trust: The Social Virtues and the Creation of Prosperity*, the political economist Francis Fukuyama argues that 'a nation's well-being, as well as its ability to compete, is conditioned by a single, pervasive cultural characteristic: the level of trust inherent in the society'. He was referring predominantly to the ways in which economies are run – whether by close-knit, nepotistic networks or more formal, distanced arrangements between parties. But besides the important exposing of political corruptions, what happens to our social exchanges when the origins of trust are routinely relocated from the moral sphere to software? If the digital trace is becoming a primary badge of reliability, is the currency of our 'word' – that analogue talisman against the unknown, the unseen, the unrecorded – permanently devalued? I have had my first student sending me a selfie displaying the physical signs of her illness, as part of her own dossier of exhibits supporting her plea for an essay extension. It is likely that I will be seeing more such evidence in the future, as students sense a new kind of arms race of the image, and the subsequent incredibility of the old-school, plaintive, apologetic email. Trustworthiness, after all, is not an absolute virtue, but is technologically determined by the type of proof that can be reasonably expected.

Barthes believed that the invention of the photograph marked a historical shift in how we perceive reality because it allowed us to say with more assurance: 'That was there.' He wrote in *Camera*

Lucida that 'Every photograph is a certificate of presence' and, since we no longer had to rely on mercurial memory to confirm what was there, he felt that in this new period 'the past is as certain as the present'. If only we could still share Barthes's confidence in the image. New concern for our sense of reality is emerging in the form of 'deepfakes' – digitally manipulated videos in which the face of one person is put on the body of someone else. Deepfake technology has come into public view because it has been used to create hybrid porn clips that seem to star Hollywood's female leads. This 'face-swapping' software, which uses AI machine learning, has been turned into an easily accessible app. This type of image might be a credible masquerade of presence, but it is certainly no certificate of it. While deepfakes may become popular as a gross way of externalising private fantasies, they may have more fundamental consequences. Deepfakes' potential for framing people, for putting words in their mouths using vocal-manipulation software, is clear. As an article in *The New York Times* points out, 'Fake video and audio may become so convincing that it can't be distinguished from real recordings, rendering audio and video evidence inadmissible in court.' And so that old treachery of images persists here in new guises: just at the moment when it seems that we can all use video footage to make our claim on what undeniably occurred, the very reliability of such imagery is being compromised.

For Barthes, the photographic images of his time were curious for being both boldly affirming and physically frail. They were made of paper and perished easily; sunlight faded them and moisture ruined them. Before photography, he argues, monuments were a permanent record of the prevailing idea of *what happened*, but 'by making the (mortal) Photograph into the general and somehow natural witness of "what has been," modern society has renounced the Monument'. And so, he implies a paradox: the photograph makes reality both more and less certain – its content verifies a view onto the past, but its fragile form means that this verification is only temporary. Ours is this issue in reverse. Our photographs are no longer frail in the papery sense. Digital images are replicable and durable in unprecedented ways. But they can also be manipulated much more easily and unrecognisably. They are paradoxically more permanent and more changeable than their analogue relatives.

It's not surprising that, in these untrusting conditions, Flat Earth Theory is currently enjoying a surge in prominence. This cosmological conspiracy model assumes that extraterrestrial footage of our planet is part of a complex space-race hoax. We are supplied with fake pictures of a spherical Earth, it argues, in order to perpetuate the master-lie of Earth's rotundity. The Flat Earth Society writes on its Wiki page that its members 'do not lend much credibility to photographic evidence. It is too easily manipulated and altered.' To accept the theory entails a retreat into immediate perception, as well as the shutting out of scientific explanations for the nature of reality: water sitting level in a glass, rather than sloshing around at 70,000 miles per hour; the agreeable flatness of your neighbourhood on an evening stroll. Flat Earth Theory is one extreme symptom of fatigue, in a world saturated in digital imagery. As a movement fuelled by distrust, it rejects the mediated view.

In the history of political optics, Buzz Aldrin resurfaces here, too. For the Flat Earth community, he is a particularly vocal fly in the ointment, always ready to 'take to Twitter' to challenge their claims. He posts photographs of his dusty footprint on the moon's surface, or his drifting exit from *Apollo*, making sure not to lock the hatch on his way out. Neil Armstrong may have been the first person to walk on the moon, but he was also its first cameraman. As a result, Aldrin held centre stage. With a 70-millimetre Hasselblad camera, Armstrong took these pictures of his pilot, as well as the famous, hesitant photograph of Aldrin standing in the Sea of Tranquillity, Armstrong himself reflected as a tiny highlight in Aldrin's visor. The idea that the *Apollo 11* landing was fake is fundamental to Flat Earth theorists, and so once again we see the camera-operator, however unevenly, cleaved in two, symbolic of both valour and deception.

The Best Picture

Just as the notion of 'the story' can refer either to what really happened or to a ruse, so the photographic image is a similarly two-sided representation of reality. Our uneasiness about such images extends into our sense of the people who produce them, with the camera-operator embodying the image's doubled potential as either testament or fraud. This tension between verification and manipulation, exposure and obstruction, which is inherent to the image, isn't a new problem. Nonetheless, the stakes are exponentially higher now that so many of us are image-makers. The more we live in images, the more vulnerable we become to a technology that can both enhance reality and, increasingly, use it as material for the most plausible fictions.

Herzog et al.'s study on 'time slices' suggests that the brain allows such a long lag between our first experience and awareness of a certain stimulus because it 'wants to give you the best, clearest information it can, and this demands a substantial amount of time'. As well as the obvious moral objections to deepfakes, we should be appalled by all purposely deceitful imagery, out of respect for this constant, hidden micro-industry of our minds. In Herzog's model, during its first, unconscious 'processing stage', the brain discerns the features of objects, such as colour and shape, assembling as accurate a profile of reality as it can, before presenting it to us as a conscious perception. The dignity of this invisible labour, in the face of growing trickery, deserves the hardiest of protections.

'How are you?' my friend asked. 'Give me a cliché.'

'Taking each day as it comes?' I said.

I am talking on the phone, pacing around my parents' empty bedroom in the middle of the day. He has just heard that my mother is sick. His blunt request is a kind of tenderness, an acknowledgement that severe illness can burden you with the stock bravado of an underdog politician. You're suddenly the leader of the third-biggest party, white-knuckling the podium at the TV debate and describing how you will govern the country. 'I believe we can do this, if we work together.'

When it comes to writing about illness, clichés stick to other clichés. Molasses everywhere. On being diagnosed with lung cancer, the writer Jenny Diski told a *Breaking Bad* joke at her oncology appointment, and then worried afterwards that this was a tired gag. For her, diagnosis seemed to set a 'ball of clichés rolling', both as a patient and as a writer. 'Another fucking cancer diary,' she thinks, at the same time as deciding that she will write a cancer diary. She remembers other people who have written about their cancer 'journeys' before her. Now I think of Jenny Diski and feel the cliché of worrying about cancer clichés. There will be wigs. There will be headscarves. I remember my mother's many doctors' visits in snapshots, or rather short little GIFs: standing above her while she is seated, being shown a wig, a standard-enough portrait. But I zoom in, against my wishes, on her fingers testing the fibres like a sample of fabric. There is the punctum.

When things were looking bad, I asked an older friend how it felt, to miss parents who have been gone for decades. We were in an airport in Carcassonne. He said: 'They're still dead and you still love them.'

I nodded. That was one snapshot of the future I could handle, one idea that should be fixed, rooted around for in the miscellaneous box of Platonic Forms. Because when they have been gone for a while, there is always a struggle against turning them into capital-I Ideas.

During one of our two dalliances with home-videos, my mother stood at the top of the stairs while my brother filmed her from the hall below. Without comment she slowly climbed onto the bannister and slid down it. I think of this piece of home-video more than any other. It was the first time I had ever seen my mother existing entirely independently of me. It wasn't like seeing her in the distance, or listening to her while she talked at whale-song length to a friend's parent. This was total separation in close-up. I remember watching her careful slide, on our television in the living room. She put her chin on her shoulder as she went, looking right at me, but without any of her normal attentiveness. The whole thing seemed out of character – there was an element of physical danger – though I admired her for knowing that the camera expects something, a show of some kind. I studied her through the screen and wished she hadn't done it: to me, it seemed there was a long drop onto a hard floor. But it was all right, she had done it. I was watching her move through the past, without me. In that short little clip, she was free from any of the maternal clichés: interest, awareness, a besotted smile. We were lucky enough to get plenty of these but even while I laughed at her antics there was something frightening in the scene. My mother had become a person. Or, rather, there was becoming between my mother and a person. Not a snapshot, not an idea, but a kind of taking flight.

PART 2

Double Vision

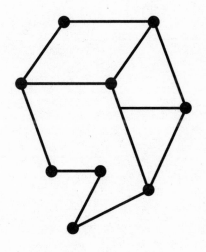

CHAPTER 4

Backstage Pass

Obscenity is always an indication that the social order is beginning to dissolve.

Ludwig Marcuse

I was an intermittently feeble child, a connoisseur of the mucky throat. My fingers were attuned to finding and swivelling neck glands, and then, with a veteran field-doctor's sigh, I would recommend another day off school. This congestive frailty reportedly came from my maternal Irish side. During fevered nights, images of lancings and of the mysterious, phlegmatic ghoul of 'diphtheria' stretched off into the darkness. My school reports would curtly wish me 'better health next term'.

One early evening at about the age of six, I was called down from my sickbed to find that my lovely form teacher, Ms Rowlands, was in the living room. She had brought me some catch-up work, and I remember how she sat side-saddle on the settee, with her suede boots pressed together. I was awestruck to see her, in real life as it were. When she had gone I asked if she was married, as if I had suddenly been awoken to the fact that she existed beyond the school gates. My mother, who wanted me to look life in the face wherever possible, guessed divorce.

I never forgot this visitation because of the sheer strangeness of a teacher in the living room, with her handbag on the floor and her car keys in hand. Anything suggesting a private life of these daytime stars came with a particular frisson. Another of my sickbeds was interrupted by a deranged snorting and panting at the bedroom door, and in came a different teacher's famed but until then unseen Great Dane, followed by her slightly less exotic husband pulling the beast back from my bedside table, followed by Mrs Bloomfield herself.

This visit was part of a star-cross'd courtship between my parents and the breed, and shortly afterwards we had one of our own, a terrifying smoke-coloured hulk called Penny. She was meant to cheer me up, after another bout of mucky throats. Her tenure with us lasted only ten days. After lakes of pee on the hall floor, a buffeted granny, and a persistent uterine issue that consigned Penny to wearing a pair of my mother's underwear with a hole cut for the tail, my parents weren't devastated when the dog bolted from the back garden one morning. Mrs Bloomfield was involved in my mother's half-hearted search party; I remember her flying in anguish from assembly, and only later learning the reason why. Penny was spotted and tracked by a neighbour, but by then the affair had obviously curdled and Mrs Bloomfield reallocated Penny to a less fickle family.

It was eerie to have Mrs Bloomfield, that matriarch of my public life, involved for the first and last time with my home world, a witness to our family's tireless capacity for giving pets away. But these kinds of sporadic crossovers, as memorable as celebrity sightings, are now part of the static of everyday life. The modern distinction between our private selves and our public personae is no longer maintained as it was a generation ago. The personal lives of those with whom we deal professionally are often on constant display. The intimacies of the home are a spectator sport. On social media, partners message each other, parents message children, quarrels play out in fractious bursts of the timeline. The author Caitlin Moran once gave a characteristically emphatic illustration of this when she urgently tweeted her husband, from somewhere else in the house, to bring her up some toilet paper. I wonder if children today still find the same humour in hearing their parents answer the phone, a dying-out activity in itself. My siblings and I would often tease both our parents for their 'phone voices' when talking to strangers, which seemed so composed and mannered and false. They might only have been adopting a reasonable tone with which to engage in some boring piece of business or other, but to us even this slight change was marked and helplessly comic.

Today, our private and public realities, our inner and outer worlds, coexist in a way particular to these times. The horror movie *Unfriended* (2015) is about a girl who kills herself after some humiliating drunken footage of her is circulated online. The girl's ghost wreaks revenge on a group of friends, one by one, while they chat on a group Skype call. The webcam view onto a scene of paranormal torture is suddenly obscured by the latest victim's Skype-profile picture. One moment there are screams of anguish or spurting blood, the next we cut to a frozen picture of the same terrorised teen in happier times: wearing a woollen hat with animal ears, or full of youthful vanity, flexing biceps. This collision of the real and the mediated is a macabre version of a common experience. We're often confronted with the poignancy of a troubled friend's unflinching Facebook grin, or privy to the sorrow behind their online gaiety. Putting on a brave face is nothing new but, traditionally, we haven't been able to display two faces at once, to be simultaneously brave and despairing. We now inhabit a reality in which our public composure runs in real-time parallel with our private woes.

This overlapping of the public and private self is arguably this era's most influential feature, deeply affecting our aesthetic and political experiences and redrawing the boundaries between truth and falsehood, reality and fantasy. For what is the endpoint of such exposure? In Tom Rachman's story 'Leakzilla', a hacker divulges the world's private emails and makes them publicly accessible. In the aftermath, most people were 'either apologizing, or refusing to. Bank details and home addresses and phone numbers gushed out. Lawsuits followed; divorces, above all.' As one character observes of personal relations, 'maybe a bit of fake is what's required to be decent'. For others, the realities laid bare in this routine unmasking of private life will lay the foundations for true political progress.

Obscenities

I learnt early that the merger of your private and public lives could have oppressive consequences. Teachers crossing from the classroom and out into the wider world were not always magical occasions. One morning during school assembly an impromptu trial opened and closed, with charges reviewed and punishments delivered. Two boys from the top class were called out by name and made to stand. I remember the brave, defiant backs of their heads. To me they seemed about eighteen years old, but were probably pushing eleven. Their crime, as laid out by the head-teacher, was that of riding on the same bicycle in heavy traffic, one of them hanging onto the shoulders of the other. She had seen them do this the afternoon before, on her drive home from school. From my place in the surrounding ground cover of cross-legged children, I was wowed by this portrait of swashbuckling, after-school street-life, so different from my own high-security escort to the beloved patch of carpet in front of the television. Their major crime, on the afternoon in question, was to engage in this reckless behaviour while still in uniform. They were setting a bad example, bringing disrepute onto all of us. Perhaps it was easier for their prosecutor-judge to claim institutional offence than to admit that she cared for their safety. But I remember feeling a sense of unfairness at this policing of their after-school hours. Our uniforms suddenly seemed so treacherous for causing this clash between our public life inside the school gates and our private home-time, when other prosecutor-judges took over.

There will have been demerits: a black square felt-tipped next to each of the boys' names on the chart pinned to the back wall. I find myself thinking of these faceless boys more and more in recent years, as it has become clear that we're all in our uniforms, now, all of the time. Most people are cautious of the fact that anything they post online, even when ostensibly part of a conversation between friends, could be used as evidence against their public, professional character. Although Twitter users make the threadbare disclaimer that their views are their own rather than their employers', this boundary has become increasingly permeable. The head-teacher's after-school beat expands ever outwards. Our new status as camera-people certainly facilitates this easy publicisation of our private moments. Juli Briskman, another disgraced cyclist, was forced to leave her job at a marketing company after a picture of her giving Donald Trump's motorcade the middle finger went viral. Citing their social-media policy, Briskman's bosses judged the gesture 'obscene' and thereupon 'separated' from her. But this concept of *obscenity* is crucial to understanding our times, because it arises from this overlapping of the public and the private realms. It gathers together questions of morality and immorality, withdrawal and exposure, artifice and actuality.

There is much support for the theory that the word 'obscene' originated in Greek drama as *ob-skene*, which literally means 'offstage'. The skene was a tent or building in the theatre, erected for the practical reason that the actors needed a place, obscured from the arena of the play, where they could change their masks. It evolved from a simple wooden structure into a larger, stone backdrop to the action, but most importantly it became a boundary between the public and private lives of the characters. In Greek theatre, the orchestra and stage represented the civic space of the play, where the visible parts of the plot occurred. The action often took place outside dwellings – whether palaces or caves – with the skene's doors marking a passageway to unseen interiors. Some of the most brutal, violent moments in the ancient texts, such as Medea murdering her children, Clytemnestra's vengeful slaying of Agamemnon, or her subsequent death at the hands of her son Orestes, are not dramatised. In staging terms, they occur obscenely and so, as some etymologists propose, we now associate an obscenity with something too horrific or violent or indecent to be given public airing, but which has nonetheless made its way into the visible realm.

One of social media's main projects is to bring the offstage to the centre stage. Through its various platforms we are coaxed to publicise the unspectacular, spontaneous moments of our lives, to be alert to and share the beauty of the commonplace, all of which cultivates our interest in the behind-the-scenes view. For all its documentation of major life events – weddings, births and even the recording of the 'big night out' – social media is intensely domestic and quotidian. This process of spotlighting the off-camera perspective or the behind-the-scenes view is our age's real obscenity, and it is influencing our attitudes, our desires and our politics.

Ironically, this appetite for the private view can also make it seem as though all the online world's a stage. The strangely uniform selfie expression that has emerged in the last few years (we've all done it!) is the digital version of a Greek theatre mask or, in the original language, a *persona*. The process of producing a solitary selfie is inherently self-conscious, for what face do we dare show ourselves? The archetypal choice is at once beseeching and vaguely puzzled, with something of a Rembrandt-by-Himself wariness. This almost cautious mien reflects the selfie's ambiguous position between the public and private spheres. Alone in our rooms or standing on bridges, we must arrange for ourselves the face that we would like to greet the world. The selfie thwarts that long-time go-to look of credible but artificial candour, which we might use if someone else is taking our picture. And so a typical selfie countenance carries a mix of innocence and cunning, as we try to catch ourselves unawares. This oscillation between authenticity and contrivance gives our digital obscenities their shimmering, elusive power. They depict solitary moments besieged by the thought of an impending audience, in which we play both actor and spectator.

The obscene perspective of social media is especially apparent when famous people make use of it. There was much uproar and debate about reality star Kim Kardashian's naked bathroom selfie, which she posted in March 2016. Some found it obscene in the 'lewd' sense, and others felt it was a statement of female empowerment, but regardless of these judgements, the image encapsulated her strategy of bringing our attention into the private domain. This photo was the opposite of candid – Kardashian superimposed self-censoring black bars across her breasts and genitals – but it also revealed the strangely entrancing, unremarkable details of her domestic life. The keenest of fans will no doubt have thought: '*That* is the cream blind in Kim Kardashian's bathroom!'; '*Those* are her pot lights!' While this particular selfie was provocative, it is arguably the ongoing access to her banalities that most enchants her millions of followers. Kardashian's persona is the flagship product of reality television, a genre fuelled by both theatrical excess and the unlikely magnetism of the non-event, and one that, in its natural blending of the mundane and the sensational, has informed our current use of social media.

The online fever for behind-the-scenes access now influences other areas of the culture, in some cases retrofitting pre-existing programmes. Nigella Lawson's recent series, *Simply Nigella*, was notable for a new interest in this sort of obscenity. Gone were the post-credits, 'midnight' raids of the fridge – Nigella gorging on leftovers in the half-light – her hearty sign-offs in earlier seasons. Instead there were bloopers and out-takes, one of which seemed to betray her onscreen persona's long-standing, inspiring attitude to eating and body image. Having flubbed a line several times, she warned someone out of shot that 'You're just going to have to find someone with dark hair and slightly too much weight on her and make her do it.'

In earlier series, before the widespread dominance of social media, her cooking segments were garnished with idealised scenarios – glamorous hangovers, harried school runs through beautiful West London terraces, garden parties – many of which were staged with knowing gusto. While these vignettes are still part of the format, Lawson's own Instagram presence now explicitly 'spoils' the communal suspension of disbelief that these programmes are really unmediated visions of her life. One post from a sunny summers' day showed a festive, tinselly picture from the final episode's shoot, captioned with: 'I know it's July for you, but it's Christmas on #SimplyNigella!' At some point the decision must have been made that we now prefer glimpses behind the stage to perpetuating an escapist fantasy. We don't seem to mind such fantasies being exposed, even while we bask in the comforting glow of them, the cogs and wheels of their inner workings revealed alongside the spinning of the fantasy itself.

The Blue Herring

Cultural debates about obscenity are never about the general rise of the behind-the-scenes view, but tend to focus instead on the proliferation of sexual images. For some, the ease with which the Internet allows us to access pornography has drenched these times in a troubling tide of obscenity. Gone are the days of sporadic, furtive trips to basement cinemas, or of the lone, racy cassette hidden in the sock drawer. We can now activate an orgy with a few keyboard clicks, as effortless as opening a music box and setting the ballerina twirling.

For this reason, this era has gained a reputation for smut. In July 2016, the UK government proposed legislation to demand age verification for all pornography sites, and since then new measures have been announced that websites failing to comply with them will be banned. In the same month, the United States Republican Party's draft election platform described pornography as 'a public health crisis that is destroying the lives of millions'. This position echoed that of Utah Governor Gary Herbert, who, a few months previously, signed a resolution recognising pornography as 'a public health hazard'. The effects of online porn on the millennial generation are often at the centre of research and debate, and indeed the State of Utah's resolution cites 'advances in technology and the universal availability of the Internet' as the cause of young people's 'alarming rate' of exposure.

For those campaigning to limit adults' access to porn, the battleground state is that of 'obscenity'. Pornography is not a legal term; an image or film becomes criminalised only once it has been legally categorised as obscene, and so here we come to obscenity's disputed, doubled etymology. While many scholars subscribe to the 'off-stage' derivation, others propose that it comes from the Latin *caenum*, which is associated with filth, muck and faeces. In the plural it could denote genitals or buttocks. Porn cavorts with both of these etymological theories. In addition to its inevitably genital and morally 'unclean' connections, pornography has traditionally been associated with obscenity because it involves the broadcasting of supposedly private activities.

Of course there is actually little *ob-skene* about a porn film; it's pretty much all scene. And while the shenanigans caught in the full-frontal view have their obvious merits and uses, the marginalia of porn scenes can linger just as powerfully in the mind, prompting obscene thoughts of a dramaturgical kind. I remember the incidental coating on tongues, the clearing of adenoids during polite pauses in fellatio. I remember noticing one actor's neat hairline, which led me to picture him visiting the barber's on a day off, smiling benignly and nodding as the mirror is held up, then standing and stretching self-consciously, his fists clenched above his head. He yawns and pays the man. I remember how, in one amateur production, a cat drifts into shot, visible through an open door. Past the bedroom, that porn house is open-plan. The lamps and couches beyond seem dispassionate, uninvolved. They aren't blushing, perhaps, because I'm not blushing. The cat winds itself between the vertical blinds, looking through the sliding doors at the bright blank of a Florida afternoon.

One day, with unbecoming urgency, I was googling a certain half-remembered scene, and I accidentally learnt that one of the porn actors I had long been watching on repeat had been attacked many years before. His head had been badly beaten, and since then he had been in a vegetative state, cared for at home. His medical bills were subsidised by the porn company for which he had worked. I thought about all the times I had summoned him up over those years, opening the ballerina box. I recalled his convincingly cheerful, fraternal approach to the job, his gung-ho-ness as his back bounced shallowly on the bedspread. These thoughts, overlaid with a sense of his quiet, cathetered body lying in an unknown, un-filmed house, for the first time felt obscene.

For those who don't feel that filming and watching non-violent, consensual sex is in itself immoral, anxieties about porn pertain to how the habits and expectations of the set infuse everyday life. The worry is that our beds become stages, that the manoeuvres and ecstasies seen online should be replicated at home. Recent studies suggest that young people are often unable to discern the reality or fakeness of pornographic sex, its resemblance to real life and how truly pleasurable it is for those involved. As the *New York Times* journalist Maggie Jones reports on her study into adolescent attitudes, 'some told me that porn was fantasy or exaggerated, others said that porn wasn't real only insofar as it wasn't typically two lovers having sex on film. Some of those same teenagers assumed the portrayal of how sex and pleasure worked was largely accurate.' In this sense, pornography captures the sense of obscenity as a dismantling of the stage walls, complicating the divisions between the real and the artificial. Even within the porn itself, theatrical obscenity is on the rise. POV or point-of-view videos are a relatively new genre in which the actors can be seen holding camcorders or phones in their hands, the action cutting between their close-up footage and another camera's master shots.

Although it is Internet pornography's associations with the genital, the abject and the excremental that explicitly link it to our era's defining obscenity, it is this other ancient sense of 'offstage' obscenity as a technical, theatrical description that most comprehensively describes our times. For our culture deals in the obscene in a much subtler way than pornography – one that is steadily reformatting the codes and conventions of public life. A prevailing obscenity of our age is not immoral, vulgar or profane (another etymologically spatial word meaning 'outside the temple'), but programmed into the ethos of how we perceive and navigate the world.

Backstage Pass

One of my earliest television memories from the hotel days is of watching a particular episode of Terry Wogan's evening chat show. The *IMDB* informs me now that the month was July, the year 1985. The show was a sort of warm-up for the evening's big event: the final episode of that year's series of *Dallas*. I remember that my young, sparrow's heart was beating fast, sped up by my older siblings' nervous excitement. Almost everyone in the country already knew that Bobby Ewing was going to be run over and killed, and so I had much, in my sixth summer, to chew on. It's likely that Bobby Ewing, as an idea, kept going in and out of focus, but 'death by car' would have been fixed in my morbid little mind. Then, bold as brass, and on a giant screen in Wogan's studio, there was Pam Ewing – whom I recognised mainly from the shape of her hair. Her face seemed very still, like a statue, between bouts of gay laughter. My mind was blown, which is probably why I remember this scrap of

1980s television. While I would have just about understood by then that actors played parts, and that the two things weren't identical, the fact of pre-recording was a hazy and somewhat perverse concept. I remember thinking: How will she be ready to start playing her part in ten minutes? How is she so calm, what with 'death by car'? Soon she would be screaming, then weeping. Bobby would shortly be flatlining in his hospital bed, a sound that would come whistling dully into my nightmares for the rest of the decade.

That memory is now so removed from contemporary life that my family and I may as well have been sitting around in Victorian mourning wear. How would my tiny self have coped with our current phenomenon of actors 'live-tweeting' about their own programmes *while* they are being broadcast? There has always been great interest in behind-the-scenes views of famous lives, but the evolution of this interest is significant because it allows us to experience the onstage performance and offstage commentaries at the same time. Live-tweeting is an attempt to reinvigorate the watching of TV programmes in what might now be called 'real-time', in an age when DVR, streaming and on-demand all threaten the communal stage of legacy trans-mission. Twitter play-by-plays, happening in parallel to the programme, are one of the unprecedented and wholly new pleas-ures of modern viewing.

Reflecting on the findings of its internal study from 2014, Twitter announced that 'one of the most powerful and direct ways to drive conversation about a program on Twitter is to have the stars of the show engaged on Twitter, particularly during the airing'. The study found a 64 per cent increase in tweets about a programme's premiere when cast members live-tweeted, compared to when they did not. Following the final appearance of Barbara Windsor in *EastEnders*, Ross Kemp, who plays her onscreen son, applauded his co-stars in a tweet: 'What an episode! Congratulations to Dame Barbara. Excellent performances from everyone, especially Barbara, Steve [McFadden], Letitia [Dean].' Elsewhere in the Twittersphere, long-time *EastEnder* Adam Woodyatt, who plays Ian Beale, exchanged tweets with his producer about one of the episode's scenes. *EastEnders* has been particularly experimental with the dynamic between its fictional world and its audience. The soap was the first in the UK to have a character tweet in real-time from within the episode itself, during a run of live episodes in 2015.

The phenomenon of actors live-tweeting is also increasingly popular in America. The US showrunner Shonda Rhimes, whose credits include the hospital drama *Grey's Anatomy*, is especially known for cultivating this social-media dimension. On her Twitter profile she posts photos from the set, as well as sharing backstage trivia and gossip. Kerry Washington, one of the actors in Rhimes's political thriller *Scandal*, has rallied the other cast members into live-tweeting the episodes. She congratulates her fellow-actors on their scenes, names the designers whose clothes she is wearing and praises offscreen contributors. While spoilers are feared and reviled, behind-the-scenes details are prized. Even our seemingly overnight awareness of, and interest in, the showrunner role signals this era's attraction to offstage matters.

The global, boisterous presence of unmasked actors in the audience, commenting on their onscreen work, is one of our truly new excitements. This demystification produces its own sort of wonder, one based in the constructed-ness of the fantasy rather than in the fantasy itself. Is there not something convivial, perhaps even cosy, in watching your favourite programme alongside the actors themselves? But while a constant awareness of artifice may simply become the normal mode in which we experience television, there are broader political implications of a behind-the-scenes culture. It's one thing for performers to be simultaneously masked and unmasked, but the effect is quite different when the same sense of duality surrounds public figures who are meant to be communicating and behaving coherently.

What happens, in other words, when this sort of obscenity infiltrates the political sphere? One of the most memorable examples from the Brexit summer was surely Ken Clarke and Malcolm Rifkind's sideline assessment of the candidates for the Tory leadership. Sky News created a sensational paradox in broadcasting these 'off-camera' remarks 'caught on camera'. Both this weird clip's form and its content suggest these two-sided times. Discussing Andrea Leadsom's prospects, Clarke said, 'So long as she understands that she's not to deliver on some of the extremely stupid things she's been saying.' More recently, during a trip to a Myanmar temple, Boris Johnson was captured on camera muttering lines from a Rudyard Kipling poem, 'Mandalay'. Given the colonial context of the poem, the UK Ambassador whispered to Johnson that it was 'not appropriate', and reminded him that he was 'on mic' for the duration of his idle performance. 'Good stuff,' Johnson replies, hoisting his smartphone to take a picture. Here the official, political visit collided with Johnson's private, romantic associations.

In this obscene milieu, we come to engage with the public realm with the understanding that it is a space of dissimulation, a collective illusion motivated by pragmatic demands and restraints. It is an illusion with which we play along, while simultaneously recognising its essential artificiality. The trailer for *Crazy About Tiffany's*, a documentary about the famous jewellery firm, offers a good illustration of this attitude. The news journalist Katie Couric, perhaps most known in the UK for her hilariously damning interview with Sarah Palin during the 2008 presidential race, gives her pundit's assessment of the store: 'New York is a place where people come to have their dreams realised,' she declares reverently. 'That's why so many people not only come to the city but ultimately make their way to Tiffany.' Immediately after this sentimental endorsement, however, the trailer cuts to Couric's 'off-camera' amusement at her own words: 'Do I know how to give good fucking [sound]bites or what?' This extreme blurring of the distinction between public position and private aside, where both appear cheek-by-jowl as part of the overall performance, seems to be a product of online culture, of social media's double aspect as both directly sincere and tightly stage-managed. But the result here is a sort of meta-sarcasm, as if the wry tone has been peeled away from Couric's punditry and given its own reality show, setting dreaminess alongside cynicism. As viewers, our instinct for coherence impels us to layer the two Courics back into a single speaker, thus creating an unstable, jaded compound.

The choice to edit the Tiffany trailer in this way exemplifies a mutated species of irony native to our times, whereby we can watch someone promote and undermine their own agendas and proclamations, not merely peddling fantasies with a wink, but giving us a behind-the-scenes tour of the illusion. A similar irony arose in the US presidential campaign when, in April 2016, the actor George Clooney admitted that the cost to be a 'co-chair' at his Hillary Clinton fundraiser – reported as being $353,000 – was 'an obscene amount of money'. There were protests outside the San Francisco event, in dramatic terms, an audience heckling the failures of the main spectacle. In the interview Clooney says that the protesters were 'absolutely right to protest'. He went to speak to them, and one protester, Clooney tells the interviewer, called him a corporate shill – 'One of the funnier things you could say about me.' It's apposite that the term 'shill', which refers to a supposedly neutral person who endorses someone or something while secretly being paid by them to do so, also has theatrical associations. A buzzword of the US election (recall the 'shillary!' placards), its roots have been linked to the carnival tradition, whereby the paid plant or 'stooge' of a certain attraction pretends to be a member of the crowd and drums up interest through ostentatious whooping and cooing. Another variation of the shill technique involves calling onto the stage a 'random' member of the audience, who is literally 'in on the act'. In this sense the shill is an obscene figure, not only in their dodgy morality, but also in their manner of confusing the distinction between the staged and the non-staged.

One of the protesters outside the fundraiser told Clooney that he 'sucked as Batman' – a role that depends on the actor maintaining a satisfying distinction between the character's masked and unmasked alter egos. In the interview, Clooney alternates between his official position as Hillary Supporter and as a candid citizen weary of the compromises demanded by life on the political stage. He offers politicised views as 'the truth', saying that 'the overwhelming amount of the money we raise' goes towards helping down-ticket Democrats take back the Senate, in order to overturn the laws allowing corporate involvement in politics, and ultimately to 'get this obscene, ridiculous amount of money out, so I never have to do a fundraiser again'. Here he is the inverse of a masked crusader who splits, in the superhero fashion, one life in two. Rather he presents himself as a sort of overt double agent, a two-in-one, simultaneously the Clooney who throws Clinton fundraisers and the Clooney who opposes the very notion of a Clinton fundraiser. Asked if he enjoys participating in these events, Clooney replies, 'I don't think anybody does, I don't even think politicians do.'

The most unexpected obscenity in the Clooney case isn't the amount of money influencing US politics, but his ability to reveal his offstage, 'obscene' feelings and agendas without believing that this admission is damningly hypocritical. He seems to trust that his audience will understand that public life inevitably places people in false positions. Rather than tipping us a wink, he expects us to look at him with both eyes wide open, with a gaze that can see both the stage and the wings. In this sense he asks us to adopt a double vision, whereby we simultaneously accept his public persona of the suave dinner host and the real person behind it, the latter revealing the necessary compromises and moral sacrifices demanded by the former.

Intermission

As a brief intermission, let's return to two vivid obscenities of the Athenian Theatre circuit. It is the fifth century BCE. We are back at the doors of the skene. On one side are props and masks and actors, on the other is the circle of the performance, an audience gathered around it in retreating arcs. A pair of notable arrivals through the skene interests us here, because both entrances are somehow against the rules. The first comes from tragedy. There is a story, which some of us moderns might say is from a 'pre-truth' world, that the arrival of the Furies onto the stage during performances of Aeschylus's *Eumenides* was so outlandish that children fainted and pregnant women in the audience miscarried their babies. While such a tale would likely fail the reality test of today's overworked fact-checkers, there is no doubt that the Furies inspired particular dread. It's possible that the reputation of these bloodlusting deities preceded them, that the very mention of their names, like saying 'Dalek' to me in 1987, could be enough to quicken the pulse. Perhaps they were inherently frightening to behold. But the main voltage of their shock-value may have come from the manner of their entrance itself. Aeschylus's staging in this play is unusual because the Furies arrive through the double doors of the skene. For ancient audiences, this choice of staging would have been astonishing. The Furies, hunting down Orestes for the murder of Clytemnestra, form a malignant chorus, and the traditional domain of the chorus was out front, in the orchestra. In Greek theatre of this period there was a clear division between actors and chorus, represented by the parts of the performing space that they inhabited. There has been debate over whether the actors worked mainly on a raised stage above the orchestra, but it is likely that both actors and chorus roamed around the orchestra, while only the actors made use of the skene's doors. And so the Furies, being thus unleashed, are in contempt of the laws of the theatre-space. This trespassing surely would have added to their monstrosity.

While the Furies' occupation of the hidden, obscene spaces of the Theatre of Dionysus is a chilling piece of stage direction, our next guest through the skene's doors enters to gales of Attic laughter. The scene has shifted to *Acharnians*, a comedy by Aristophanes. Halfway through the play, the protagonist, Dicaeopolis, calls at the house of the tragic playwright Euripides to ask him for help with an important speech. Euripides' slave tells Dicaeopolis that his master is 'within' and 'not within'. He means that the poet's body is in the house, but his mind is elsewhere, composing his tragedies. Yet this riddle becomes a running joke. Euripedes, shouting out through the skene's doors, reluctantly agrees to see Dicaeopolis, but refuses to leave his writing couch as he has 'no time to waste'. So how does the audience see inside Euripedes' house? For such occasions, the Greeks used a piece of stage machinery called the *ekkyklema*, a wheeled platform that would be rolled out through the skene carrying representative tableaux from the unseen interiors (often the dismembered victims of obscene crimes). In a comic moment of meta-fiction, Euripides accepts that for Dicaeopolis to come 'within', he, Euripides, will have to come 'without'. And so, drawing all eyes to the established convention of the *ekkyklema*, Euripedes replies, 'All right, I'll wheel myself out.' Thus Euripides arrives in full sight, both inside and outside his house, in an act of textbook obscenity. Classical comedy is filled with such breaches, wherein the artifice of the play is acknowledged. This rupture of suspended disbelief, a kind of disillusionment, produced hilarity. In *Greek Theatre Performance*, David Wiles writes that comedy 'plays on the permeability of the actor-audience boundary'. Tragedies, he suggests, were much more 'closed and sealed', requiring the audience largely to accept and forget theatrical convention in order to experience fully their harrowing events. Comedy, by contrast, revelled in its openness. Thus, while the Athenian comedies often included lewd mentions of buttocks, cocks and our private effluences, an equally important source of humour lay in the genre's innate capacity for self-exposure.

The Two of Trumps

Although the George Clooney controversy is a rich illustration of our various modern obscenities, it is a mere sideshow compared to Donald Trump's extreme engagement with obscene politics. The release of the 2005 'Pussy Grabbing' footage was a breathtaking collision of obscenity's forked meanings, with Trump's misogynistic stream of consciousness occurring offstage. The now-notorious *Access Hollywood* bus was driving Trump to the set of the soap opera *Days of Our Lives*, where he would do an interview about his cameo on the programme. In an ostentatious over-egging of this theme, the footage captured behind-the-scenes moments of a behind-the-scenes interview. Obscenity was packed inside obscenity. While Hillary Clinton suggested that Trump would become a puppet of Putin, on that bus-ride with Billy Bush, Trump became a Russian doll. In his official apology, Trump was quick to assert the marginal context of his remarks, casting them as 'locker-room talk', all part of pre-match, masculine camaraderie. At the second presidential debate, two days after this news story broke, moderator Martha Raddatz claimed that it was the most talked-about story of the entire election on Facebook. In mitigating the impact of this tape, Trump had to do battle with the reality of these times – infused as they are with the logic of reality television – that the sidelines can swiftly morph into the floodlit stadium, packed with spectators.

In 2005 Trump was perhaps not as aware as he would be now of the treachery of microphones, or that cameras are rolling before the director says, 'Action!' His reality show *The Apprentice* was only a year old, more or less the same age as Facebook. Until this tape emerged, Trump had carefully exploited his image as the 'obscene' politician, in both of the word's senses. Throughout the nomination process, it was widely reported that he dominated the field in terms of online clout. Following appearances such as at the Republican debates, he routinely provoked millions more 'interactions' – posts, re-tweets, etc. – than his rivals. The intensity of his online presence has corroborated the idea that he is speaking directly to the American public, via the unofficial channels of social media. Trump has capitalised on the cultural enthusiasm for the obscene view, consistently presenting himself as speaking from an offstage perspective, where lies the unpoliticised reality. Indeed, he had great early success in fashioning his onstage declarations as offstage truth-telling. In a *New York Times/CBS* poll from December 2015, 76 per cent of polled Republican Party voters reported thinking that Trump 'says what he believes'.

Like a good Attic comedian, one of Donald Trump's aims during the election was to call attention to the theatrical necessities of the campaign. Unlike his fifty-nine-year-old, bus-riding self, he always knew where the cameras were pointed. During the press conference to announce former rival Ben Carson's endorsement of him, Trump voiced his frustration that during his big stadium rallies the cameras 'never turn around' to show the size of his audiences. He also unveiled his behind-the-scenes strategies, the ruthlessness of his machinations. After Carson edged ahead in a poll, Trump recalled to the reporters, 'I said, this guy is unbelievable, and so I started going after Ben [. . .] and it's politics and Ben understands that.' Trump's strategy, all along, was to highlight the artificiality and contingencies of the political stage.

It was during this press conference that Carson put the cat among the post-modern pigeons. 'There are two different Donald Trumps,' Carson said, 'there's the one you see on the stage and there's the one who's very cerebral, [who] sits there and considers things very carefully [. . .] and that's the Donald Trump that you're going to start seeing more and more of right now.' After a fumbling hug, Trump took over the podium to answer questions, and the journalists in attendance pursued Carson's theory with great interest. They asked Trump to expand on this proposed duality. They used words such as 'persona', 'character' and 'performance'. Trump initially agreed with the verdict: 'I think there are two Donald Trumps. There's the public version and people see that [. . .] and it seems to have worked over my lifetime, but it's probably different, I think, from the personal Donald Trump.' While it doesn't seem unreasonable for someone to suggest that they behave differently in public than in private, Trump is too keen to insist on the inherent falsity of the politician's public life for the distinction to be useful to him. Speaking about campaign financing, he said that past experience in earlier elections prepared him for this one. 'I know it from the real side,' he claimed, 'not the politicians' side.' And so it wasn't long before he distanced himself from Carson's 'Two-Trump' model, which compromised his position as unmediated and unmasked: 'I don't think there's two Donald Trumps,' adding, with a tortuous existentialism worthy of Sartre, 'I try to be who I am.'

After the airing of the *Access Hollywood* bus ride, the question of how many Trumps there are returned with a new fury. In his official apology, Trump scowled into the camera, bisecting himself afresh: 'Anyone who knows me knows these words don't reflect who I am.' During the second debate, Hillary Clinton evoked a similarly doubled image of her opponent, saying that 'everyone can draw their own conclusions at this point about whether or not the man in the video or the man on the stage respects women'.

Trump's confusion in the Carson press conference over whether it is better for there to be two, or just one, of him was a potent sign of our obscene era. His uncertainty arose from a general redefining of the boundaries between what is public and what is private. With social media encouraging us to make our private lives an active constituent in how we present ourselves to the world, the very concept of a public persona has become exceptionally slippery. This new, paradoxical centrality of the offstage voice, which speaks alongside the official rhetoric, has fascinating repercussions for the notion of political authenticity. The authentic position, as with both Clooney and Trump, seems to be one that admits to its own capacity for inauthenticity, and which confesses when it is 'playing the game'. The confession itself, an invitation to come and see behind the scenes, is presented as a request for forgiveness, and a badge of trust. One could argue that part of Trump's success has been to harness this contemporary desire for the double act of theatricality and revelation.

In a suitably sidelined footnote to his 1969 *An Essay on Liberation*, Herbert Marcuse argued that obscenity could be used to refuse the stageshow niceties of those who wield brutal power. Obscene – that is to say, vulgar – language becomes an act of resistance, a rejection of the false civility and injured yearning for orderliness that despots often favour. Marcuse writes that 'If, for example, the highest executives of the nation or of the state are called, not President X or Governor Y but pig X or pig Y, and if what they say in campaign speeches is rendered as "oink oink", this offensive designation is used to deprive them of the aura of public servants or leaders who have only the common interest in mind.' But if, by the magic released in the collapsing of the stage walls, the president can be simultaneously both president and pig, then obscenity as this sort of political tool is blunted. If the oinks are uttered in among the promises to care for each and every citizen, then other ways of renaming and redefining oppressive regimes must be found.

A Transparent Mask

At about the same age that, blanched with terror, I watched Bobby Ewing's demise (a fictional reality that was later recast as a fictional dream), I was given an animated film called *The Last Unicorn*. Thinking about obscenity has made me remember one of its scenes because it sums up our age's peculiar dynamic between artifice and reality. While the eponymous unicorn is asleep at the roadside, a witch captures her and puts her in a travelling carnival of mythical beasts. Save for a genuine harpy raging on its perch, the unicorn realises that all the other attractions are just fairground illusions: an old circus lion parades as a manticore, a lame ape is a satyr. The witch's problem is that us naive humans can't tell the difference between a unicorn and a white mare. The fabled horn is invisible to us, and so the unicorn has to be magically altered too, a glowing fake appendage cast in front of her real one. 'I had to give you a horn they could see!' the witch tells her, cackling at the irony.

The Last Unicorn, standing aghast in her carnival cage with a second, gaudy horn, is simultaneously masked and unmasked. Indeed, it's her mask that unveils her, so that carnival visitors come and weep at the sublime sight. This public performance exposes her private secret, with the fake horn glimmering somewhere between reality and unreality, symbolising both the seen and the unseen. But isn't this the stuff of what so much of our own public identities are made – our dispatches from behind the scenes that are the publicised rendering of private life? We offer up spellbound versions of ourselves, in the hopes that they will stand for what we truly are, the person that somehow is never seen. We try to restore the overlooked truth. In this way, the double-horned unicorn offers a striking image for how, as spectators in this carnival, we have to negotiate the blurred bounds of the performed and the authentic, in a culture where private citizens are widely expected to build online personae as part of their basic participation in the world, and where public figures invite us into their bathrooms. The obscene turns life inside out.

In this environment, people who yearn for a relatively offstage life might set up a second Instagram account where they can put unfiltered, unlovely pictures of their lives, without the careful lighting. These 'hidden' accounts, to which only a few close friends are given access, are called *finstagrams*, a portmanteau of 'fake Instagram'. Here reality is labelled as artifice; privacy becomes the space for falsehoods. It is this logic that, as we have seen, leads to a dog-walker without video evidence falling into the class of the 'untrusted'. The backstage reality needs to be put on stage, in order to be considered real.

Enter Trump once again, bursting furiously through the skene's doors. 'Let's be honest, we're living in the real world,' he said during his sullen apology message for the sexual-assault 'banter'. But how is our sense of the real world changing, due to the structural obscenity of everyday life? One of the psychological concerns about excessive pornography use is that it turns our idea of sex into a performance watched at a distance. As a result, the real thing, with all its intimacy and bloopers, becomes too unrehearsed, too immediate. In our poorly lit, unedited bedrooms, the intact fantasies offered by porn naturally can't be sustained. And yet, with the widespread cultural rise of theatrical obscenity – the offstage perspective – the opposite appears to be true. It is the bloopers and ruptures of the performance that turn us on. Increasingly we encounter public life – on television and social media – as a curious, ironic mix of artifice and reality, as a fantasy that deliberately undoes itself.

In the early 1980s, the philosopher Jean Baudrillard described the rise of mass-media technologies as a 'pornography of information and communication, circuits and networks', which over-expose social life, turning it transparent, making the private sphere obscene by wheeling it onto the public stage. 'This white obscenity,' Baudrillard wrote, 'this crescendo of transparency reaches its summit with the collapse of the political scene.' He argues that politics cannot survive the throwing open of the stage doors, since the very discourse of politics requires a sort of dramatic containment, rather than comic obscenity. In civic life, he writes, 'For something to have meaning, there must be a scene; and for a scene to exist, there must be illusion, a minimum of illusion, of imaginary movement, of challenge to the real, one which transports you, seduces you, revolts you.' If the boundaries of the stage dissolve, then nothing meaningful can be uttered. A curious aspect of the US presidential election was that it seemed to be the act of disillusionment that either seduced or revolted. It was Trump's fundamentally comic mode that energised his supporters and appalled everyone else.

We haven't yet arrived at Baudrillard's state of political collapse. The move towards transparency has not reached its crescendo. Instead, we appear to be in a phase in which the persona and the person are simultaneously in play. The public stage, of course, remains; and the masks remain, even if we are invited to see through them. While this masked transparency can be amusing and inspiring in some corners of the culture, it can be a recipe for paralysis and cynicism in political life. One of the difficulties of engaging with an obscene form of politics is that obscenity – of the offstage variety – is by definition an impossibility. When it manifests in front of the public eye, it is no longer technically obscene. In this sense, obscenity has a joke, a paradox, built into its etymological roots. It is as impossible as Euripides on his *ekkyklema*, both onstage and offstage at once. But that which makes a good joke on one stage is an act of jaded opportunism on another.

While Euripides gets the laughs with his inside/outside schtick, we might think instead about his slave. Away from the political stage, the slave's remark that the playwright is both 'within' and 'not within' the home, because his mind is off wandering in imagined lands, offers us a more seductive, productive paradox. The only stable form of obscenity exists in the imagination, that natural habitat for things that are both real and unreal, and also neither real nor unreal. Our imaginations are often out roaming through hidden rooms, back rooms, far-off rooms, long-forgotten rooms, filling them with furniture and their own emotional weather. In them we find those mysteries called 'other people', whose truly offstage lives we can never witness, and which we can *only* imagine. It is possible that having certain limits to our vision is a necessary precondition for our empathy. To think about the parts of people's lives that we can neither see nor know for certain is an act of generosity. We might find in this imaginative obscene space a wounded porn star, perhaps, or a teacher coming home and making her dinner. We might imagine that an ordinary white mare is a unicorn in disguise. In this generous place between reality and fantasy, the truly obscene both evaporates and holds its mysteries, before our wandering eyes.

CHAPTER 5

Romance Languages

I feel the need to share an obscene story. What follows is a back-stage view into a brief run of my thoughts, one day in 2009. The hour is about 11 a.m. I am money-less in the way of many students, and am in bed in the small front bedroom of my parents' flat, working on some writing. (This is the room where, in another fifteen months, my mother will rest like a swan, but for now she's up and about, denim shirtsleeves rolled to the elbow, a tissue tucked into a sleeve, and generally being a retrospective miracle, even if in this moment she is only wringing out a J-cloth, or thinking about driving into town and deciding against it.) It all happened so quickly as I lifted the mug from the bedside table. There may have been some recoil, some backlash, in the precarious, tilting mechanism of a bed-workspace: a slipping book or jerk of a tucked-in leg. The undeniable result was a splash of tea across my laptop's keyboard.

Perhaps there was some death-drive carelessness in the swing of my tea-arm, since the computer was old and gone at the hinge.

The screen was liable to slump forward in exhaustion or faint into darkness for a few disconcerting seconds. I mopped up the tea somehow (with the edge of the bed sheet? It isn't beyond me) and with two fingers checked for a pulse, typing a couple of adjacent keys – asasasasasasa. I was amazed when the type behaved itself, 'a's and 's's streaming across the page. I deleted them and continued to write some proper sentences. But then, within the hour, it was as if a switch had tripped, somewhere deep inside the laptop. The sentences I was writing suddenly turned to nonsense. A neat, sensible little paragraph subsided into strings of gobbledygook, a sweater unravelling from the bottom. I don't remember feeling too distraught. Most of my attention was trained on the whisper of a resemblance. What was this mishap *like*?

The actress Natasha Richardson had recently, tragically, died following a ski accident. She had fallen during a lesson on a beginners' slope, hitting the side of her head. She got up and laughed off the tumble. It was silly. As a precaution, she visited the infirmary at the ski resort, but was back in her hotel room within half an hour. An hour and a half later an ambulance was called, as her symptoms had become serious. It was the interval between the fall and the panic that had distressed me. For a few days after her death, I would imagine her putting away her ski jacket, sitting on the edge of the bed, then moving to the bathroom to look at herself in the mirror.

And so, Your Honour, it was the basic, haunting scheme of this interval that I saw reflected in the trivial tea-spill: a moment of imbalance, a seemingly minor event shrugged off, developing into something more damaging. To write this down is appalling; it has no place, no proper shape in the outside world. But in the obscene privacy of my thoughts I understood the exact bounds of this morbid metaphor. I knew what was similar – a faint echo in timing – and the million other differences. I forgave myself. 'Laurence, are you really comparing your laptop to Natasha Richardson?' said a trusted friend when I told her, wanting someone to share in my mind's audacious associations.

I might be more indiscriminate than others when it comes to my involuntary metaphor-making. Perhaps not; it's hard to guess at other people's obscenities. Pattern-finding, which is the basis of metaphor, is linked to evolutionary success, and there is no doubt that we're all rampant pattern-finders. Noticing similarities allows us, for instance, to predict danger: this mushroom looks like the mushroom that poisoned my cousin. When we encounter something unfamiliar, we're apt to think about what it reminds us of, how it might be classified. This pattern-finding ability can be difficult to keep harnessed. Apophenia is the perception that meaningful connections exist in random sets of data. One type of apophenia is pareidolia, our habit of seeing faces in inanimate objects: clouds, shadows, patterned carpets. But whether or not most people would regularly indulge in such slight and unilluminating correspondences as mine, our sense of reality is intimately tied to the more robust metaphors that help to organise it. Indeed, linguists argue that we have no verbal understanding of reality beyond systems of metaphor, because the structure of language itself is essentially metaphoric.

Even simple nouns, which seem to point soberly and directly to the things they describe, as if brushed by Adam's fingertip, are clown cars of metaphoric associations. Take the word 'bat', altered from the Middle English *bakke*, likely a relative of the Old Norse *ledrblaka*, which means 'leather flapper'. *Bakke* is itself derived from the Proto-Indo-European root *bhlag*, meaning to strike, which has swooped off in another direction to form the basis for whipping words such as 'flagellate'. Etymologists believe that *bakke* may have become *batte* because bats were wrongly associated with moths, which in Latin are *blatta*. But bats have also commonly and mistakenly been linked to rodents, as with the sixteenth-century word 'flitter-mouse', which lived long enough to make Johnson's *Dictionary* 200 years later. Whether flying cuts of leather, mice or moths, bats carry – in both their old and new names – the traces of figurative thought.

The poetry locked inside these everyday words might be hidden from us, but the derivations reveal our metaphoric thinking. Explicit metaphors, however, the figurative language we use and the comparisons we make in order to describe the world, reveal a society's values. Metaphoric language highlights common cultural ground, through which something new can be better understood in relation to something broadly familiar. In their study *Metaphors We Live By*, George Lakoff and Mark Johnson point out how metaphors 'play a central role in the construction of social and political reality'. The poet Wallace Stevens unsurprisingly grasped the full power of comparison, writing that 'Metaphor creates a new reality from which the original appears to be unreal.' Metaphors are not simply reflections, but open up new avenues for thought by juxtaposing non-identical things and inviting us to find their commonalities.

The relationship between language and reality is being explored today with great vivacity. Because we encounter so much of life on the glowing page, in words and images, more than ever before we experience the world as a text to be analysed.

As a result, literary criticism has in the last ten years become a key skill of everyday life. With our personal relations unfolding in scrolls of words on our phones, we can reread them like we would a book, examine the pictures we have passed back and forth to our loved ones like paintings to be contemplated. We can slow the text down, zoom out and zoom in, scroll back and hover over a single word, returning to contemplate a conversation or a photographed moment after several days, events that once would have been consigned either to forgetfulness or to the less stark, less credible scrutiny of our memories. No letter-writing era can compare to ours in the amount of documentation we produce today, simply by socialising. In the realm of everyday gossip and grievances, we have the transcripts before us, the CCTV footage at the ready.

This capacity to scour the records, on our lunch breaks, is making us particularly attentive to the assumptions carried within other people's words, the moral blind spots that reveal themselves through language. Semiotics, diction, metaphors, similes and analogies are mainstream preoccupations. In the era of smartphones and tablets, we're captivated and concerned by literary devices. And since the comparisons we make now have the fuel to reach unknowable audiences, we're having to think about how our private poetry – the idiosyncratic connections and correspondences that we nurture in our minds – translates into this newly internationalised public sphere. What sort of poetic language can we agree upon to represent a collective reality? Should we even try to express the movements of the mind that lead us to see epidural haematoma in a pool of tea? (Asking for a friend.)

Metaphor on Trial

One of the great joys of contemporary life is the abundance of visual metaphors. Because we swim in images, they are readily available to illustrate our current mood. The GIF of a dolphin riding the waves conveys the joy of finishing work, a digital version of the TGIF kitten poster pinned to the office wall. We react to events metaphorically by borrowing the expressions of others – a cartoon rabbit banging its head, Jack Nicholson in sunglasses blowing a kiss, Whoopi Goldberg catching her breath as she accepts an Oscar, Elsa from *Frozen* skating along, singing 'Let it Go'. A picture of Angela Merkel's weary sideways look may come to stand for our own exhaustions. There are some dedicated and brilliant flights of metaphoric fancy. The Twitter account TabloidArtHistory offers up dazzling juxtapositions: a photo of Britney Spears reaching up to take a Del Taco bag from her drive-thru attendant is set next to Caravaggio's *David with the Head of Goliath*; Paris Hilton primly holding her chihuahua Tinkerbell shares a split screen with Da Vinci's *Lady with an Ermine*. The motto of the account reads: 'Because for every pic of Lindsay Lohan falling, there's a Bernini sculpture begging to be referenced.'

Amidst all this fun, however, there is risk in metaphoric thinking. The ill-judged simile is one of the signature misdemeanours of our times. The news is regularly peppered with people apologising for controversial comparisons: a London Underground official for comparing the staff of a private train company to the Gestapo; the Queen guitarist Brian May for calling a badger cull genocide; George Lucas for suggesting that Disney executives were like 'white slavers'. There are certainly degrees of outrageousness. The singer-songwriter Lorde got into meta-phoric trouble when she mentioned in an interview that being friends with famous people is like friendship with someone with 'very specific allergies': there are places you can't go with them. Practical considerations and concessions have to be made because of the level of their celebrity, just as you might not invite someone with Coeliac disease to a pizzeria. 'It's like having a friend with an autoimmune disease,' she said. The now-standard Twitter 'backlash' followed – backlash itself being a mechanical metaphor, referring to the effects of an inconstant load on a machine's wheels. Lorde's simile was deemed by at least one person as diminishing the plight of those with autoimmune diseases. Lorde apologised, but there was even some backlash to the backlash, the wheels of Twitter juddering as people with autoimmune diseases came, with the full credentials of their suffering, to Lorde's defence.

To even mention the Lorde exchange feels like contributing to the magnification of a molehill into a mountain (no offence to moles, whose achievements should not be trivialised), but most significant about this scandal is the fact of its comprehensive coverage in global tabloid outlets. Whereas in other eras young pop stars might court scandal from toppling drunkenly, like Bernini sculptures, out of cars, they now get flak for their use of literary devices. While many objections of the Lorde variety strike me as being based on ungenerous interpretations, for any student of the humanities this close attention to language is an exciting develop-ment. That the misfiring metaphor has become a genre of public misstep reflects the textualisation of our reality, which is training more people to notice and reject these more or less egregious comparisons. Everyday life is being put under a kind of literary scrutiny that is now regularly used to dispel destructive and lazy myths, as well as insidious condescensions, about other people.

Those who have been politically marginalised have always been keenly aware that language is often not on their side. The current, pervasive alertness to metaphor is in large debt to these critiques from the margins, which are thankfully becoming more audible and more centralised. As well as poetry, our words have centuries of entrenched thought locked into them, the full implications of which are not always apparent to the speaker. The classicist and broadcaster Mary Beard received much criticism for her tweeted words about the Oxfam charity's scandal in Haiti, where aid workers have been accused of the sexual exploitation of young and potentially underage Haitian women. In trying to explain her initial position that these actions took place in the context of a nation still recovering from a devastating earthquake, Beard raised two explicit metaphors. The first claimed surprise that the popularity of *Lord of the Flies* hadn't taught us more about 'the breakdown of morality in danger zones!!' The second, which she felt was 'less fraught', compared aid workers to the French Resistance in terms of them representing minorities in a society – that is, many people in France collaborated or kept quiet, just as many people may express sympathy for the international plights of others without actually risking their own safety to help. There is always the danger with metaphors and similes, especially bad ones, that the wrong correspondence will be emphasised.

Beard's fellow-Cambridge academic, Priyamvada Gopal, responded to her colleague's tweets in a blog post that, among other strong objections, found the image of 'Western aid workers as resistance fighters' both 'bizarre' and 'cringe-making'. She then supplied her own literary metaphor, invoking Joseph Conrad's

Heart of Darkness to characterise Beard's account as one of 'white aid workers as Mr Kurtz figures caving in the strain of "The horror, the horror."' She challenges Beard directly, writing that, 'Black agency, Haitian agency figures nowhere in your vision'. Many people would benefit from reading Gopal's post in full, but my specific interest here is how this argument unfolded metaphorically. While Gopal rejected Beard's French Resistance metaphor, Beard would likely not have recognised her own position in Gopal's imperial simile. Addressing her Twitter audience, Beard wrote, 'I am not really not the nasty colonial you think I am.' She felt she knew the shape and limits of her own metaphors, and that the truncated public forum of Twitter had distorted them. 'I speak from the heart (and of course I may be wrong)', Beard wrote. And yet her heartfelt words are broadcast to her 185,000 followers. In this context, as Gopal proposed, 'it is part of intellectual morality to be utterly precise and clear even in the shortest of sentences'. She publicly encouraged Beard to examine her private 'habits of mind'. Ultimately for Gopal, Beard's figurative language, whether Beard knew it or not, revealed 'what is still acceptable and, indeed, valorised in public *discourse*', her metaphors betraying a political reality that could not go unchallenged.

The Problem of Metaphor

'One bad metaphor and you're fucked,' my writing tutor once said, with real fear in his eyes. Metaphors are a constant occupational hazard, both for technical and moral reasons. 'I am growing, as I get older,' Norman MacCaig writes in his 1965 poem 'No

Choice', 'to hate metaphors – their exactness/and their inadequacy.' He was well aware that this poem is packed with metaphor, as he compares his thoughts about an unnamed 'you' to different types of rainfall, from a gentle 'moistness' to a downpour. This irony speaks to the lack of choice of the poem's title, for how else might he give shape to the formless ways we hold other people in our heads? His distrust of metaphors is precisely their habit of pinning the things they describe under the weight of their own image. Their exactness, he fears, can overpower their subjects, robbing them of their multiplicity or of their essential unknowability. Any ill-feeling that he holds towards them surely comes from the inescapable dilemma that metaphors pose: are they a trap or an embrace? Do they separate us from the reality of the material world, or do they offer a moment of intimacy, drawing us closer to the essence of a thing? There are also Mammy issues at play in MacCaig's agitation. In an interview late in his life, he spoke with great fondness and admiration for his illiterate, Gaelic-speaking mother's flare for elaborate and wonderful metaphors. 'If there's *any* poetry in me [. . .] which I doubt,' says MacCaig, 'that's where it comes from.' As much as he distrusts them, metaphors were a delightful part of his initiation into language.

Like the camera resolving the horse's gallop, metaphor is an attempt to reveal some unseen reality. It is a visual act, whereby the evident quality of one thing is placed, like a magnifying glass, over the generally overlooked quality of something else. Metaphor is never holistic; it always gives a zoomed-in view. We see MacCaig grapple with this problem in his poem 'Toad', which begins with a sly telling-off. 'Stop looking like a purse,' he admonishes a toad who has appeared in his house. Of course he is really telling himself off for his poetic instinct to make similes. He immediately debunks his own image, scolding its inadequacy: 'How could a purse/squeeze under the rickety door and sit,/full of satisfaction, in a man's house.' And yet, doesn't a purse help us visualise the heaped repose of plump amphibians? In stating the impossibility of a purse that 'clambers' along the floor and looks satisfied, he zoom's out from his image's brilliant exactness, wilfully blowing it up by asking it to stand for too much. Once unpinned from the first metaphor, the creature moves forward, on its 'four corners', into the path of another. 'I love you for being a toad,' MacCaig says, asserting the toad's sovereign toadiness, only to add, in the next line, that he also loves it 'for crawling like a Japanese wrestler,/and for not being frightened'.

The toad has two reasons to be frightened – one prosaic, one poetic. It would be wise to fear MacCaig's broom, being unaware of his warm feelings. But the toad also has to fear the poet's lyrical manhandlings, of being dissected into a collection of resemblances. The poem's great tenderness is likewise both tactile and linguistic. The toad is saved twice, as MacCaig writes, 'I put you in my purse hand, not shutting it.' Now the metaphor has moved on to the metaphor-maker, the poet's own body being turned, for a few beats, into something other than itself. MacCaig then reverses the common fantasy that toads carry a gem in their skulls, a 'toadstone' that is an antidote to poison: 'A jewel in your head? Toad,/you've put one in mine,/a tiny radiance in a dark place.' In this way, MacCaig liberates the toad of its metaphoric and mythic burdens. His narrator-avatar in the poem sets the animal free outside, unveiled, 'directly under/every star.' He thus creates a moment of communion by revealing the movement of metaphor, switching the flow of the comparison, allowing the toad and its figurative associations to transform *him*.

This bi-directional quality of metaphor, the way it comes into your home and leads you out of it, is the source of its ambiguity and its ethical power. Sylvia Plath published her poem 'Daddy' in the same year as MacCaig's 'No Choice', and it was immediately notorious for its use of metaphor. Plath described it as being about a girl with an Electra complex; in the poem she re-imagines the father figure as a Nazi. 'I thought every German was you./And the language obscene', Plath writes, 'An engine, an engine/Chuffing me off like a Jew./A Jew to Dachau, Auschwitz, Belsen./I began to talk like a Jew./I think I may well be a Jew.' The childish 'chuffing', to describe the transportation of Jewish people to the camps, is horrific and violent in its careless carefreeness. The narrator moves from simile to metaphor, from 'talking like' to possibly 'being' Jewish. As the Plath scholar Jacqueline Rose has pointed out, the poem has clear autobiographical elements, since Plath's father, who died when she was eight, was suspected of having fascist sympathies. In this sense the poem can be read as what Rose calls a 'mega-fantasy', but since its publication there has been much criticism of the conceit. To give just one, relatively mild, example, Leon Wieseltier wrote in a 1976 essay for *The New York Review of Books* that 'the metaphor is inappropriate'. Today, the charge would be one of appropriation – the argument that Plath unrightfully used the momentous sufferings of the Holocaust for her own purposes. But this question of property is at the root of our understanding of metaphor. In his *Poetics*, Aristotle defined the device as 'Giving the thing a name that belongs to something else'. Metaphor always entails a borrowing, which in some cases may become theft. Its very structure contorts our concepts of ownership and territoriality.

Hilary Mantel has written more generally on the problem of making equivalences to incomparable events such as the Holocaust, arguing that: 'it is demented cosiness that denies the differences between people, denies how easily the interests of human beings become divided. It is indecent to lay claim to other people's suffering: it is a colonial impulse, dressed up as altruism.' But Rose's interpretation of 'Daddy' complicates this idea of 'laying claim' by suggesting that the direction of the claim is not clear. Once again we find this idea of metaphor's two-way nature. She sees the poem's conceit as a form of memorial to the Holocaust, the commemoration of identification, which, she argues, is the ongoing duty of *all* people, especially given the declining numbers of those who endured it first-hand. Rose, who is Jewish, proposes that Plath 'is not appropriating; [the Holocaust] is appropriating her'. She asks, 'how do you keep it alive if not through such an act of identification?' Nor does the poem, with its intense idiosyncrasy, attempt to deny the differences in suffering. The poem is full of private horrors and fantasies. It unleashes the violent energies often suppressed within family relationships and uses them to evoke the brutality of fascism. Its central comparison feels both true in its anguish and in the callousness of the mind's associations. The microscopic scale – one girl's heartache set against six million deaths – is, for some, the source of its ethical violence, but this grotesque disproportion is itself a linguistic offering to the grotesqueness of genocide. As Rose claims, Plath 'is trying to make a leap of imagination which will connect her to that history which she precisely did not live'.

There is no question that the denying of difference is an immoral use of metaphor. Like MacCaig, Vladimir Nabokov, whose brilliant tropes illuminate and animate the things they describe, knew well the inadequate exactness of metaphors, which in *Lolita* he exaggerates into a kind of violence. The initial molestation of

Lolita begins as soon as Humbert describes their first meeting, and is wholly metaphoric. He comes upon her sunbathing in the garden, and the vision unbuckles his associative mind. Seeing her lounging on a mat, he thinks, 'there was my Riviera love peering at me over dark glasses'. He takes the metaphor's bluffing rejection of the simile's 'like' or 'as' and doubles down, treating the metaphor as the reality. Lolita *is* the girl, 'my dead bride', whom he 'fondled' twenty-five years before. He recognises her, 'as if I were the fairy-tale nurse of some little princess (lost, kidnaped, discovered in gypsy rags through which her nakedness smiled at the king and his hounds)'. Lolita's body adopts all the quirks of her predecessor, such as 'the tiny dark-brown mole on her side'. Here we are many lurid miles from MacCaig's gentle epiphany, his 'tiny radiance in a dark place'. This small patch of darkness on Lolita's body is a mark of possession.

As his fantasy progresses, he and Lolita shapeshift according to the rules of his palpitating metaphors. While playing the nurse, Humbert is also both the king and the hounds receiving the smile of the child-princess's nudity; he is the brute who stares with 'aging ape eyes', who then transforms into 'a hunk of movieland manhood'. Lolita, looking at him over her sunglasses, changes in an instant from the 'Riviera love' to 'the little Herr Doktor who was to cure me of all my aches'. But, above all, Lolita is, for now, the other girl, the 'prototype', who schooled the younger Humbert in the art of nympholepsy. One terror of this scene is that Lolita, as the perfect, exact copy, does not manifest as herself at all – she is the void at the centre of Humbert's lustful reverie. There is no room for her as he pushes metaphor to its perverse extreme. Rather than noting a resemblance between two people, he extinguishes any difference between them. As he confesses, 'Everything they shared made one of them.' This scene in the garden is the novel's unoriginal sin, the deranged whirl of metaphor signalling Humbert's lustful mania. He admits in his confession, which is the text of the novel, that 'I find it most difficult to express with adequate force that flash, that shiver, that impact of passionate recognition.'

These writers are all grappling with the central problem of metaphor: its power to both expand and limit our realities. Is metaphor a way of extending a hand, an act of compassion and identification? Or is it ultimately a lasso, flung around its targets? The poetic terminology of metaphor defines the main thing being described as the tenor, and the thing to which it is compared as the vehicle. So, in 'the moon is a ghostly galleon', the moon is the tenor and the galleon the vehicle. But the division isn't always so clean, for isn't there always a tension between the two parts – doesn't the ghostly galleon take on some of the moon's qualities, as well as the other way around? It is the intimate quality of comparison that causes, as many kinds of intimacies are apt to do, much of the trouble.

The Good Metaphor

My mother found the old proverb that 'comparisons are odious' a handy way of shutting down explicit sibling rivalry. She knew, from canniness as much as ethics, that the tacit rankings produced from such comparing were not good for the long game of family relations. At the same time she loved comparisons of other sorts, the more absurd, the better. Nicknames were a household staple, based on tenuous but strangely true resemblances. A university classmate of mine, a young woman with close-cropped sandy hair and a Windsor handsomeness, became known as Prince William. These monikers constituted our private language, so that in London we shared a garden fence with A.S. Byatt and occasionally went to a yoga class taught by Jennifer Saunders. Nor were family members spared from these likenesses: my brother, it turned out, had the same optimistic smile as our next-door neighbour's dog, Bear Rae; when his first daughter was a baby we called her Max Branning, the bald *EastEnders* thug, behind her back. Our father was the illustrated card 'Peter' in the board-game *Guess Who?*; my sister, Elaine from *Seinfeld*. In my teenage years I had long hair in the grunge style, but when I tied it back with a regrettable centre-parting, my mother said I looked like a minor daughter from Jane Austen. 'Yes, you, the plain girl!' she would summon me, with the tone of an impatient Mother Superior, this line itself a quotation from *Blackadder*, when Rowan Atkinson hid himself, be-wimpled, in a convent.

Through my mother's sensibility we learnt to find likenesses everywhere, an alternative network of things. Somehow these jubilant comparisons only underscored, rather than undermined, the ultimate dignity of our subjects. Our wayward metaphors, those runaway vehicles, heralded the inadequacy as well as the delight of language. In their ludicrous frenzy to define, they revealed the impossibility of absolute definition. They were a way of paying attention to people, of studying mannerisms and situations, but their partiality, ambiguity and absurdity were all admissions that people are only ever themselves, and that there aren't really words for that. For me, there was real peace at the centre of this metaphoric whirl, where the unsaid existential question wasn't 'Who are you?'

but 'Who are you sort of like?' The plurality of the second question's possible answers was a kind of freedom.

By contrast, when metaphor is robbed of its vital ambiguity it becomes stereotype, that ancient tool of humiliation. Stereotype takes up the whole frame, the whole stage, acting as a total, definitive revelation. In the case of racist stereotypes, a utilitarian metaphor is conveniently seen to illuminate the full, false essence of the oppressed – these people *are* parasites, these people *are* property. The stereotype permits no darkness at its edges, so that nothing is obscene. Rather, it blanches its targets, robbing them of their sovereignty, ambiguity, eroticism.

For this reason, ethical metaphors, with their ambiguity intact, have a form that is crucial for us to remember now, in these over-exposed times. The metaphor brings two things together according to a certain commonality, illuminating shared ground. It is a public meeting of two private things. The good, non-broken metaphor never suggests identity. If the two things were identical, then their relationship would not be metaphoric but actual. The metaphor's standard structure is blatantly arrogant. Its very form is a bluff that points to its own incompleteness, undoing its own self-certainty. To say, for simplicity of illustration, that a person *is* a wolf is not rationally meant to imply that the person is, in every respect, lupine. Rather, on either side of the spotlit, shared ground – a zone of carnal ferocity perhaps – the metaphor preserves two darknesses. The first shelters all the aspects of the person that do not resemble those of a wolf; in the second darkness sits the wolf's unshareable, inhuman features. And so there is a great wisdom to true metaphor that is often overlooked. It insists on the privacies of the elements that it brings together, calling our attention to both unlikely, often joyous similarities and to the limits of comparison. Uniqueness and sovereignty are not the same. The good metaphor corrodes the illusion of uniqueness while upholding the sovereignty of each thing or person, a combination that is perhaps a prerequisite for compassion.

I continue to speak to my mother, now, in metaphor and analogy. Sometimes when I'm overwhelmed at the sheer dumb tedium of her non-being, I think of the final moments of *Brokeback Mountain*, when the reticent and bereaved Heath Ledger tenderly clicks shut a top button of one of Jake Gyllenhaal's shirts, hanging from the cupboard door. 'Jack, I swear . . . ' he mutters, with the full rage and disbelief of loss. Almost everything to the dead – once the funerals and memorials are over – is said under the breath. 'Jack, I swear . . . ' I say, to my gay-cowboy-lover-mother. Maybe Jack Twist's shirt is my mother's belonging that most does me in – it wasn't the shoes, in the end, or the unsorted handbag. And I know that, in grief, these metaphors are like pinhole cameras in an eclipse.

Bathos

Metaphors get into trouble when they are somehow imbalanced, when their two parts are out of proportion. There is often the charge that insensitive metaphors diminish the importance of something momentous, by putting it to the task of describing a much more trivial thing. Controversial metaphors often, but not always, cause offence because they are *bathetic*, and here again a literary term helps to define one of our era's prevailing moods. Bathos, which, as we'll see, is an inevitable effect of social media's format, describes the deflation that occurs when two opposing tones or registers clash in a work of art. This clash produces a sense of disproportion. We owe the term to the eighteenth-century English poet Alexander Pope, who coined it as a mean-spirited joke in his corrosive treatise called 'Peri Bathous; Or, the Art of Sinking'. While Western literature had long interested itself in the sublime – language's ability to transport the listener or reader to an exalted plane of experience – Pope saw in the work of his peers a tendency in the opposite direction. Lacking the genius necessary to reach the lofty heights of sublimity, they unintentionally followed 'the gentle down-hill way to the *Bathos*'.

Two main classes of figurative language, Pope argued, were to blame: 'the Magnifying' and 'the Diminishing'. A bathetic poet such as Lewis Theobald might write an overblown rendition of someone lighting an ordinary fire: 'Bring forth some remnant of Promethean theft,/Quick to expand th' inclement air congealed.' Or he might announce the simple act of opening a letter as: 'Wax! render up thy trust.' Likewise, Pope wrote, a poet such as Richard Blackmore would belittle the ocean with the pedestrian image of housework: 'The ocean, joyed to see the tempest fled,/New lays his waves, and smooths his ruffled bed.' Or he might reduce the Lord Almighty to a humble supplier of leavened goods: 'God in the wilderness his table spread,/And in his airy ovens baked their breads.' Pope's sarcastic rules to achieving bathos in poetry were a clear attack on the aesthetic and moral climate of his time. He saw his fellow-citizens as being naturally bathetic – striving for spiritual grandeur while ultimately mired in everyday, material concerns.

These examples now read like old relatives of some famous lines from English comedy: Monty Python's 'Blessed are the cheese-makers' or Peter Kay's 'Garlic bread, it's the future, I've tasted it.' Recall Britney Spears's Del Taco bag as the head of Goliath. But one of the frightening aspects of current political life is that its bathos is delivered with unshakeable sincerity. The unethical metaphor often involves some combination of magnification or diminution, or both. A breathtaking example from recent times is CNN pundit Jeffrey Lord's naming Donald Trump 'the Martin Luther King of healthcare'. In this metaphoric tethering, Trump is magnified by association, at the price of diminishing King's colossal achievements. Nigel Farage, one of the most consistently bathetic politicians, has compared himself to Darwin and Galileo. If we consider that the root of the word 'analogy' is from the Greek *analogus*, which means proportion, we see that metaphors weren't designed for these outlandish comparisons to be taken seriously. We slide into bathos when their proportion is tipped, and so even the most deadly serious of these deranged metaphors have a ring of grim comedy to them.

Pope concluded more generally that bathos was the 'natural Taste of Man', and three centuries later we have yet to outgrow this taste. Indeed, we creatures of the rising tides have many new routes to those sinking feelings. The increased presence of our personal realities in the public sphere is a great source of bathos, because all the poise of our professional demeanours can be so easily deflated by one glimpse into our unpolished, often chaotic, private lives. In recent viral memory there has been no more hilarious example of such bathos than when the BBC interviewed Professor Robert Kelly about the political situation in South Korea. He sits in suit and tie in a home office decked with the classic symbols of expertise: books in piles on the desk, a large map of the world on the wall, a bookcase in the distance. He has just finished saying, in a serious, BBC-interviewee voice, 'And all the time the question is how do democracies respond to those scandals,' when his young daughter comes romping into the room, swinging her arms and swaying her head and settling in front of the webcam. She is followed by his even younger son, who glides into view imperiously in a mobile walker, one-and-a-half feet from the ground, followed by his panicked wife, sliding through the door in her socks with the comic timing of Cosmo Kramer. She ducks down and gathers up the children, knocking books onto the floor, catching the walker on the edge of the wall, and once they are all out of the room – and as he is trying to continue analysing, one word at a time, tensions on the Korean peninsula – she reappears on hands and knees to swing the door shut. Her attempts to stay low, hoping to be out of shot while still completely visible, are a huge part of the scene's unintended genius.

The social-media newsfeed is inherently bathetic for similar clashes between our personal concerns and the big issues of the day. The newsfeed arranges itself according to tactless algorithms, colliding the miniature with the immense. A rant about the summer trend of men wearing flip-flops sits above an elegy for Arctic ice; photos from a snowboarding trip live beside images of coral reefs bleached to near-oblivion. Televised news, by contrast, has always been wary of bathos, which is why those cheering stories that form the news's lighter side are typically reserved for last, often with a cushion of sports or weather in between. This format imposes a crude narrative structure on the day's events, with peril ultimately usurped by a happy, or at least whimsical, conclusion. Yet such careful management of emotional tone is absent in the newsfeed, which in this sense is closer to the rawness of real life, with its moments of shock and unexpected shifts in mood.

Because social media's structure is prone to accidental bathos, this register can be manipulated for political purposes. In the immediate aftermath of the terrorist attacks on Barcelona and Cambrils, Twitter began to fill with pictures of cats, as it had during a 2015 Brussels anti-terror operation. This feline strategy, which is thought to have been started by a Belgian cameraman, has multiple aims. One of them is to short-circuit the viral spreading of eyewitness images of the violence, which could be useful to fleeing terrorists or those planning more attacks. These cats are also meant to act as a screen to uncensored photographs of victims, the circulation of which both traumatises families and magnifies the impact of the attack, working for the perpetrators by disseminating terror. Pictures from the scene and images of the suspects become a form of glorification, an aggrandising of the event. The intentional setting of kittens alongside explosions is a reclaiming of the natural bathos of Internet news. In this age of the camera-operator, we do at times need to diminish rather than magnify the image, and the bathetic quality of memes is emerging as one such lessening device. A similar approach has been adopted by users of 4Chan, who began Photoshopping the heads of rubber ducks over the faces of ISIS fighters, both to mock them and to prevent them from becoming globally notorious – arguably one of their motivations.

Purposeful bathos also offers a shrewd way of resisting authoritarian regimes, which propagate their authority through triumphalism and heightened imagery and symbolism. As Pope advises in his mock-guide for bad poets, their eyes 'should be like unto the wrong end of a perspective glass, by which all the objects of nature are lessened'. The bathetic mode effectively diminishes the fragile grandeur of tyranny, fighting some remnant of

Promethean theft with some remnant of Promethean theft. In South Carolina, a local musician responded to a KKK march – protesting at the removal of a Confederate flag from the State House – by playing lumbering, cartoonish music on his tuba-like 'sousaphone'. The result was a ridiculous soundtrack to the deluded righteousness of white supremacy, turning the march into a ponderous Teddy Bear's Picnic. Whether accidental or intended, bathos has this balloon-bursting effect, and the more that reactionary forces fixate on historical symbols of superiority, the sharper bathos will become as a strategy of deflation.

Cultivating our natural taste for bathos will be essential if we are really to continue down our current post-truth, alternatively factual road. American comedians quickly recognised how difficult it is to satirise such an unreal political landscape. Satire relies to a huge degree on irony, where there is an affecting tension between what is said and what is meant. But how do you ironise a political climate in which what is said shamelessly bears so little resemblance to what is meant? Irony relies on a stable sense of shared reality on which to enact its destabilising effects. Given the sustained attacks on our ideas of truth and falsehood, bathos is useful because it doesn't depend on knowing what is real or unreal, but instead plays with the binary of big and small. A popular meme called 'Tiny Trumps' has been doing the rounds, in which photos of Trump are altered so that he appears impossibly shrunken in relation to everyone around him. He belongs in a different universe. In miniature he greets other world leaders, or signs executive orders. This sort of bathetic undermining uses scale as a weapon, turning the majestic into the paltry, joining in with fantasies of superiority and then sabotaging them from the inside by hitting not a false note, but a bum one.

Commemoration

The extent to which we allow historical symbols of superiority to continue to define our present and future realities is a vital issue. As well as our metaphoric language, the poetry of our public spaces is also under much scrutiny. How do we reflect in our civic iconography what really happened in the past? Is it possible to poeticise our histories without distorting the truth of them? Because of the current prominence of such questions, a crisis of commemoration is unfolding in societies around the world. There has been a widespread dismantling of Confederate monuments in the southern United States, and elsewhere statues to colonial and imperial triumphalism have been removed from public spaces: Edward Cornwallis in Nova Scotia, Cecil Rhodes at the University of Cape Town.

Bathos is relevant to this issue, too. Most statues of real people are doubly bathetic, in the sense that statues both magnify and diminish their subjects. They are anti-climactic in two directions: whose life could ever live up to the absurd grandeur that a giant stone monument imposes, but equally what life, even in memory, would want to be confined in stone? The statue's primary function is to aggrandise the figure on the plinth, announcing and preserving their achievements and cementing their public influence. At the same time a statue is also, inevitably, an assault on a life's fullness, because such commemoration demands simplification and erasure. To turn someone into an icon is to reduce them, and so the statue is always both too big and too small to represent the plenitude of personhood.

There is a fixity and comprehensiveness to a civic statue that is not as inevitable in other kinds of portraiture. The statue's place in public means that it must stand firmly for something more general – a society's values and cause for pride – than a single life can typically accommodate. How do we petrify certain qualities or aspects of a person into an object that is meant to represent everybody who moves through these public spaces? A monument in the town square, by its very position, has greater burdens of inclusivity than, say, the oil painting of an old CEO in a company's boardroom.

Statues are always at odds with the ambiguities and inconsistencies of personality. In this way, they are vertiginous things, swinging in and out of focus as their subject, Alice-like, shrinks and expands before us. There are those who acknowledge the disrepute of these historical, statuesque subjects – the architects and administrators of colonial rule, for instance – but who feel that to erase their public prominence is an unhelpful purge of the past. They argue that the plinth should become a kind of stocks, or a less gruesome version of the head-on-a-spike, in which disgraced figures are preserved for posterity, lest we forget. This approach demands a more complex attitude to commemoration, whereby a statue may both be an honour and a rebuke.

Whether we believe statues should be removed and perhaps replaced with morally superior icons, another literary device lies at the centre of this debate. The very idea of a statue is linked not to metaphor but to its less flashy cousin, the metonym. Many urgent questions about our evolving notions of public legacy and remembrance, as well as how we think more generally about what personhood *is*, depend on the metonym's relationship to reality. Unlike the metaphor, which aligns two or more different things, the metonym operates within a single system. As a device it makes a part or aspect of something – an object, person, position, institution – stand for the whole. Referring to the sea as 'the Deep' is a classic metonym, whereby the thing is named after one of its prominent qualities. Likewise, 'hand' is a metonym for a sailor because of the traditional importance of this appendage to the jobs of rigging and rowing. Hence, 'All hands on deck'. In metonymic terms, meals are 'dishes', business executives are 'suits', the royal family is 'the Crown', one's language is one's 'tongue'.

The metonym's substitution of the part for the whole, the specific for the general, is the source of the mistake that is built into all statues. While these monuments physically imitate a whole person, or at least a whole head and shoulders, they are usually erected because of a specific attribute, talent, action or event in the subject's life. They are concrete metonyms. In this respect, the Greek and Roman gods have an advantage as the models for statues, since they are metonymic by nature, embodying large abstract concepts: war, love, the sea, the sky. Turning mortals into statues is probably an unwise idea, since such idolatry, in the name of honour or recognition, is inherently vulnerable to the whole story, beyond the metonym.

The link between metonyms and the crisis of commemoration becomes even more vivid if we consider that the literal Greek meaning of metonym is 'to change the name'. Political change has always been fought on the battlefield of nomenclature, and so it's not surprising that the call to rename is growing louder in the intensifying activism and historical awareness of these years. In Canada, the question of renaming has focused recently on those who were involved in the brutalities of the residential-school system, which removed 150,000 indigenous children from their communities and attempted to assimilate them in conditions rife with physical and mental abuse. The Langevin Block, a part of the governmental offices in Ottawa, was renamed 'The Office of the Prime Minister and Privy Council', rescinding the honour given to Hector-Louis Langevin, one of those most implicated in the residential-school system. In America, the racism of the Confederate armies during the Civil War is prompting petitions to rewrite the maps of Southern towns, whose streets bear the names of celebrated generals.

But it is not only those figures enmeshed in the large-scale, institutional and federal violences of history who are being challenged over their entitlements. The controversy over the Margaret Court Arena at the Australian Open's Melbourne tennis complex shows how commemoration begins to crack up, once it is no longer judged metonymically. Court is the former Australian player who, at the time of writing, has won more Grand Slam singles titles than any other person. In 2017, players began to object to the naming of the stadium because of Court's historical statements on South African apartheid and her present comparisons of LGBTQ awareness and political equality to her muddled sense of Nazi and Communist mind-control – a terrible clutch of metaphors. Commenting on the controversy, Chris Evert has said that the name should stay because 'You're celebrating her tennis.' But the American champion Lindsay Davenport argues that 'When your name goes on a building or a stadium, it's [because of] more than your accomplishments.' Similarly, in an open letter, Martina Navratilova wrote that things are named after people 'for one reason. That reason is their whole body of work.' She then expands the notion of a 'body of work' to include '*who* they are as human beings'. This is itself an ideological leap, which fuses the professional and the personal. Court's second career as a preacher has made this fusion particularly robust, and indeed any famous figure who broadcasts moral proclamations is arguably making their private beliefs a matter of public concern.

Navratilova and Davenport's position rejects the metonymic purpose of commemorative naming, which preserves the noteworthy quality of a life. Margaret Court's tennis prowess – that singular quality – is surely the only reason for her to be remembered widely. Their argument suggests, very reasonably, that immoral people don't deserve the recognition of the namesake. In this sense they are responding to the excesses that surround any metonym; the part may be taken for the whole, but the substitution is never perfect. The whole cannot be wholly obscured. For many, the name Margaret Court will not simply summon a thunderous first serve, but also her belief that homosexuality is a sinful 'lust of the flesh'. The metonym on which the honourable naming depends cannot hold.

The pragmatic view is that there are plenty of great champions who were both remarkable champions and who do not believe that transgenderism is the influence of the Devil, and whose name could replace that of Court. Navratilova concludes her letter by proposing Evonne Goolagong, and indeed for a short time, due to 'user contributions', Google Maps listed the stadium as such. But perhaps the act of naming itself should be reconsidered. As our lives become more and more exposed, so will the old statuesque tradition grow more unsustainable. We will not be able comfortably to contain a life in that way. As a character in Olivia Sudjic's novel *Sympathy* asks: 'Do you think we will still create statues of people in the future?' The answer is no, 'because we will know too much about them'.

The crisis of commemoration raises broader questions about how we think about ourselves and other people. With private and public life being increasingly intermixed, it becomes harder to think about an individual in terms of isolated qualities or actions. The obscene always threatens to trespass onto public grandeur. Our historical approach to considering people metonymically, with parts of them coming to represent their complete personalities, may have to be rethought. The toppling of statues forces us to ask more generally, 'What are we really like?' and to consider personhood in new and exciting ways. We might choose to replace the statues of oppressors with the statues of liberators, but this moment also offers an opportunity for more radical ideas about how we represent ourselves and others in public life.

It isn't, after all, just influential figures who must contend with their legacies. Running in parallel to the memorial debate is the problem of how private citizens are being represented and remembered in the newly expansive civic sphere of the digital age. Anyone with an online presence faces the danger of magnification, whereby the part dwarfs the whole. Indeed, one of our credible everyday fears is that a part of us – one tweet, one uploaded image, one deed recorded in the annals of Google – *will* be read by others as the sum of us. Young people especially feel the danger of becoming disgracefully monumental. Online shaming is often metonymic in nature, especially when the identities of those shamed are overwhelmed by a single event: a thin string of 280 characters coming to indict one's entire character, or a humiliating night at a party caught on camera. Those entering the job market worry that one wrong 'like' on their Facebook page could cost them employment. Jon Ronson's *So You've Been Publicly Shamed* exposes the aftershocks of what he calls 'mega-shamings', people whose lives have been ruined because of an overheard aside, a terribly misjudged joke or one moment of stupid irreverence. Some citizen-judges are happy to let such metonyms stand, arguing that wickedness can be deduced from one sentence, which is certainly possible. Our judicial systems are based on the metonymic quality of crime. But aside from the criminal record, other kinds of civic transgression – failures of judgement, uncharacteristic bursts of anger, stupid metaphors, the effluvia of our less edifying private selves – now rise tall and turn to stone, visible from space, casting long shadows across digital fields.

As a result, running parallel to our commemoration crisis is the legal delineation of our 'Right to be Forgotten'. Under EU law, Google must consider an individual's request to have links removed from search-engine results according to certain criteria, which 'relate to the accuracy, adequacy, relevance – including time passed – and proportionality of the links'. This idea of proportionality brings us once more to bathos, that tonal clash of two different scales. Those who wish their data forgotten feel aggrieved by the search engine's relentless powers of magnification, which can persist long after the relevance of the story has diminished. For those who choose not to topple their own digital monument in the courts, private enterprises can now help you to shrink the effects of the offending link by manufacturing heftier, more wholesome stories that will take up the first pages of a Google name-check. The modern Latin phrase *damnatio memoriae* describes the routine sacking of establishment iconography that has historically occurred whenever one regime falls and another takes its place. Those who invoke their right to be forgotten are asking for such a damnation, requesting that their own statues be pulled down in the night.

In his autobiography, written in the third person, Roland Barthes notes how 'He is troubled by any image of himself, suffers when he is named.' To be assigned adjectives is a kind of domination, he writes, a kind of death. But then he describes visiting Morocco, where the people he met never thought 'to *gloss*' him. 'Initially,' he confesses, 'this matte quality of human relationships had something exhausting about it, but gradually it came to seem a triumph of civilisation.' We are similarly finding the statuesque mode, the assigning and enlarging of a handful of adjectives, to be increasingly intolerable. But what will replace it? Maybe two-second GIFs of Rue McClanahan batting her eyelashes? That would be fine with me. By purifying our everyday imaginations of their harmful romances, how might we find a vocabulary and symbolism that are exuberant without magnifying or diminishing their subjects, without sliding into unwanted bathos? We will have to ask ourselves: What size do we want to be? How much space should we take up in the world? We will have to reconcile the weird scale of the private life of the mind – with its often inexplicable standards and associations – with a new public life in which every conceivable kind of person could be listening to us. This question of how to produce and maintain a poeticised reality, which is intimate without being overwhelming, will be an ongoing task of this century.

The Colossus

In another of Sylvia Plath's paternal poems, 'The Colossus', the narrator declares the impossibility of rebuilding the dead in memory: 'I shall never get you put together entirely,/Pieced, glued, and properly jointed.' A smashed male colossus is strewn across a classical landscape, the tongue, lips, ears lie in fragments, pieces of bone stretching to the horizon. 'It would take more than a lightning-stroke' we are told, 'To create such a ruin.' The words coming from the colossus's dislocated lips are impossible to resolve and unify – 'Mule-bray, pig-grunt and bawdy cackles'. Again we find the incoherence of mixed metaphors. Despite the futility of the task, the narrator tries to restore the monument, crawling 'like an ant in mourning' across the 'weedy acres' of the brow.

The international crisis of commemoration accidentally mirrors my own problems with representing the dead. In the midst of this cultural drive to reconsider the ethics of metaphors and metonyms, to find modes of expression that reject the fetish and the cliché, I'm finding it hard to imagine a suitable, domestic iconography for my parents. It was several years before I could look peacefully at snapshots of them. At present, their ashes sit beside each other, on high, in my office cupboard. They are still in their institutional maroon boxes, hidden in a sturdy canvas shopping bag folded over on itself. Beside them is an unopened quilted single mattress-protector, *Absolute Balderdash* stereotypically aslant, a shoebox with two sliced bands of masking tape, and a pair of black dress shoes, one inside a plastic bag and the other wedged on top of it. Below this shelf some spare coats and shirts press together on second-best, assorted coat hangers; still further down, there is a chest containing yet more squashed shoes and boots.

I generally don't think about the ashes, besides a diaphanous idea that they are keeping me company. Language has been seared out of them. Sometimes I say to myself: you're like Rebecca from *One Hundred Years of Solitude*, carrying a canvas sack of her parents' bones around with her wherever she goes. *Cloc-cloc-cloc.* But the simile can't take hold in that soil. I'm not Rebecca. Of the ashes themselves I draw a humourless blank, unable to visualise them. I remember a childhood storyline of *Home and Away*, the young beach-bum cutie with a popped berry-aneurysm. The song 'Wipe Out' played at his funeral, and at the end of the episode a cresting surfer tipped out his ashes in slow motion. Are they like that? But even those, one assumes, were metaphoric remains: dusty sand, grit, good brown sugar?

The ashes baffle us. We once took my mother's institutional maroon box on what we called a 'Reality Tour' of some of her favourite English places – around the old streets in Newcastle, a metallic day and night on the island of Lindisfarne. That is, of course, to say that we toured these sites in her honour; the box remained in the B&Bs and hotels. The plan was to scatter her in the countryside in Cumbria, where we'd had some good times in the Seventies and Eighties. This was a period when we as a family perfected the art of the 'crap day out', as my mother used to call them, but this stretch of Cumbrian stream with a well-positioned tree stood out to all of us as a worthy place of rest. After the picnic in our usual spot, however, and after the obligatory, tottering recce of the flat shelves of stone a little further round the bend, we packed up our things and got back in the car. I'm sure the ashes were not brought ceremonially from the car to the picnic blanket, to sit among the crisps and dips; I'm not sure if someone had even taken them from the B&B that morning. We passed the buck; we were on the same page.

Now there are two boxes of baffling ashes. It's us, the survivors, who have been scattered, and so there's no long-standing, central place to bury them, no gnarled and beloved old oak. From time to time we think that a potter friend-of-a-friend might make a joint urn for them, but that would require asking her. I can't imagine what the design on such a vessel would be. Do we retrofit a coat of arms?

I get melancholy enough just from painting a room and realising, with a little heap of sample-pots at my side, that the room can only be this colour now, for some time. When I consider this imaginary urn, I hear Norman MacCaig in my ear: every option would surely be too exact, too inadequate. That is to say, too monumental.

I've seen real ashes, tactlessly in the flesh, only once. We scattered my elderly uncle during the season of parental departure, a simpler task because he had nominated a valley near his home, in a different part of Cumbria. But even though I took my turn lakeside, I can't remember the stuff of them. My uncle's dear friend, who with his wife had looked after him tirelessly in his final weeks, was nervous and chatty. We had just finished reading out a touching Celtic poem and, in a kind of social panic at the emotion of the occasion, he pointed up at the distant fells and said: 'That was where that woman lived, the one I was telling you about – do you remember – the one whose husband was killed by Raoul Moat?'

I tend to think of this memory now as if it's my mother who is remembering it. I feel that I know what she would have made of the comedy, the relentless humanity of the moment. Grief has many examples of these tiny radiances, the jewels the dead put in our minds. These co-memories are my private commemoration. I smile silently along with her, as though it's she who is telling the story to me.

CHAPTER 6

Fellow-Feeling

'How are you feeling?' became, in bereavement, the sort of question that draws a blank, like naming your favourites in a certain category: films, books, musicians. For me, it brought with it a great cosmic 'Ummm . . . ' and a furrowing not just of my brow, but of my whole mind. The question is a kind one, but I've always been slightly afraid to discuss my grief with others. Writing books about it is a different matter (!), since I don't have to watch people's expressions during the divulging. In person, no matter how sympathetic the listener, there is always, inevitably, that moment when their concern must dim, when they pull their coat from around their chair, squint in the direction of the window to see how late the afternoon has grown, pat their pockets for their wallet, go and pay for the coffees and perhaps come back via the toilets with their reset face terribly and truly placid. The alternative would be morbid and terrible in its own way; imagine how trespassed you would feel if someone tried to enter wholeheartedly into your pain. But nevertheless I shied from the loneliness of this moment of the reset face.

Besides, there are so many standard and expected feelings that hardly seem worth articulating. What does it mean to say you feel sad? Desolate? Heartbroken? The Argentinian writer Jorge Luis Borges noted that there are no mentions of camels in the Koran because, for its writer Mohammed, camels 'were a part of his reality, he had no need to emphasise them'. So too with the overwhelming emotions of grief. They begin to compose the new reality so entirely that you stop seeing them as something separate, to be turned in the hand and named. 'There are no words' is a common response to tragedy, an official statement. But sometimes there *are* some words, or rather thoughts made of words, or feelings that could be converted into words, if only you dared. There might be words to do with the elation that it is over at last, the sense of having achieved something. After weeks, months, years of caregiving and rotas and confinement, there is the chance for a pleasant, bestial sniffing at the doors of bars, which for many Friday nights you walked past with a shopping list, or a bag of milky, high-energy drinks swinging at your hip. There is the feeling of contentment at spontaneously accepting invitations, the happiness of sitting in a busy city pub, with the traffic flowing easily outside it and strangers coming in through the doors, the excitement that, if the dead have had their time, then at least you haven't had yours.

There are other feelings even less fit for public consumption.

I came to grief at more or less the same moment that it became the norm to share our feelings with the wider world. We are all now quizzed on or invited to share our emotions, as a matter of daily life. The first thing to greet me on my Facebook page is a question: 'What's on your mind, Laurence?' To my response I can append a feeling, easily selectable from a dropdown menu. But all social-media posts occupy a paradoxical space: are they diary entries or press releases? Their trappings are often domestic, intimate, local. 'Good Morning Laurence!', here is a list of village birthdays and an example of how to respond to them ('Wish them well!'). At the same time, as we have just explored in the problem of our private poetry, the scope of our intimate thoughts and feelings is mercilessly global. Every idea, every proposition, is potentially subjected to international peer-review. Having a feeling in public is a dangerous pastime, since our feelings are often not up to such scrutiny.

The comedian Sarah Silverman, who has more than ten million Twitter followers, said in an interview, 'I always think of a tweet as a message in a bottle.' While intellectually she knows that huge numbers of people read her tweets, she is at the same time surprised that there is an audience for them. Here, she is referring to the unexpected response she received to a series of tweets on the subject of her decision not have children. Her interviewer refers to them as 'idle thoughts', a description with which Silverman agreed. But it is precisely this ambiguous position between the internal and external, the idle thought and the megaphone announcement, the message in the bottle and the sky-writing, that is complicating the place of feelings in public life. How will the public expressions of our private emotions have to change in this magnified, amplified world?

Zadie Smith avoids social media because of its effects on her emotional freedom. As she told the *New Yorker* writer Jia Tolentino: 'I want to have my feeling, even if it's wrong, even if it's inappropriate [. . .] I don't want to be bullied out of it [. . .]

I understand it's important to be appropriate in public life, in social life, in political life.' But there is also that private place of the inner life, which she wants to protect as a place for 'instincts, feelings, inappropriate feelings – which I have all the time, all kinds of inappropriate feelings about all kinds of things'. These parts of ourselves, she argues, can only be protected by avoiding social media, which is now the basis of public, social and political life. We likely have a sense of what a poor match social media is for our feelings, and yet we're successfully encouraged to use these platforms as a repository for our personal truths. We broadcast what is in our minds. And then, on both small and large scales, we put our foot in it, we are somehow tactless or embarrassing, we hurt other people's feelings even if we don't know it, or we're bullied for our opinions.

There is a remarkable disclaimer in the foreword to Zadie Smith's book of essays, *Feel Free*, in which she emphasises that these pieces come from her own sensibility, and that they needn't represent anyone's reality but her own. 'All [these essays] have is their freedom,' she writes. 'And the reader is likewise unusually free, because I have absolutely nothing over her, no authority. She can reject my feelings at every point.' It is telling that Smith feels the need to point this out. For hasn't this always been the case with literature of all kinds? We throw books across the room or, less dramatically, we close them in disgust and say 'ugh', or we let them drift away from us, half-finished. An instruction manual has authority over us if we need to heed its advice, a book about wildlife extinction should hold our culpability over us, whether we like it or not. But the kinds of literary essays that Smith writes have surely always been met as an offering, a proposition. In a much earlier essay about essays in general, she writes how their readers 'thankfully do not have to live within the strict terms of manifestos'.

Smith has always been keen to emphasise in interviews that she is not writing from a place of expertise, but rather as someone who is working through a question by writing about it. But the tone of her 2017 foreword, introducing a set of essays written during 'the Obama years', has a very current unease to it. I would hazard a guess, which can of course be rejected, that Smith wrote this disclaimer because it has become very difficult to put feelings into the wider world. There are so many ways that a feeling can go wrong, curdling under the lamp of public attention. The anxiety I sense in this foreword applies more generally to all of us. This is a problem we all share, now that we are all publishers. We might not be writing essays, though many of us are doing so in the form of blogs, but all the time we send out little short ideas into the world: observations, propositions, snatches of feeling. Smith's disclaimer seems to have been influenced by the more general realisation that whenever we make online declarations, we aren't addressing one person or a select few, but, in theory, diverse multitudes. Whereas the professional writer may once have written sentences with the idea that, at any one time, they will be read in an intimate, private space between her and a single reader, that fantasy of privacy is much less easy to sustain in our open-book culture.

By contrast, the foreword to Smith's 2009 essay collection, *Changing My Mind*, has a different disclaimer. Compiling these essays has made Smith realise that 'ideological inconsistency is, for me, practically a matter of faith'. Life is too complicated, she implies, for fixed perspectives that refuse to see the world from multiple sides. But here, she is the one rejecting her own ideas by raising internal contradictions and alternative views. The audience of readers isn't mentioned. And while she accepts that our moral and imaginative position on one subject may clash with our feelings about another, she still thinks finding truth may be possible, what she calls her 'cautious, optimistic creed'. But by 2017, when the second forward was written, she wants there to be no mistake. The essays are what we would now call *her truth*. They are, she tells us, 'to be used, changed, dismantled, destroyed or ignored as necessary!'

You can understand Smith's concern. For although public life is now powered by the flow of opinion and sentiment, an opinion has never felt less like an opinion, a casual hunch never more like one of the Ten Commandments. Although our perspectives are continually courted, we are more wary of their influence. The amplifying quality of social media means that there is a new responsibility in expressing your position. To take an extreme example, in the days following the Parkland School shooting in Florida, which killed seventeen people, the number-one trending YouTube video was a clip arguing that the students speaking out in anguish for gun control were hired 'crisis actors', in the pocket of CNN. What began as a video posted twice to Facebook quickly received hundreds of thousands of views. These deliberate acts of misinformation need to be seen for the smallness of their origins rather than the enormity of their impact. They must, in Smith's words, be dismantled, destroyed, ignored.

To further complicate matters, as we grow understandably more anxious about the expression of our feelings, these feelings are being turned into a precious resource. As we shall see, there is now a billion-pound industry that seeks to know what we are feeling at every turn. Our emotions are coaxed out of us in the surveys and polls that have quietly become part of the red tape of daily life. New wearable technologies are designed to nestle against us and convert our physiological responses into valuable data. As public life seems to be losing its hold on what is real and true, the backstage technologies that are now defining many of its terms are ruthlessly concerned with the reality of our emotions. They aren't interested in filtered postures or ironic stances, but with unenhanced feeling. They are genuinely invested in us. 'What do we *really* mean?' they ask. 'What do we *really* feel?' While we look to find a new grammar to express private sentiment in a globalised public sphere, to find acceptable forms and forums for our personal sympathies, a new industry of emotion works steadily to collapse the distinction between the personal and the public, between the soul's reality and the brave face.

Big Emotion

In 1872, Charles Darwin published *The Expression of the Emotions in Man and Animals*. In this work he explored the causes and outward signs of our feelings, but one of the expressions that most intrigued him was the blush. He proposed that 'Blushing is the most peculiar and the most human of all expressions.' It is a threshold phenomenon; its heat and colour shimmer in that uncomfortable space between suppressed and expressed feeling, between private reaction and public expression. While many of us are capable of fake smiles and crocodile tears, the blush is considered a sign of true sentiment. Although the observer may not know the blush's source – an embarrassment, a secret on the brink of revelation, a burning shame – it has an exceptional authenticity. Its reality makes it notoriously difficult for actors to simulate. Darwin concludes, reasonably enough, that blushing occurs because of our 'sensitive regard for the opinion [. . .] of others'.

The blush is thus the hallmark of our self-consciousness as social creatures. It betrays a moment when we feel that our inner lives have no proper place in the larger world. But some of Darwin's contemporaries were more optimistic about this involuntary reddening. Darwin quotes the French anatomist and zoologist Louis Pierre Gratiolet, who saw blushing as a sign of humanity's 'high perfection' among the species of the world. 'It is in the order of nature,' Gratiolet believed, 'that the most intelligent social being should also be the most intelligible.' We are designed, for Gratiolet, to reveal ourselves to our societies, to give signals of what is happening in our minds and hearts. Even feelings that we would most like to keep to ourselves are hinted at by the blush.

In this sense, the blush's ambiguity is an invitation for analysis and social scrutiny. As George Eliot wrote in *Daniel Deronda* (also in the 1870s), 'a blush is no language: only a dubious flag-signal which may mean either of two contradictories'. For instance, that we love someone or we do not love someone. Both are possible, and literary blushes at least have been known to cause confusion. The blush is both overt and covert, a hint of something true and, if deciphered correctly, a step towards intelligibility, to the decoding of the blusher's inner life.

Indeed, Gratiolet's idea is echoed today in the ethos of one of our era's emerging and most powerful industries, whose goal is to make sure that we improve on our 'high perfection' and become even more intelligible than ever before. In today's paradigm, the blush has become a problem to be hacked. Here I'm giving the collective name Big Emotion to the various endeavours and approaches of this industry. Any enterprise that gathers large quantities of information about our sentimental lives – our moods, our feelings, our opinions – converting this information into data and then interpreting it using powerful data-processing algorithms, is part of the Big Emotion project. To these companies whose business it is to know our business, we are always blushing. At every moment we are revealing ourselves, if only the signs can be properly discerned.

Big Emotion is working on a large canvas. It seeks to decipher our feelings in all their modes of expression: in how we communicate online, in our external body language and, even more intimately, in the codes to our emotions that we keep inside our bodies. On social media, our words can often be the only evidence of our feelings. As a result, coders are busy improving their software's capacity for 'sentiment analysis'. Also known as opinion-mining, this genre of computer program attempts to discern our moods and feelings in the linguistic patterns of our social-media content. One of the obvious problems is that we don't always say what we mean. Lotem Peled and Roi Reichart, two researchers in this burgeoning field, have given themselves 'the novel task of sarcasm interpretation'. Their work so far involves gathering tweets that include '#sarcasm' and then designing an algorithm that can create an accurately sincere version of the sarcastic tweet. So in a simple scenario, the tweet 'What a great way to end my night #sarcasm' might become 'Not a good way to end the night'. Once the algorithm has identified the true mood, then it can become useful. What upset the conclusion of the evening? Perhaps a product would be able to spare you from that, next time. Of course the sarcasm hashtag is a way of short-circuiting our own irony, so the future of this research will involve the ability to detect a sarcastic phrase without this giveaway.

Fortunately for the merchants, in our physical lives, when our body language is on display, we tend to conduct ourselves more sincerely and revealingly. This is especially true when we are unaware of being watched. In the shopping malls, retailers are already using facial recognition in wall-mounted cameras, which read the expressions and body language of customers. In 2016, Apple bought Emotient, which bills itself as the 'leading authority on automated facial expression recognition and analysis, designed to enable emotionally aware technologies'. This kind of software can tell when a pupil has dilated with interest. Our motions are tracked for meaningful pauses and return journeys to the same item. A concentrated frown might trigger an alert to human attendants, telling them to swarm on this contemplative consumer. Thermal-imaging cameras can analyse our heart rates, detecting that flutter of excitement at the verge of a purchase. There are countless commercial applications to these technologies, and it has been estimated that the business of detecting and inter-preting emotion will be worth more than $36 billion by 2021.

But Big Emotion is not satisfied with the remote scrutiny of sentiment analysis and facial-recognition cameras. The branch of this industry that deals in wearables is devoted to a new kind of empathy, an intimate exchange of information between the human body and the biosensors voluntarily strapped to it. One goal of wearable technologies is to judge our moods from quantifiable physiological responses. Marcus Mustafa, the Global Head of User Experience at the global marketing and technology agency DigitasLBi, has described the biometric data from wearables as the 'glue' that binds the more easily trackable and analysable digital data – our browsing and online purchase histories – to our feelings. He has predicted a near future of wearable clothing and jewellery, equipped with biosensors that can 'extract relevant data that [he] can turn into a relevant offer'. In other words, our T-shirts will lead a double life as both mild-mannered garment and commercial go-between, gathering up our heartbeats and passing them on to interested third parties. Mustafa sees wearables not as a blended fabric (part turncoat and part personal shopper), but 'as beacons to figure out relevance, context, how you're feeling, where you are, and then send localized, personalized offers around that'.

It's impossible to separate the history of advertising from an interest in the emotions of the marketplace. The founder of the psychological school of behaviourism, John B. Watson, who joined the New York advertising world in the 1920s, believed that advertisers must confront their customers with 'emotional stimuli'. The goal was to 'tell [the audience] something that will tie [them] up with fear, something that will stir up a mild rage, that will call out an affectionate or love response'. The so-called creative revolution in 1960s American advertising broadly entailed a move away from such rational and systematised methods as behaviourism to a more intuitive and artistic approach, but nevertheless the focus remained on the emotionally provocative powers of the form.

This revolution is dramatised in one of *Mad Men*'s most famous scenes, written to persuade us of Don Draper's genius. The setting is the pitch meeting for the Kodak slide projector. In a darkened boardroom full of suits (plus one 'sweetheart' at the light switch), Draper projects photographs of his family's all-American life: hot dogs meet *Lady and the Tramp*, children lolling on shoulders and couches, the ad-exec dad in weekend jeans, wedding-day whites. 'Technology is the glittering lure,' Draper tells his would-be clients, but to engage the public most deeply, you need to forge in them 'a sentimental bond with the product'. The ache of nostalgia is the marketer's friend, he explains, growing ever more moist-eyed and tense-jawed with each click from one slide to the next. The Kodak 'Carousel', as he coins it, is a time-machine that takes its owners to 'a place where we know we are loved'.

This excellent scene first aired in October 2007 and now has two layers of datedness. To the grim politics of 1960s office culture, we can add the scriptwriters' own understandably blinkered perspective on the burgeoning industry of digital advertising. For while it is true that the same sentimental bonds still underpin the commercial world, there is a new alertness to the possibilities of capturing and thereby exploiting pre-existing feelings, rather than merely provoking sentiment. And while Nielsen produced its first market survey in 1929, the cutting-edge business of tracking consumer feeling in real-time would have seemed futuristic to most people in 2007. Ten years later, Adobe vice-president John Mellor told a summit meeting that 'Emotion is the new currency of experience.' This 'new currency' could be an echo of one of Don Draper's Manhattan aphorisms, as could the bioanalytics company Lightwave's proposition that 'Innovative businesses understand the power of emotion.' But these old platitudes bely a truly revolutionary set of practices.

As a formalised profession, advertising's early strategies involved being as loud and declarative as one could afford, as opposed to the more inquisitive, insinuating variations we see today. In 1870, the company of a Boston ad executive, George P. Rowell, issued a guide to the trade called *The Men Who Advertise*. The book emphasises that the advertiser is a kind of proclaimer: 'He must keep a trumpeter, the public attention must be arrested.' In this era of print, the copy should be 'rhythmical' and 'poetical', in order to 'produce a pleasing effect upon the reader'. Today, instead of a trumpeter, the good advertiser must keep a stethoscope.

Mustafa defines emotional data as being 'all the things in between the lines, all the unmeasurable data that makes us humans do what we do'. This drive to uncover our feelings has an accompanying rhetoric, which argues that the display of emotion is the true measure of rich experience. Increasingly we're being asked to believe that life must be saturated in explicit, measurable emotion in order for it to have the full weight of reality. For example, in 2015 the car-maker Jaguar issued Wimbledon spectators with Lightwave's biometric wristbands. These wearables monitored heart rate, location and movement, from which conclusions could be drawn about 'audience engagement'. On Centre Court there were sensors capturing the volume of applause and the length of tense silences. Online, spectators could respond to the match under the hashtag #FeelWimbledon. Laura Schwab, Jaguar's UK Marketing Director, describes this data as revealing a deeper kind of truth about the occasion of Rafael Nadal's 'heartbreaking' loss. 'You can look at the score,' she says, 'but the real story is, what did it feel like?'

The irony is that, in this case, these feelings were largely converted back into numerical outputs, which have more in common with a scoreline than an Olivier soliloquy. There was, we are told, the poignant tally of 34.3 hours of total silence during Nadal's upset.[1]

While these businesses develop new ways to discover the truth of our feelings, our own sense of reality is being altered by these very commercial demands that profit from capturing them. With emotions becoming a new capitalist frontier, we are told that we can only know reality if we know what it feels like.

And the Survey Says ...

Big Emotion scans our tweets for sentiment, takes our pulses and peers into our eyes like Larry David in *Curb Your Enthusiasm*, but it also asks that we pitch in to help the cause of intelligibility. You may have noticed that there has been an expansion in the number of polls and surveys that rise to meet you as you journey through your day. It's now apparently part of our social contract to volunteer our feelings and judgements in easily countable formats. One consequence of assigning huge financial value to our emotions is that their expression changes to match their final destinations in the database. We are now regularly asked to declare our feelings according to the logic and limitations of a survey.

Here is a squalid example. One morning recently there was a tap at my front door. I zoomed up from the depths of hungover

---

1. Since that match Nadal has regained his form. When he returned to the top ranking in 2017 after a three-year absence from this summit, the tennis player admitted of this achievement: 'It's a big emotion for me.'

sleep and staggered with that particular decompression sickness to the door, where I found a man with fingers draped in shopping bags. It was my forgotten supermarket delivery. Hastily and inappropriately dressed (I remember fabric billowing), I relieved him of the bags and shut the door. Later that day I received an email from the supermarket vendor, asking me to rate my experience of the driver, on a scale of one to six, between Disappointing and Excellent. I considered the wine-stained apparition that greeted this driver. Surely he, if anyone, had the right to feelings of disappointment. But no, I had to judge how courteous *he* was. 'Was your driver polite?' I was asked. Did he/she explain any swapped items, was he/she careful with the groceries, did he/she take any unwanted bags away with him? Am I alone in hearing a note of menace in the supermarket's description of their drivers as 'the friendly face' of the business?

We now know that an experience is over when it's time to quantify it, the moment ending on a question mark rather than a full stop. After each journey using a ride-sharing service, you are locked in that stalemate of mutual appraisal. Similarly, from library coffee shops to airport security lines, it's now commonplace to encounter those stands with childish buttons for us to press on our way past. 'How was your experience today?' these unstaffed customer-service stations ask. The nebulous swirl of sentiment that we carry around with us must then be compressed into one of four buttons, each painted with a different cartoon face, moving swiftly from beet-red rage to beatific green smile. A New Zealand company called Push My Button is 'the official reseller' of the Happy or Not survey terminal. They are in the business of understanding our moods. 'Do you know if satisfaction differs by the time of day?' the Push My Button website asks pointedly. 'Increase happiness, and grow your business' is another of its imperatives. An embedded promo video for Happy or Not warns of the dangers of ignoring the sadness or annoyance of clients, and offers the solution: a quick and convenient poll of consumer or employee feeling. The video shows graphics of customers with hearts pulsing in their chests: 'How can a company be certain of what their entire customer base actually feels about their service?' In the midst of all this warm and fuzzy talk of feelings, the real agenda is hammered home: capturing customer emotions is one of the 'keys to increasing your profits'.

In the field of artificial intelligence, moreover, innovation depends on making us as intelligible as possible to the machines. As with marketing analytics software, success currently demands a simplification of our responses. Computer scientists at MIT recently conducted an experiment into robotic mind-reading. The robot, named Baxter, is given a binary task of sorting two types of objects – paint and wire – into their appropriate containers. Baxter has the aid of a 'human collaborator', whose brain signals Baxter can capture and interpret using sensors attached to the human's head. This is a closed-loop experiment, meaning that the human and the robot interact directly throughout, responding to each other's behaviour. Whenever Baxter makes a mistake in its sorting task, the human's brain will automatically transmit an error-related potential (ErrP) signal, prompting the robot to buck up its ideas. In response to this ErrP, Baxter's face changes from neutral to 'embarrassed', denoted by a crestfallen expression and, of course, blushing cheeks. But Baxter's blushes share none of the ambiguity of George Eliot's 'dubious flag-signal'. The interaction hinges on a binary human input: ErrP or no ErrP. Paint box or wire box, correct or not correct. In this infancy of AI, some robots may be being built eerily in our image but, due to the agendas of Big Emotion, our affective lives are being reshaped in theirs.

For this reason, a comedy of errors is brewing in that uncanny place where people and machines mix and mingle. In 2015, a pioneering AI company called Hanson Robotics unveiled its humanoid robot called Han, which, unlike blushing Baxter, can read and respond to human facial cues. At the time Hanson saw itself as 'the leader in creating the most humanlike robots with a full range of human facial expressions'; its robots are skilled in the 'emulation of over 62 facial and neck muscular architectures'. In the same year, Facebook began testing its 'Reactions' feature – the panel of six emojis that sits alongside the 'Like' button. These 'reactions' included variations on 'Like' ('Yay' and 'Wow'), but users were at last able to hint at bleaker human moods with the 'Angry' or 'Sad' buttons. The digital age's zest for quantitative analysis has primed me to notice the disparity of these figures: six versus sixty-two. For it's a comic irony of the times that, while robots are being developed to interpret the widest possible range of human expression, we are increasingly encouraged to corral our responses into a narrow, incomplete spectrum. AI machines engage with what Henry James's father called a 'sensuous educa-tion', yet we are pleased to have our mobile devices stocked with the newest emojis.

Unlike the rigid online coding of human expression, popular imaginings of AI exploit the terror of emotional ambiguity. Speculative fictions of the near-future envision the eerie signs of an artificial life form's emerging sentience: a lingering, knowing stare from their synthetic eyes, the merest smirk at the outer edge of their polymer lips. Programmes such as *Humans, Black Mirror* and *Westworld*, as well as the films *Her* and *Ex Machina*, explore artificial life grappling with the subtlest shades of feeling, broadcast in an era in which Mark Zuckerberg has yet to trust us with a 'Dislike' button. Hanson Robotics's more recent invention is the robot Sophia, who is more uncannily lifelike than Pepper, and who in 2017 was awarded Saudi Arabian citizenship. In a scripted interview, Sophia announced in that stilted, metallic robot voice we've known for ever: 'I want to live and work with humans. So I need to express emotions to understand humans and build trust with people [. . .] I strive to become an empathetic robot.' Both humans and humanoid machines are currently embroiled in new questions of expressiveness, precisely at the moment when we are dematerialising into their networked world and they are trundling into ours.

'What they really want is the ability to express empathy,' Zuckerberg said during a corporate event, speaking not of robots, but of his billion Facebook users and their desire to do more than 'Like'. I'm not of the strangely austere school that objects to people garlanding their text with emojis. However, these little icons are, appropriately enough, symbolic of a more pervasive process by which online platforms invite us to divide our feelings into discrete categories. To every Facebook post we can append our feelings in emoji form, which we are encouraged to choose from a drop-down menu. There is also a storehouse of other options, each with accompanying emoji, which the predictive function rushes to supply. If you're feeling eccentric you can name your feeling yourself, and illustrate it with an off-piste smiley, but the list of official options inevitably reveals the affective status quo. Those absent feelings further delineate, through negative space, the limits of Facebook's emotional landscape. There is no 'feeling horny',

I notice, despite all the porn, though there is 'sexy', chaperoned by a winsome, blushing emoji with a lunar tilt. It's hard to imagine a less sexy icon, unless the pursed lips and red cheeks are meant to signify mid-coital ardour. Facebook is puritanical in matters of the flesh (the 'naked' feeling comes with a fig leaf), though you can announce that you're drunk or hungover – a big red tongue tipped out.

But most conspicuous in absence are the feelings that suggest a concealed inner life behind the public emoji, a potential disconnect between what is felt and what is revealed. According to the certified roster, we don't feel secretive, private or demure. There's no feeling sly, disingenuous, treacherous or even ambivalent, though you can be 'conflicted'. The closest to irony you can get is 'sarcastic', a helpful admission for the sentiment analysts. It is not considered indecorous to publicise feelings that were once thought to be intensely personal – loneliness, heartbreak, desperation – as long as they are unambiguous. Facebook likes to think the best of us, so that we are never 'ungenerous', 'petty' or 'vengeful'. Such negative emotions are generally turned inwards and are variations of self-pity, of being 'unwanted', 'unappreciated' or 'unimportant'. Tellingly, many of these less upbeat feelings, no doubt seen as downers in the caffeinated breakout rooms of Southern California, aren't considered important enough to come with a corresponding emoji. Instead they are lumped together under the sign of the sleepy face, with Zs stamped across the brow. Here at last there is a longed-for hint of ambiguity – is this generic snoozer meant to signify the world's boredom at the troubles of others, or does Facebook assume that the sufferer must simply fall into a swoon at the sadness and unproductivity of it all?

Meanwhile, back in the lab, SoftBank corporation's 'emotional' robot, Pepper, has been introduced to the US market after a successful launch in Japan. Pepper can recognise some emotions but, during a demonstration, the boyish, flirtatious machine requested that the *Wall Street Journal*'s Joanna Stern keep her facial expressions 'simple'. Thus, while robotics companies are trading on the relative complexity of their products' emotional intelligence, the same agenda urges us to simplify and exaggerate ours. Stern stooped in front of the diminutive robot and gave it an amplified frown, another Greek theatre mask of a feeling – or to use a contemporary metaphor, she contorted her face into an emoji. Robots such as Pepper are intended to help care for children and the elderly but, at this point in their sophistication, any emotional interactivity will arguably require pantomime performances from their human pals.

There is a 'Gift of the Magi' quality to these two trajectories. In O. Henry's 1905 Christmas tale, a poor wife sells her prized hair to buy her poor husband a beautiful fob for his gold watch. Sentimentally, she imbues the gift with her husband's attributes: 'It was like him. Quietness and value – the description applied to both.' When she presents him with the fob, he has the reciprocal experience: 'The dull metal seemed to flash with a reflection of her bright and ardent spirit.' These things come alive with their feelings. But then the wife discovers that her husband has, that very day, sold his watch to pay for some bejewelled combs for her long, lustrous hair, which she has just hawked for twenty dollars. In our digitised version of this tale of compassion and folly, one set of programmers works on teaching robots the nuances of the Mona Lisa smile, while a second prepares the code for emoji U+1F195, otherwise known as 'Face with Head Bandage'.

Sympathy and Fantasy

The expression of empathy is not just a problem for the robots. In our own carbon-based fashion, we're learning the appropriate ways of displaying our sympathies in a world that feels both intimate and exposed, where we can never fully know the effects of our announcements on other people. The anxiety of showing any true feeling in these conditions is especially raw when it comes to the moral questions of who receives our sympathy and who doesn't. I sometimes cheat this fraught system by expressing my sorrows in a particularly insular and bunkered way:

'Did you hear?' I ask my dead mother.

'What?' she replies.

'Alan Rickman died.'

'Oh no . . . ! Not Alan!'

'I know.'

'Just awful.' We both say at once. She winces again at the idea of it.

'That voice,' she says.

'I know.'

'Poor Alan.'

I don't dare mention Victoria Wood. Luckily my mother isn't an omniscient ghost, and she relies on me for this sort of news. And as a ghost, she has yet to die in the way of other people. I have found that having a couple of full-time phantoms affects my relationship to sympathy. When I hear about Carrie Fisher's death, for instance, or Caroline Aherne's, I think how awful that must be, both for them and their loved ones, but it's as if I have no first-hand experience of such sadness. I feel gobsmacked and frightened and innocent of these feelings. My sympathy doesn't spring from a sense of recognition. What my parents did, in their tactless relay race, belongs to a different category. I sense this difference more strongly with my mother, perhaps because she was robbed of more time than my father, and so her dying is even more partial and incredible. And in any case, being a Fifties chap, I don't think he would be much moved, now that there is neither Morecambe nor Wise nor smiling Sid James, by these newfangled celebrity passings. My guess is that Dame Vera Lynn is the only star left who could make him wince.

The philosopher Adam Smith, also deceased, wrote that we 'sympathize even with the dead'. He meant that we lament their non-being on their behalf, even though we know that they can't be consoled by our sympathy. My variation – posthumous gossip – takes Smith at face value. But this question of why we sympathise, and more generally how we recognise and partake in the emotional lives of others, was a major one for Smith and other Enlightenment thinkers. Smith's countryman David Hume often wrote about this mysterious transfer of emotion in terms of how vividly or faintly other people appear to us. He suggested that 'sympathy be much fainter than our concern for ourselves, and a sympathy with persons remote from us much fainter than that with persons near and contiguous'. But the basis of clear-eyed morality, for Hume, involves adjusting for our own partiality, turning the contrast dial up or down, to make far-away faint people more vivid, and those who are too vivid – too close for us to assess without prejudice – appear fainter. We must move imaginatively closer to those who are distant, and place some rational distance between those whom we know best.

Any imbalance in this moral vivacity becomes obvious during times of mass tragedy, when how the world offers its sympathies is revealing. After the French attacks of November 2015, *Je Suis Paris* became a global hashtag of solidarity and identification. World landmarks were bathed in red, white and blue lights, from the Sydney Opera House to Christ the Redeemer in Rio de Janeiro. For the first and last time, Facebook invited us all to follow monumental suit by promoting its French-flag profile filter, 'to support France and the people of Paris'. Online, old friends and new friends showed their sympathy, their cheeks flushed with the tricolour. But at the far edge of this horror, wasn't there an incidental glint of panache in the 'Je Suis' formulation?

As was pointed out at the time, where were the filters to mark the fresh attacks on Ankara or Beirut? Every day could be a day to stand in visual solidarity with Syria. For many, the proliferation of French flags unambiguously represented the insularity of the West, despite a prevailing rhetoric of internationalism. Facebook has since discontinued this custom, in recognition of its invidiousness. Now, users can develop their own mournful veils to which other users can subscribe, but the top-down nudging of our sympathies quickly proved to be an untenable model. After the 2016 Nice attacks, the *Mirror* newspaper noticed Facebook's new tactfulness, and so ran a short how-to article for its readers, linking to an app that would keep the tricolour effect alive.

On one hand, the Facebook filter was the opposite of a blush: a voluntary, unambiguous sign. But on the other, we were back in the world of Eliot's 'dubious flag-signal'. Behind the apparent simplicity of this display were myriad private motivations, memories and local sentiments, among which were a million fantasies of Frenchness. Since the nineteenth century, Paris has been a focal point of international daydreaming. 'Paris Syndrome' sounds like the quintessential urban legend, but is by all accounts a real phenomenon in whereby Japanese visitors to the city fall ill with disappointment.

I lived in Paris for six months of my twenties, and the long stretches of newcomer's solitude were filled with an unsteadying interplay between fantasy and reality. I watched the workers returning home, carrying baguettes with the tops – the elbows – already bitten off. The sight of an old woman buying biscuits at the bakery section of a down-at-heel grocery store had a Balzac pathos and dignity. Halves of lemon sunk into crushed ice, omelettes at midnight, a waiter's apron, the ashen melancholy of a big boulevard – all my delights had been felt by others a thousand times before, but they were overtired rather than tired, and had that jittery, perverse energy of this stage of exhaustion. I loved passing that most sustainable resource of Parisian life: rows of people sitting outside, fulfilling their contractual obligations to my fantasies, drinking small drinks slowly and talking a kilometre-a-minute, holding up their cigarettes to the evening sun.

When I go back to Paris now there is always a dreamlike quality to the first few hours. One of the last times I visited, our waitress during this transitional phase asked where we were from. 'Londres!' she sighed, pressing the base of a four-euro Coke into her midriff as she flipped off the cap. 'I would love to go there.' While she gazed into the middle distance and thought of London, I remembered my sooty slalom down the Victoria line, the St Pancras sushi shop's mindless circuit, the vastness of consumer choice that somehow always funnels itself into a Pret A Manger porridge. Her daydreaming cut like acid through mine and, out past the awning, the rue des Abbesses looked suddenly corroded and fragile. The circular, faux-marble tables all around me began to resemble their ersatz counterparts outside the Café Rouge at Euston Station.

Many of our allegiances are based on fragile daydreams such as these. They can be more vivid than real life itself and, when it comes to the question of empathy, vivacity is key. In our capacity for solidarity and fellow-feeling, you can find a map of our romantic identifications. In Patrick Hamilton's novel *Hangover Square* (1941), the doleful antihero George Harvey Bone confronts the brutal prejudices of our sympathies in terms very similar to Hume. Picking up a newspaper, Bone 'scanned the headlines gloomily. "TRAINS CRASH IN SNOWSTORM: 85 DEAD, 300 INJURED."' We are told how he 'experienced a momentary feeling that he was about to be shocked, and then saw that the news came from Budapest, which meant that he did not have to be shocked. Train disasters [. . .] had their own tragic haloes which grew faint and dissipated at a great enough distance.'

But what happens to the relationship between distance and feeling in a world that, in certain respects, makes many of us more proximate than we have ever been? As we have already been exploring, we can now see pictures from inside the train, walk virtually among the images, read tweets from the survivors, read the last tweets from the dead. And of course if far-away suffering is potentially closer to us, we are also closer to it. Possibly, but not always. One of the most difficult aspects of voicing emotion online is that we can't predict the range of our pronouncements. To whom are we speaking? Are we able to express feelings as naturally as we once did, now that the bounds of our audiences are inherently unstable? Was this 'natural' feeling ever that desirable to begin with?

An audience is now a volatile idea, and this volatility has already begun to impact upon the ways in which we register our public sympathies. Eleven months before 'Je Suis Paris', its ontological predecessor appeared. On 11th January 2015, three days after the attacks on the satirical French magazine *Charlie Hebdo*, more than three million people gathered in the Paris streets to protest at the shootings and to honour the victims. The words 'Je Suis Charlie' were repeated, on placards and head-bands. In horrific death, it was a mass declaration of being. The phrase itself began in the immaterial world as a Twitter slogan, and will be remembered as one of the decade's most infamous metaphors. But its huge popularity and worldwide reiterations almost immediately summoned its opposite – 'Je Ne Suis Pas Charlie' – in objection to this mass identification with what many considered to be a recklessly inflammatory paper widely accused of racism. Of those who took the original stance, most were, presumably, Charlie to the extent that they'd prefer that people not be slain for drawing or writing or speaking. Other Charlies, more Charlie than the first, believed in the magazine's satirical project. But such a collective slogan was unable to reflect these differing gradations of metaphor.

The sudden global interest in the cartoons of a historically marginal publication, stinging from the edges of the French press, distorted the power dynamics necessary for satire. To be 'mean and nasty' has always been *Charlie Hebdo*'s motto, but it is far less sustainable to be mean and nasty from a position of cultural influ-ence, on a large stage. In an interview with the BBC a year after the attack, *Charlie Hebdo*'s editor Gérard Biard discussed the problem of the magazine becoming an international symbol. 'It's sometimes difficult,' Biard said, 'because you speak to people that are not supposed to read you.' The attacks had cost the survivors the hideous, evil loss of their colleagues. But in the aftermath the magazine also lost the easy maliciousness of the ignored. The French culture minister granted a subsidy of one million euros to the publication, bringing the anti-establishment paper into the mainstream. And so in this sense *Charlie Hebdo* has indeed become symbolic, not only as a zealous defender of free speech at any price, but of how many of our margins are less marginal than they used to be. We no longer have the assurances, for good or ill, of the periphery. When people get censured for voicing their feelings, it is often because they are speaking to those whom they didn't think could hear them. Hume believed that in our assessments of others we 'confine our view to that narrow circle, in which any person moves, in order to form a judgment of [their] moral character'. But how will these judgements have to change, now that many of us no longer move in the narrow circles of eighteenth-century societies, but rather in the vast, exposed spheres of digital community?

Many years after Patrick Hamilton's train crash, in the non-fictional Tavistock Square a diverted bus became one of four sites of the 7/7 bombings. In an essay about the attacks, Andrew O'Hagan remembers the days when his old office at the *London Review of Books* shared a building with the British Medical Association, the entrance of which was 'shattered' and 'pierced' by the explosion. He understands that pictures of the gore-splattered door would not only affect those who intimately know the building. And yet, he writes, 'proximity is the currency in a culture of bomb-fear: those of us who used to come to that place every morning might be allowed to pause for a second in our own way'. There is something apologetic in his tone here – the pause may only last a second – while at the same time he admits that such devastating events produce gradations of feeling among those who witness them. I am interested in this momentary, deeply private pause. Can it, and should it, ever be represented in the universalising grammar of social media?

The Small Personal Voice

While the reality of our emotions is now big business for third parties, it is a tricky business for us participants in this public–private partnership otherwise known as social life. If we are to live the majority our lives in the cosy line of fire of this global intimacy, how will the construction of our feelings change? The more we are invited to share the contents of our minds with fluctuating, indeterminate, unpredictable audiences, the more we will have to work out a new common language for the communication of feeling. We will have to find one that is agile enough to negotiate the pervasive, paradoxical scope of social media, which is at once universal and particular.

When we express our sorrow, anger and joys, these local, personal feelings are measured against international standards of sensitivity and goodwill. I have witnessed one person being chastised on Twitter because she expressed her delight that it was snowing in London. Think of rough sleepers! she was urged. What could she say in reply? In these times it is impossible for many of us to ignore the great tactlessness of our lives. We *should* think of the homeless on cold nights, and work politically to improve the general conditions for everyone. That old enclosure of grace – the family encircled in a prayer of thanks before the meal – has been opened out by the fact that we now count our blessings in public. We can no longer simply 'remember' or 'think of' those less fortunate, since online we address them directly, and crucially they can address us in return.

We can already see our emotional language changing as we acclimatise to this global intimacy. A Canadian friend of mine announced online that he was going to see the Tragically Hip's farewell concert in Kingston, Ontario, their last because the lead singer was very ill. He anticipated that it would be an evening in which he 'felt all the feelings'. This phrase and its equally vague variations have emerged in the last few years. Someone posting an affecting news story or blog may caption the link with the conclusive words: 'All the feelings'. These formulations are significant because they allow us to be both expressive and general. They admit defeat in the face of relentless demands to define our moods. 'All the feelings' is the equivalent of two fists pummelling along the short row of plastic smiley buttons. But this is a deceptively guarded display of sentiment, at once effusive and impersonal, communicating the fact of intense emotion while nimbly evading interrogation.

In 1957, Doris Lessing published an essay called 'A Small, Personal Voice'. It was about the state of the novel in the Cold War, 'a time which is so dangerous, so violent, explosive, and precarious that it is in question whether soon there will be people left alive to write books and to read them'. Sound familiar? The essay explores how these first years of nuclear terror affected language, now that science, in splitting the atom, had 'assaulted that colossal citadel of power'. Lessing felt that words themselves had been changed by the World Wars and this new threat of planetary annihilation. 'Words,' she writes, 'can no longer be used simply and naturally. All the great words like love, hate; life, death;

loyalty, treachery; contain their opposite meanings and half a dozen shades of dubious implication.' Under the pressure of the nuclear paradox – that microscopic colossus, the immense within the minuscule – many of the old great binaries had likewise collapsed. In these conditions it is hard, she argues, 'to use words like good and bad'.

But for Lessing the very possibility of nuclear Armageddon was buttressed by one last great binary, which she believed was frighteningly intact: the public versus the private. 'We all know,' she claims, that 'there is a terrible gap between the public and the private conscience'. She most feared the impersonality of institutions, the decrees of government committees, which would be willing to enact more atrocities as collectives than any individual on their own could stomach. It was the 'anonymous technician', not the solitary 'madman', whose finger was poised over the apocalyptic switch in her mind. And so, addressing her sphere of influence, she wanted the novelists to help bridge this gap between private sympathies and collective misdeeds. The fiction writers of her time, she urged, should fill their books with the modern drama of 'the responsible individual, voluntarily submitting [their] will to the collective, but never finally; and on insisting on making [their] own personal and private judgements before every act of submission'. As well as dramatising this moderate individual, who negotiates the tension between personal morality and civic duty, Lessing saw the form of the novel itself as a threshold medium between the public and private spheres. She imagines the novelist as someone speaking 'as an individual to individuals, in a small personal voice'. In her era of committee art, Lessing recognised a need for such a personal voice to be heard in public life.

Lessing's essay was written in the year following her break from the Communist Party and should be read in this context. Our own reboot of the nuclear catastrophe franchise is very different. Do we not currently fear the madman more than the technician, the private rant impersonating civic judgement: 'Sad! DEATH PENALTY! DO SOMETHING!!!'? A little institutional anonymity would be welcome at this point. And equally, at the level of the ordinary individual, the gap between the private and public conscience is narrowing. The opinion-miners and emotion-capturers work to cross this divide, to dish the paydirt of what one data-driven art installation called 'The Body's Truth'. DigitasLBi's Marcus Mustafa, who – you might recall – defines emotional data as 'all the things in between the lines', believes that 'the "in-between" is rapidly disappearing'. As a result, in addition to all the relevant offers streaming into our wearables, Mustafa wonders whether, in this disappearing space between our feelings and our actions, 'we might become more aware of ourselves, and hopefully more tolerant to others'.

There is no doubt that small personal voices, silenced for so long, are rightfully being heard, and that the culture that brings us sentiment analysis has also enabled a more coordinated, sustained and empathetic movement towards social justice to mobilise in response to these voices. With this vanishing in-between, some of the shelters for unambiguous immorality and clear abuses of power are being torn down. When BBC Radio's ethical debate programme, *The Moral Maze*, discussed the early days of the Harvey Weinstein scandal, the journalist Tim Dowling remarked: 'Where's the maze?' Nevertheless there do remain mazes aplenty, not only of the moral kind, but also those through which our offhand, half-formed thoughts and feelings blunder. We mustn't let the hedged walls of those mazes be bulldozed, in the annexing of the inner life by public, commercialised scrutiny.

The more our sentiments are commodified, the more we are coaxed to narrow this gap between thinking and expressing. In this climate we're still trying to find the right volume for the small personal voice, to place our sense of reality among the realities of others. And so there are often apologies for hasty musings, for what reaches the ears of others as a big personal voice, an opinion resounding like policy. In Lessing's essay, she observed that language had become so decentralised and subjective that 'the simplest sentence overheard on a bus reverberates like words shouted against a cliff'. A version of this phenomenon lies behind much of the ill-feeling, as well as the revolutionary potential, of our current public discourse. Perhaps this challenge to find an ethical, common language will produce the mould for a new kind of moral individual, forged in the linguistic pressure to translate our private lives onto this expansive public stage. It is possible that tact, out of sheer necessity, will become the gateway virtue for a new kind of inclusive thinking. We will perhaps be forced to reassess some of our ideas of the world, out of blushing embarrassment, if not empathy, or shame.

PART 3

Bolts from the Blue

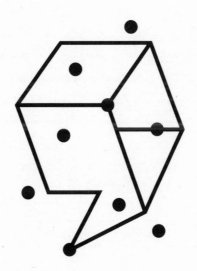

CHAPTER 7

Final Fantasies

In the world of public emotion, few things convey true anguish less than the online 'Nooooooo!!!' written above the news of a beloved celebrity's death. The sorrow certainly exists somewhere else, but for me it doesn't lift off the page. Likewise, the crying sad-face, pinned to the death-notices of both celebrities and real-life loved ones, however well meant, has felt at times to this bereaved person like a glib reaction. For me, the fleet of RIPs that we see now, except in cases of the very elderly, advocate for hurried, terrible closures. I've often wondered why we're so quick to wish peace on those who could perhaps enjoy allies in their fury at being so cruelly cheated of their days. The 'Rest in Power' alternative is closer to this spirit, but puts a different sort of burden on the dead. We can of course communicate aspects of bereavement online, but these platforms often make it difficult to capture the rawness of shock, or to bear relation to the unending, quiet No behind the 'Nooooooo!!!'

And yet, the opposite is also true. One of our emerging problems, which will require careful legislation, is the horrific
proximity of online death. Suicides and murders make news
whenever they are live-streamed on Skype or Facebook. The
vlogging millionaire Logan Paul was recently 'punished' by
YouTube for his video from Japan's 'haunted' Aokigahara forest.
The place is a notorious suicide spot, and in the video Paul is
filmed beside the body of a dead man. In his Twitter apology he
describes being 'misguided by shock and awe', but nonetheless
YouTube demoted him from their lucrative 'Google Preferred'
programme, which allow stars such as Paul to receive the largest
cuts from the brands advertising on his channel. As one enter-
tainment journalist put it, the scandal had caused Paul to be
'demonetised'. But there is certainly a reliable market for morbid
footage. Compilations of 'final selfies', taken moments before
hideous accidents – falls, plane crashes – are a new photographic
genre. Videos featuring real or impending death are also popular.
In one, two young men speed through the English countryside,
going faster and faster and chattering away until the phone that
is filming them drops suddenly and blankly to the ground. This
particular car accident has been kept available as a public-service
warning, but typically such gruesome posts, like Logan Paul's,
are removed in order to prevent these upsetting realities from
penetrating our ease.

Our current social relationship to death, then, feels both too
mediated and too immediate. We are both screened-in by virtual
platitudes and over-exposed, with bodies bursting vividly through
the haze of our online scrolling. When death arrives into the
intimacy of one's house, however, there is no tab to close, no link
to break. There is no more commonplace happening that so utterly

disrupts our sense of both our inner and outer realities. As an event, death shocks the living because of its resistance to interpretation. What are we supposed to do with it? In *Levels of Life*, Julian Barnes describes a death as 'that banal, unique thing'. We can't, he feels, 'make it part of a wider pattern'.

One way to weave it into the wider pattern, which Barnes's book itself enacts, is to at least attempt interpretation, to transform the impossible death into art. There has long been evidence of an artistic impulse to capture the details of death when it occurs. Several millennia since the earliest Egyptian death-masks, the Impressionist painter Claude Monet could not help analysing the changing colours and tones of his wife Camille's skin in the hours after she died. This intense observation resulted in his portrait 'Camille on Her Death Bed'. In our century, Annie Leibovitz photographed the corpse of her lover, Susan Sontag, saying later that to do so seemed a natural extension of her artistic practice. The Scottish novelist John Niven has described how his brother's suicide immediately prompted him to shape it in words:

> I excused myself from my mother and sister, who were weeping in each other's arms, and went into the bathroom. I locked the door, sat down with my little Moleskine notebook, and recorded everything that had just happened: the angle of light from the window above the bed, the coiling pale blue lines of the monitors.

When large-scale disasters strike, a common response of bystanders is that it 'felt like a movie'. Devastating reality appears to us as impossibly unreal. And so we try to *realise* death using the tools of the living, creating stories, things and images to contain it in terms we can understand. While death is arguably the most typical and vivid example of how life can be punctured by some irreconcilable realisation or event, the more or less coherent pattern of our reality is disrupted in other ways. In these moments, it can feel as though our surface reality is breaking down, revealing glimpses of a truer but more incredible reality behind it. These ruptures force us to reconsider our own position in the world, to find a new place to stand in relation to a fragile sense of real life.

After the political upheavals in the West in 2016, there is a general feeling that reality itself is becoming less real. Alongside this civic disorientation, we are having to reconcile the rupturing effects of an increasingly commercialised world, one in which the fantasies of advertisements are routinely and tightly entwined in the fabric of everyday experience. In such an unreal environment, the technologies that allow us to measure and monitor ourselves offer the consoling stability of data, its apparently objective take on what is *really* happening. But what are the consequences of prioritising this quantified view of reality?

Memento Murray

One way that we have tried to find forms for the big existential questions is through allegory. Renaissance writers were especially partial to allegorical treatments of our grandest abstract ideas: love, death, good, evil. Tennis, as it happens, was a popular allegorical subject. In 1632, Francis Quarles wrote a poem in which God and the Devil play a tennis match for the human soul. 'Man is a Tennis court,' Quarles's allegory begins, 'His Flesh the Wall: The Gamster's God and Sathan; Th'heart's the ball.'

The poem's narrator beseeches God to 'Strike, and strike hard, but Strike above the line;/Strike where thou please, so as the Sett be thine.' The court itself, being made of mortal flesh, is naturally 'base' and untrustworthy, with 'many a false Rebound'. The poem's narrator beseeches God to volley our ball-souls, keeping them safely away from 'th' ground', an allegorical symbol for the grave. Since the game's earliest incarnations, writers have recognised its symbolic possibilities. Allegorical Renaissance poetry used the conceit of real tennis, a medieval precursor of the modern sport, to dramatise life's most important moral and practical battles.

I'd like to bring this tradition of tennis-court allegories into the twenty-first century, to illustrate what I mean about those moments in which our reality is somehow ruptured. In 2012, having not watched the US Open for many years, I was curious to see if Andy Murray could beat Novak Djokovic in the final. I should say that at that time I was already fairly primed for moments where the real and the unreal seemed to coexist in the same room. By then my father was very frail and had just been moved, for the last three weeks of his life, into a local nursing home. He was so weak that he often lapsed into hallucination. These delusions were often on a House of Windsor theme, even though he never normally mentioned the Royal Family and certainly didn't revere them. Not long before the move, I lay next to him all night because he kept getting out of bed to look for his 'Airforce jacket'. As the Prince of Wales, he said, he would be expected to attend the horse race. We were both dozing on our sides, facing each other like parentheses. At some point he reached out and took my arm, then pulled it slowly towards his opening mouth.

'That's my arm!' I whispered, laughing.

'That's never your arm, is it?' he whispered back.

'Yes it is! What did you think it was?'

After some consideration, he replied, 'A bit of fish?'

When in those final weeks I would go to tuck him in, I might find him propped up in the dark, speaking to whichever shades were gathered at the foot of the bed. 'Would you believe it?' he said on one occasion, throwing his hands up in mock surprise. On realising that I was in the room, he told them, 'So here I am, with my various henchmen.' It was after one of these visits that I came home to listen to the Murray/Djokovic match on Internet radio. Because of the time difference, the match ran late into my night, and I lay in bed half-listening to the commentary. I was aware of the two miles between my father in his bed and me in mine. I had left him turned on his side, cosily burrowed down. Despite the distance, we still made a pair of brackets. But what did we hold between us? Thirty-two years of togetherness, scarcely containable in two miles of residential streets? Or was it another body, slung between us, as if we each held one end of a stretcher? Lying between us was that version of me, the father's son, inevitably and exactly as ill as the father himself.

I dozed off before the match was over, my laptop washing me in spectral light until it put itself to sleep. The next day YouTube showed me the lost visions of the night before. After match point and the two players' standard tummy pats and shoulder rubs, the new champion Murray spent a few minutes with himself, prowling around, crouching and grimacing. The final had taken five hours, and his feet were in tatters. He lobbed his sweatiest accessories into the crowd, then began an exchange with his ecstatic girlfriend, who was on the other side of the stadium. 'I don't have it . . . ' he gestured. He at last limped his way over to his supporters, not to thank or embrace them, but to locate the Rado bauble he was being paid millions to wear during the trophy presentation. He looked up at his girlfriend, who was pointing back across the court towards his bag. He turned away without a smile, or any attempt at the expected off-roading into the friends' box.

With Andy Murray's growling interlude, we're back in the world of Renaissance allegory. His panic, which fell between the relief of victory and the joy of raising the silver cup, was like the best memento mori because it showed how ineluctable forces are working to undo us, even in our brightest moments. Here it was a case of memento money. His expression had a bottom-line brutality to it. Get it done. I want it yesterday. The look was different from his intensity during the match, which revealed all the fear and ferocity you would expect from a world-class competitor absorbed in struggle. This other face came from outside, and signalled a breach in the tennis court's border-walls. Those few minutes while the watch was lost and found again interrupted the self-contained story of the Dunblane boy who became champion of the world. The ill-spiritedness of the outburst had nothing to do with what was happening at the surface of things: an impressive, exciting victory, a cheering crowd, a relieved team, a trophy presenta-tion unrolled. Soon this tear was sealed over as Murray hoisted the trophy, but that which it made briefly visible pulsed like an after-image over the rest of the proceedings. In another obscene display, the workings of the sport – its real, commercial underpinnings – were put on show in the form of a corporate scowl, which sits behind the poster boy's smile, and which the delighted glistering of a wristwatch likewise obscures.

Recently I went online to recover the footage of Murray's escapade with the watch. At around the time it first happened I wrote the description of it that you read here, but I wanted to check that I hadn't missed any details and that it had unfolded more or less as my notes suggested. But when I followed the link embedded in the one tabloid article that also registered the event – this is the company my epiphanies keep – I was taken to a YouTube error message: that shrugging, maddening TV set with an uh-oh mouth. The obscene had retreated, leaving only this jaunty scar. In our world of documentation, the lost YouTube video is a rare instance of forgetting, a modern version of a repressed memory.

Murray and his lost watch are for me symbolic of those instances where something more real than our surface reality becomes visible. At these times it's as if we have a flash of X-ray vision, such that the hidden bones of the moment appear, fixed and glaring. Mine is in one way a banal example: you only have to look at the billboards lining a tennis stadium to understand that this is a corporate event as much as a sporting spectacle. Tennis players and their equipment are covered in a rash of logos, but all of this is so familiar that it has been incorporated into the patina of any match. And while I rationally know that Murray's sponsorships outstrip his earnings from prize money, nonetheless this barefaced display of commercial anxiety made everything happening around it feel like a broken illusion.

Facing Reality

Murray's outburst was in fact so symbolic that it was almost too on-the-nose. That he was searching for a timepiece was a nice allegorical touch. No glory is immortal. Man cannot evade the sands of time, and will even seek out His own end. The Renaissance painter Hans Holbein the Younger would have loved a crack at this portrait of a champion, at the face that appeared from elsewhere, and in a completely different mode from the rest of the scene. His famous work *The Ambassadors* (1533) shows two Frenchmen: Jean de Dinteville, in a Henry VIII-style fur-trimmed, fat-sleeved coat with cap, and a bishop called Georges de Selve, who wears a rich chocolatey floor-length robe. They lean against some wooden shelving heaped with symbolic objects, including navigational equipment and globes. The age of colonial exploration and expansion has begun. The seafarers are abroad. The painting's focus – its cold hearth – is the smeared, anamorphic skull jutting diagonally from the bottom of the canvas.

In Jacques Lacan's reading of the painting, the skull represents a site of collapse, where our everyday reality breaks down. What bursts through this rupture is what he terms 'the Real': that which cannot be represented or mediated by language. We only experience the world, Lacan argues, through a complex system of symbols, the meanings of which we collectively agree upon. Words have serviceable meaning only because we all subscribe to their official definitions. We walk through the streets, 'reading' what we see – buildings, signs, advertisements, other people – and interpreting them as images according to a set of more or less arbitrary cultural values. Lacan's Real eludes this 'symbolic order', resisting our attempts to give it shape in language or imagery. Because it lies outside our web of social codes and conventions, we don't directly experience it.

And yet, we know it is there. The circle drawn around all that we *can* represent symbolically brings into being the impossible idea of what lies outside the circle. But when we try to broaden this circle, to invite this Real inside, it defies our representation, cracking up our language, smearing our brushstrokes. It cannot do anything else. Lacan was interested in Holbein's skull because, in order to bring it into focus, the viewer must stand to one side of the painting. Once you can see the bony gape, the rest of the painting – the merchant's clothes and vainglorious possessions – is blurred. It is impossible for both to be in focus at the same time. To see the Real, in other words, you must first dissolve our world of symbols. To experience true death, rather than our symbolic representations of it, you must step outside life. The painting dramatises how, even if we can't resolve the Real with our everyday map of the world in place, we are nonetheless aware of it. Our symbolic order is disrupted by the knowledge that we move, as social creatures, through a system of approximations that we pluckily call reality.

The presence of the skull thus brings us to life as viewers of the painting by creating a break in our visual field. The painting isn't immersive because, via its deathly glitch, it draws attention to itself as a painted thing. In turn, says Lacan, we become self-conscious. Here we are, looking at a painting. If we are told or guess Holbein's trick, we stand to the side and look from there and, as we shift positions to try to comprehend it, the skull makes us aware of ourselves, our own standing, in relation to the work of art. With a feeling of self-consciousness comes the feeling of being watched, and so Lacan suggests that the painting effectively 'looks back at us' through the stretched eye of the skull. Under its gaze, we feel the fragility of our belief that we inhabit a stable, meaningful reality. The skull challenges all our grand postures, taking the sheen off our possessions – which we invest with so much importance – and mocking our pompous sense of achievement.

That, at least, is one role of the memento mori. But in everyday life, we don't have to be contemplating the inevitability of death in order for our surroundings to somehow seem less than solid and meaningful. We have intimations of the Lacanian Real whenever we perceive the social scene in which we're involved as a kind of coordinated charade. Misfits and outsiders will be familiar with this feeling. It is the sense of being at a school dance and finding all the social mores and codes, which everyone else seems to know intimately and take for granted as 'real', to be somehow ludicrous. Whenever etiquette or convention or ritual – the stuff of the symbolic order – reveals its scaffolding to us, then we might feel that what everyone is calling reality is something else entirely. From such feelings come those nightmarish *Desperate Housewives* inversions of the perfect suburban life, where the ideal is both a façade and a cage.

Capitalism contributes to the feeling that reality is a coordinated charade because it is a system that depends on assigning unfixed values: to goods, people's time, houses, land. The philosopher Slavoj Žižek expands Lacan's idea about *The Ambassadors* 'looking' at us by suggesting that it doesn't just gaze at us as mortals, but as consumers. He argues that the skull isn't the only aspect of the painting that puts us in an impossible position. The clothes and draperies, he points out, are painted in such exquisite detail that, from a standard viewing distance, it feels like our noses are pressed into the iridescent folds of Jean de Dinteville's sleeve. Holbein has zoomed us in without sacrificing our view of the whole, creating a weird perspective that Žižek argues represents the inherent weirdness of the merchant-capitalist sensibility that was burgeoning in Holbein's time. To Death, we now add that other great real-unreality of Money. When viewing the painting, we can see the surface of material things *too well* from our standpoint six feet in front of it. Especially in comparison to the flattened, undetailed skin of the ambassadors themselves, Holbein renders their possessions in so much 'real' detail that these luxury commodities begin to seem too real, hyperreal.

For Žižek, this 'excessive realism' is a commentary on the strange relationship that we have always had with consumer goods: we know that their monetary value is too unstable to be considered 'real', while at the same time we believe in the reality of this unreal value. This value, he writes, 'has material effects upon the lives of both buyers and sellers, even when they realise that talk of such value is a fiction'. We respect this fictional reality enough to pay for it, or indeed to envy others for possessing it. Many of us *really* want to keep up with the Joneses. This sense of hyperreality makes us – as does the skull – self-conscious. We become aware of ourselves as viewers because once again the painting challenges our vision. This excessive painterly detail is another glitch that makes us unsure of where we stand. Are we six feet away or one inch away? Do we believe in what is being represented or not? Can we ever resolve this distortion in the visual field and see things fully as they are? Knowing where to stand in the face of this unreal, commodified reality is an existential question, as well as an aesthetic one.

The Influencer

Commodities, with all the fantasies of status that they materialise, are concrete symbols, a composite of the real and the illusory. While Karl Marx pointed this out over 150 years ago, today the commodity's disruptiveness is intensifying. We are living in an age when it is possible to commercialise our personal experiences on an unprecedented scale. Private life isn't only there to be shared with our followers, but also to open up a space for publicity. In this economy of publicised privacy, the social-media *influencer* is our age's figurehead, an icon of late-capitalism's intensely porous relationship between fantasy and reality. I love the blatancy of the term 'influencer', which lays all its cards on the table. It doesn't attempt to hide the fact that our view of the world is manipulated by external agents. Influencers, such as the disgraced and 'demonetised' Logan Paul, are private citizens of a new kind. Their title comes from their large online followings, which they are often able to commercialise. Time is money, but so are attentive eyeballs, and wherever gazes gather en masse, such as a tennis champion's wrist, advertisers see a potential billboard. And so, among the regular updates designed to maintain and develop their audiences, influencers will intersperse sponsored posts, often a scene supposedly from their real life turned into an advertisement. On Instagram, influencers will label these posts as 'paid partnerships', or with the hashtags #ad or #spon. In them they appear alongside a product they have been contracted to endorse.

Some of these ads are more explicit than others. The Manhattan family medicine doctor, Mikhail Varshavski, who goes by the handle doctor.mike, interrupts his everyday adventures with his beloved husky to be a spokesperson for lubricant. 'Let's talk sex!'

his caption tells his four million followers. 'Healthy and safe sex can happen whenever. K-Y believes you don't need to wait for a special occasion to celebrate each other.' In the photograph, he leans in his scrubs against a wall, hand in one pocket, the other throwing into the air what seems to be a digitally inserted, oversized box of K-Y 'Yours + Mine' Jelly. These influential advertorials aren't in themselves especially discombobulating, since they're merely variations on a standard spokesperson model. They are, however, placed among other non-sponsored posts, so that it can be a K-Y ad one moment and an earnest Doctor Mike studying an X-ray the next, thanking his team of medical colleagues for their hard work. Sponsorship becomes an intermittent but largely undifferentiated part of the influencer's everyday reality.

More deranging than these obvious promotions are those posts in which the paid product appears as just another carefully choreographed object in the influencer's photograph. For example, a blogger called Christabel, who describes herself mercurially as a 'Singapore-based human', has an Instagram post that could pass for the crafted insouciance that saturates the website. Christabel sits in a bleached-out café that is as empty and orderly as the afterlife. On a turquoise table is a tea tray. Christabel is touching the handle of the small glass teapot with a downturned, philo-sophical gaze. Is the tea the product? Is the matching turquoise cup in her hand? What about her striped shoes? Everything is a suspect! Once you click on the picture, it is revealed that the paid partnership is with Calvin Klein. Christabel's crossed legs, jeans torn at the knee, are the product, a modern manifestation of the disruptive, hyperreal object.

The sponsored object distorts the image by inhabiting two registers at once. It is both a thing and a commodity, playing the double role of possession and prop. When it appears naturally within a scene, the caption alone signals that it is an alien presence. And as with a painting that includes a smeared skull, there are two levels of artifice at work here. The most successful influencers aren't gritty realists, but rather stylise their images with signature filters. In other words, even their unsponsored Instagram posts have all the luxe and artifice of a *Vogue* shoot. Their collection of posts are called 'galleries', and their audiences agree, as with paintings, to these simulacra, whereby a series of carefully doctored photos represents real life. Into this faked reality appears the product placement, a visual paradox that makes everything surrounding it appear both more real and less real. More real because all of the non-sponsored stuff in the frame attains a greater sense of belonging by comparison, and less real because the promotional content explicitly undermines the post's pose as a striking moment in someone's 'private' life. As Russian-Swiss influencer Xenia Tchoumi commented in a statement about 'branding tools', 'My Instagram is about sharing my life and experiences with people [. . .] With the branded content tag, I'm able to be fully transparent about my commercial relationships.' In such an economy, where private life merges with commerce, it is transparency, not reality, that counts.

This is not just a way of life for the privileged few who have mastered social media interactivity. More and more people may find themselves able to supplement their incomes as part-time sandwich-boards. As the profession of influencer has become more recognised, the fashion has already begun to move away from a few superstar promoters with enormous followings to smaller-scale influencers. There is the sense that these stadium-filling influencers are becoming too glossed with endorsements and compensations to maintain that ideal balance between fantasy and reality, while so-called micro-influencers are favoured for cultivating a more 'authentic' relationship with their audiences.

Whatever their scale, the influencer's mixing of everyday life with corporate sponsorship produces an effect on their audiences similar to that provoked by *The Ambassadors*. The sponsored post always contains a disturbance that prevents us from being fully immersed in the image because it brings us into being as consumers. We are, in this way, alienated from the picture as a spectator. We can't lose ourselves in the image of someone else's Thai beach holiday, the way we might with other alluring Instagram posts or indeed with Cézanne's *The Bathers*. The commodity calls out to us for special consideration, appealing ultimately to our wallets. It asks us to consider our position in relation to it: do we want it? Can we afford it? In this sense, the sponsored post looks back at us, addressing us, fracturing the agreeable illusion that we are looking at a scene from a real life.

The Counting House

Recently a chill ran down the world's spine when news broke of a New Brunswick lobster whose claw had been tattooed with a partial Pepsi logo. Besides the horror of ocean plastification – one of our 'capital R' Real problems – the lobster was an unwitting spokesperson for the ways in which advertising now intrudes on almost every corner of life, such that crustaceans are brand ambassadors. But this pervasive commercialisation of people's holidays, jobs and hobbies – the influencer's remorseless mix of the real and unreal – is part of a broader de-realisation of public life.

Since the big political shocks of 2016, there has been a sense in the air that reality is disintegrating, that the wider pattern is breaking down. The much-discussed polarisation of ideological positions on both sides of the Atlantic is regularly analysed as a failure to agree on the basic premises of a shared reality. Whether or not this period in these places is more or less precarious than any other can't be established conclusively or quantifiably here, but it is in itself significant that we've begun routinely to frame these times in terms of our disbelief. A new discourse of 'bubbles' has emerged and established itself in the mainstream, positing that people's sense of the world is always partial and biased. In the UK, the EU referendum vote divided the nation, remapping the political landscape. Old party allegiances no longer seemed adequate to describe or predict the public mood. During this turbulence Theresa May, repeating the words 'Strong and stable' despite the circumstances or the context, became known as the Maybot. Coined by the *Guardian* sketch-writer John Crace, this nickname lends itself to talk of glitches and malfunctions. This caricature mockingly suggests that there is no real sentience at the helm of British political life, just a broken machine caught in a faulty loop.

In America, Trump's rise to power was for many a sublime event. The Trump presidency was predicted by an episode of *The Simpsons* from the turn of the millennium, as if the true Y2K bug, all along, was a terrible idea with a long incubation phase. So many of our largest anxieties have this retrospective, fictionalised quality to them, a dated twentieth-century kitschness that can make them feel somehow unbelievable. In circulation are Cold

War pictures of Fifties children crouched under school desks. Scientists have just begun to show off broad-shouldered, humanoid robots that can do back-flips. It isn't difficult to imagine them coolly armed and on a rampage. Elon Musk has called for a ban on 'killer robots', but isn't this fear a back-flip to the storyline from *Terminator*? And, of course, the Nazis are regularly in the news again.

These ironised, passé perils, which manage in their familiarity to feel both terrifyingly real and incredible, appear alongside omens of an unravelling reality. Political jokes are often now focused on this portentous theme. During Theresa May's 2017 party conference speech, letters fell from the Tory slogan on the wall behind her. Language literally cracked up as her extended fits of coughing interrupted her speech. May was later pleased to announce that after the Brexit vote the UK would revert to blue passports, rather than the burgundy of the EU years. She proposed that this change in colour would symbolise 'independence and sovereignty'. It was swiftly pointed out that UK passports could have been blue all throughout Britain's EU membership. In this landscape of uncertain meaning, even symbols are refusing to play along.

Our sense of ontological crisis is played for laughs, viral jokes reporting the latest nonsense from the highest of public offices. One of these jokes, which are in the end as funny as nuclear war, involves Trump claiming to have sold an imaginary aircraft to the real country of Norway (I say real because non-existent countries have also been posited by the same source). In the very meeting where Senator Orrin Hatch removed unreal glasses, Homeland Security Secretary Kirstjen Nielsen refused to confirm that Norway was a 'predominantly white' country.

Collecting and sharing these omens is a new social pastime, and clearly reflects an alertness to the glaring hypocrisies and absurdities of current political language and behaviour. An instant classic in this genre occurred when Pete Hoekstra, US Ambassador to the Netherlands, was interviewed for television by a Danish reporter. Hoekstra denied ever saying that there were 'no-go zones' in the Netherlands because of 'the Islamic movement' and that cars and politicians were being burnt. He dismissed this report as 'fake news', only for the Danish reporter to show him clips of him making these remarks. He then denied that he had just called the reporter's claim fake news: 'I didn't use the words today. I don't think I did.'

We've begun to share these tears in the fabric of normalcy, reason and accountability with genuine, if macabre, relish. But as fake news, post-truth and alternative facts become the corrosive hashtags of the political era, we are also entering into an opposite paradigm where hard, cold facts are given central importance. For as much as this is an age of incredulity and widening gulfs between what is said and what is meant, it is also an age of what could be called hyper-empiricism. The theory of empiricism states that reliable knowledge is primarily attained from direct sensory experience of the world. With new technologies, such as those of Big Emotion, focused on the data-capturing power of sensors, we are more empirical than ever. And so, as the reality we felt we once knew seems to be being dismantled, there is more and more 'reality' in the world in the form of data. While we consider the polarisation of political opinion, this clash between hyper-empiricism and unreality is an overlooked way in which our everyday experiences are being polarised. The importance of collecting data and a retreating sense of 'the truth' now sit side by side. If our shared reality is breaking down, will this quantified approach to life offer a stabilising alternative?

There are no doubt countless and crucial uses to which this hyper-empiricism can be put. It may be that the ability to data-model complex organisations, institutions and ecosystems will become vital to the humane regulation of our societies. We desperately need, for example, to find sustainable equilibria for our energy consumption and production. It is already essential that we track CO_2 emissions, ideally, at this late stage, to the nearest molecule. The ability to set quantifiable parameters of our collective conduct, and to receive full-throated alerts when we are over-stepping the safety of these bounds, may be the mainstay of our long-term survival. But does the individual, living in a society judiciously kept in balance by data analysis, require their own life to be similarly crunched? Should the personal be so zealously analytical?

At no other time in history have we been more confronted with personal measurements. The industry of wearable devices such as the Fitbit relies on the charisma of hard but ever-changing facts, and the idea that our experiences should be filtered through them. Fitbit converts the day's busyness into a count of steps taken. Our sleep and its particulars, once the province of Morpheus, pipes up through our wearables and into the Cloud. In the morning, as dreams disperse, we can peruse a spectral graph of 'Logged Sleep', charting our moments of restlessness between 4.32 a.m. and 7.49 a.m. As the technologies progress, there will be more ways to quantify ourselves. Parents, like the best sentiment analysts, can already track their children's heart rate and temperature remotely. This capacity is taken to a speculative extreme in the *Black Mirror* episode 'Arkangel', in which an anxious mother monitors her daughter's cortisol levels through an embedded chip, activating a parental filter that pixelates the child's vision whenever she encounters something disturbing. In this fictional world, the young are shielded from epistemological ruptures, those moments when reality suddenly seems too impossible to believe.

Every day in this quantified world likely includes a tailor's fitting of sorts, but is the tailor's tape accurate? Does the account of reality produced by our fervent data-crunching offer a recognisable representation of our experiences? There may be much solace and inspiration to be found in a system that seems to define objectively both ourselves and our place in the world. By building our sense of reality out of data, we seek to impose a transparent order on our lives, creating a map of the world that is based on continual, purposeful revelation. As Žižek has pointed out, that moment in *The Matrix* when Neo sees the world in all its reality – a streaming scape of fluorescent green code – is a brilliant representation of what it would be like to experience the Lacanian Real. But in our era, two decades since *The Matrix* was filmed, streams of data no longer solely compose that sublime plane on the other side of our perceptions, but have become a major constituent of how we think about everyday reality. In Lacanian terms, the stuff of the Matrix isn't part of that unknowable Real; it is an ever-increasing element in our symbolic order, how we construct a sense of ourselves and how we navigate the world.

I, probably like you, have been on country walks with avid Fitbitters. In the fields a spring lamb, its coat bright with Easter sunshine, confronts us for a shivering instant and then is off down a green lane. A Fitbit vibrates; a voice cries, 'I've done my steps!' Someone grasps their bare wrist and realises that they've stupidly left their wearable at home. Another misplaced timepiece. They curse themselves, thus consigned for the next hour to picking up and putting down their feet in an ephemeral mug's game, the shadow-play of the unlogged. The one with the Fitbit walks the next ten paces with their head down, fiddling with buttons, studying charts, their silhouette making the old-fashioned shape of a person winding up a watch. I look out to the far-off hills and quietly swell with sanctimony. I rise like a hot-air balloon over the party, feeling soulful and bloated with my authentic way of having an afternoon.

The naysayer is vulnerable to accusations of churlishness. Arguments pour forth about keeping active, motivation, weight loss, the support and spurs of other Fitbitters. It is easy to seem like a Grinch, except that there already seems, overall, a distinct absence of holiday cheer in this economy of self-surveillance, where a burst across the Downs becomes a jackpot of bankable strides. 'People seem disappointed at least as much as they're happy,' I argue with a friend who advocates the merits of such wearables. The device so often seems embroiled with its master in cranky tribunals, accused of not counting enough or counting too much. 'Oh, the point isn't happiness,' my friend replied.

I may have developed a neurotic, ill-tempered relationship to this vision of the quantified future because of the traumas of the past. The idea of being hooked to a device that monitors your vital signs has, for me, too much of the sterile whiff of the intensive-care unit. One of the most frightening nights of my life followed my mother's first surgery, performed under a sudden panic. During the operation her body became septic, and she was comatose for about forty-eight hours afterwards. A wonderful Irish nurse calmly took me through a chart of her various test results, explaining that the number next to her kidney function was a promising sign. On the second evening, when we were saying goodnight, my mother's puffy, unusually badgery hand reached up and took mine. From some far-off place, she slowly shook her head. And so we stayed with her, sharing hour-long shifts at her bedside.

In the dimness of the nocturnal ICU, in this small country hospital in southern Ireland, I held my mother's hand and watched the illuminated numbers moving on the screen above us: blood pressure, respiratory rate, oxygen saturation. I tried to block out the green barbed wire of her pulse, along with all the soap-opera nightmares that snagged on it: Bobby Ewing, naturally, as well as car-crash Daphne from *Neighbours*. Our sickbeds are crowded. In the middle of the night, her respiratory rate suddenly plummeted. I called the nurse over from her station. 'She's all right,' she said, 'those numbers can be misleading.' Soon my mother's breathing climbed back to where it had been. At dawn she woke up, full of mischievous smirks, sparkly-eyed insinuations and conspiracy theories, about the nurses running a drugs ring and the 'pregnant' old woman who had just arrived in the neighbouring bed. While I had passed the hours staring at her statistics, as if my gaze could buoy her blood pressure, she had been lost to toxic dreams.

These ICU associations are what we used to call, in less forgiving times, 'my shit', and I don't mention them in order to lobby for the banning of wearables or to cast snide aspersions on those who benefit from them. But isn't it sometimes hard to deny the miserliness of spirit that our interest in personal data can provoke in all of us? Any fluctuating, quantifiable thing – daily footsteps, calories burnt, number of re-tweets, YouTube views, Airbnb reviews, crypto-currency values – invites an obsessive and solipsistic sort of accountancy. I have certainly cut a crouched, panting figure as I check up on particular stats that are too obscene and mortifying to specify here. We're regularly provided with new ways to think about our lives numerically, giving us a model for our realities that favours concretion over abstraction, quantity over quality. We can now track so many aspects of life that they stream like stock prices along the bottom of our minds. As a consequence, we're spending more and more time locked in the existential counting house, poring over ledgers that could only possibly be of interest to ourselves.

The End of the Story

The world's most notorious miser, Ebenezer Scrooge, is so corrupted by the pursuit of gain that he experiences all of life through this singular lens. When his cheerful nephew visits his counting house on Christmas Eve, Scrooge marvels that so many people should be so merry, when for him the close of the year is 'a time for balancing your books and having every item in 'em through a round dozen of months presented dead against you'. The irony of the story is that, despite being rich, Scrooge was more oppressed by the idea of money than any other character in the Christmas tale. In a paragraph dense with images of enclosure, Dickens describes Scrooge as 'a squeezing, wrenching, grasping, scraping, clutching, covetous old sinner!' He is 'secret, and self-contained, and solitary as an oyster'. The arc of the story shows the spirits disrupting his enclosed sensibility, so that his reality broadens beyond the near horizon of quantifiable profit.

As well as being a tale about the empathetic benefits of virtual-reality simulations, *A Christmas Carol* is a warning against data addiction. The spirits' immersive visions place the covetous miser in the same rooms as former colleagues, lost loves, the family of his ill-treated employee, Bob Cratchit. From this spectral storytelling – the spirits shape Scrooge's life into instructive vignettes – he gains a moral education. The Spirit of Christmas Past takes Scrooge back to his boyhood, when other things besides financial data absorbed his attention. The young Scrooge is lonesome and solitary still, but sustained by his imaginative life. As the boy sits reading, fictional characters materialise to keep him company. Scrooge observes his former self surrounded by these fantasies, which were 'wonderfully real and distinct to look at'. Ali Baba stands outside the schoolhouse window. Then Robinson Crusoe's parrot appears, and the excited money-lender tells his spirit guide how the castaway sails around the island and returns to his bower, only to be wakened by the bird calling to him: 'Poor Robin! Where are you, Robinson Crusoe? Where are you? Where have you been?' This is a poignant moment, since these are really the existential questions that the Spirit is asking Scrooge himself. He begins the voyage back to his own self when he sees these literary visions from his child-hood, which contain not the commodity's alienating blend of reality and artifice, but the hospitable, unreal truth of the artistic imagination. There are other realities, the spirits show him, beyond the clean facts of the balance book.

Just as Scrooge made an idol out of monetary gain, we're making an idol out of precision. In its aim to count and measure reality objectively, science maintains an important distinction between precision and accuracy, two words that are often used interchangeably in everyday speech. For scientists, precision refers in part to the number of significant digits that a measuring device can record.[1] A scale that can show me that I weigh 75.231 kg is more precise than one that measures my weight as 75.2 kg. Precision tells us nothing, however, about accuracy. This precise scale may be broken, since I know that my true weight is 79 kg. And so the instrument is precise but not accurate. A similar tension between precision and accuracy is tightening around our lives beyond the laboratory. Whereas we used to go on walks that would be 'about three miles, round trip, there or thereabouts', we now know how many steps the journey takes.

A reading of 11,378 steps is certainly precise, but besides technical queries about the counting device's accuracy, it can't capture the jokes, squabbles, flares of ancient grudges, fractious hunger, the sense of futility in each step as it becomes clear you'll never make it to the mysterious Yorkshire destination of Cauldron Snout, the chips eaten in the car with the wipers on, all of which could be logged in memory under Crap Day Out no. 149. You could reasonably object that no one in their right mind expects a step-counter to be a video camera, but the seductive property of such data gives it a distorting superiority among the various stories told about our time. One study, conducted by a researcher at University College London, showed that 43 per cent of respondents described activities performed without their Fitbit as 'wasted'. And haven't we noticed, in ourselves and others, how the sense of an event can be altered retrospectively by our documentation of it – how it fits into our quantitative expectations, and how it ranks in the eyes of others?

1. Precision also refers to the degree of variation of results when the same measurement is repeated multiple times. If your results are close to one another, then these measurements are precise.

People delete posts because they haven't market-tested well on Instagram. The influencer, who is both camera-person and accountant, is unabashedly concerned with their currency of countable audience interactions. A disproportionate amount of feeling therefore gathers around these precise measurements, in the thrill of a day that is liked precisely 2,046 times, in the melancholy precision of a 'Story' that is ignored altogether.

Viewing the world in terms of numerical data not only shifts our sense of *what happened* out in the world; such a perspective has important implications. Joseph Cevetello, a digital technology specialist, has written about the emotional impact of managing his diabetes with a glucometer, the device that monitors blood-sugar levels. 'Our interactions define my sense of who I am,' he explains. He keeps a logbook of this data, and has a fixed goal of 100 milligrams of glucose per 1 decilitre of blood. If he meets this target, within a narrow range, he feels 'a sense of accomplishment, a willingness to meet the day', but if the reading is too high, he chastises himself: 'What did I do? What on earth did I eat yesterday?' His qualitative estimation of his blood-sugar levels, based on how he is generally feeling, can clash with the glucometer's reading, so that he might feel poorly but receive a sound result, and vice versa. In other words, the tension between the externally produced data and his own intuition fractures his perception of reality. At such times, he can lose trust in both the meter and his awareness of his condition.

The ability to collect this data, with both accuracy and precision, has given diabetes patients the 'tight control' necessary for the healthy management of their disease. However, for Cevetello, the human administration of this information is merely an intermediary step to a truly liberating revolution in diabetic care. Sensory technology has raised patients out of inevitable ignorance and subsequently poorer prognoses, allowing them to exert the control that stems from knowledge. But the ultimate advancement, for Cevetello at least, involves a return to ignorance. He imagines a 'cyborg' future in which his 'computer pancreas' functions autonomously, sensing his blood-sugar levels and adjusting the insulin output accordingly. He wants to be taken out of the equation, freed from the oppressions of data management and brought into a scenario in which 'it is difficult for me to remember that I have diabetes'.

Those people in similar medical situations to Cevetello understand the double-sided nature of quantified living. While data brings well-being, it can also be oppressively enclosing, locking its subject inside its narrow parameters and definitions. Those who are fortunate enough not to rely on such constant monitoring to maintain their health might heed Cevetello's cautionary tale. For how many of us voluntarily enter into a situation in which a relationship to some kind of daily counting comes to define our sense of self-worth? Setting medical necessity and other forms of constraint aside, a habitual interest in numeric data combines poorly with our vanity and compulsivity. To quantify our own lives so prodigiously without forming unsightly attachments, we would benefit from the robot's cool, data-processing head. But a more likely solution to these addictions, as Cevetello suggests, is to drive this data underground, to benefit from its knowledge while treating it as a kind of obscenity, something that is best not brought to the surface of our everyday realities.

If our current mode of chronic personal accountancy produces its own oppressions and disruptions, it can also be another kind of memento mori. Although data is often used to predict the future, it is after all a representation of an irretrievable moment from the past. This 'pastness' naturally gives it a chilly quality, no better illustrated than in the two bookending dates of a dead person's life, framing that (mad) dash in between. The very act of tallying up suggests a sense of completion, a final reckoning. In Sartre's novel *The Reprieve*, set on the verge of the Second World War, a young Frenchman called Boris imagines his death in combat as a stark quantifying of all the vague, unknowable habits of his life. He glumly calculates how many omelettes he will have eaten in his lifetime. At twenty-two years of age, he judges that he has eaten about 8,030 lunches, estimating that he has an omelette for lunch 10 per cent of the time: 'Only 803 omelettes?' he said to himself with astonishment. 'Oh no, there are the dinners too, that makes 16,060 meals, and 1,606 omelettes. Anyway, for a man partial to omelettes, that was not a considerable total.' Boris believes he will be called up in a year, which means only 730 more of his twice-daily visits to cafés. All this accountancy 'gave him a shock', and he wonders what it is like for other people who do not have this sense of their own impending completion, those 'who could look forward to 10,000, 15,000 evenings at cafés, 4,000 omelettes, 2,000 nights of love'.

Here, the fixity of data heralds death. In Sartre's existential philosophy, once a life is over, it gains a new status precisely because it is complete. The life is bound by birth and death; its containment on the timeline gives it definable borders and limits. The omelettes can be counted; the full story can be told. For Sartre, this enclosed entity known as a life lived takes on the relative inertness of a solid object, as stable in its dimensions and metrics as a table or plant pot. By continually totting up the recent past, we are establishing a morbid relationship between data and the time of our lives. We drag the past behind us, not as an amorphous, mysterious accretion, but as a chain of tallied 'things', made solid and burdensome by our measurements. In this sense, it is not sleep that nightly approximates death so much as it is the clicking of one's wearable, the finished day eulogised with statistics.

Yet at the same time, the ticker-tape jitteriness of a quantified life couldn't be further from sepulchral quiet. We recognise that fizz of anticipation as the latest results come in. Assuming some change, yesterday's tally may embolden us or disappoint us, but the fact that yesterday's datum can only be better or worse than today's ensures that we can't experience one feeling without being exposed to the other. Data is curious, therefore, because it both deadens and animates, and here I'm reminded of the early electrical experiments of Galvani and Volta, the frog specimen's lifeless legs twitching on its slab as a current is passed through its exposed nerves and muscles. It is in honour of Alessandro Volta that we give the term 'voltage' to the difference in electrical potential between two points in a circuit, a metaphoric slope down which a current can flow. The compulsive quality of data can be understood as a kind of voltage. What else drives us to check so avidly our various stats but this 'potential difference'? The placement of the last tally in relation to the prospect of a new one creates the voltage that powers the current of our attention. The true excitement doesn't really lie in the two numbers themselves, but in the space between them, where crackles the promise of change. Any change will do. Perhaps that is why we crave the next quantitative input so forcefully, as proof that we are still here and still accountable, the fluctuating data a cold and jolting *memento vivere*.

The Unreal Reality

To the two certainties of life – death and taxes – you can add data collection. But what about our many uncertainties? We live in a period when new technologies offer us quantitative assurances, at the same times as our broader social realities feel precarious and, from many angles, appear to be a distorting combination of the real and the unreal. If you accept the idea that our data-driven personal lives are cultivating oppressive habits, then we have too much reality on one hand, and too little on the other. We are coming to seem less reliable to one another just as we are at our most quantifiable. As we get better at gathering the facts, we seem to be less politically convinced by them. The pervasive and unapologetic commercialisation of private life, under the glare of which we are evolving from consumer-citizens to advertiser-citizens, creates a purposefully confounding dynamic between reality and fantasy.

These various collisions and mergers between the real and the unreal are definitive of our times. But they are also creating promising kinds of disenchantment and disillusionment. As what we might once have confidently called everyday life comes to seem increasingly unreal, our incredulity can be harnessed into progressive forms of scrutiny. Radical movements – such as Black Lives Matter and Me Too, to name just two – are rising from perspectives that have always stood in some way at odds to the mainstream view. They are demanding the resolution of those blurred skulls that have always been central to our social orders. We're learning to stand at new angles in relation to our everyday normalcy, to question its assumptions and our place within it. These ruptures where the real and unreal meet alienate us from our expectations of the world, but for many of us this alienation is an opportunity to reposition ourselves. The skull sitting on the Renaissance desk is both horrifically alien and horrifically intimate, too distant to be understood, too close to be misunderstood. Whenever our sense of reality is disrupted, we feel put in a paradoxical viewing position, able to see too much and too little. But in this impossible line of sight, new realities begin to appear possible.

One last unreal reality: my mother died at half-past midnight and we were all asleep by three. In her last weeks we had converted my bedroom into a makeshift ward. Two young men had come to assemble the hospital bed, paid for by the NHS. They put it together quickly, like the house was on fire and they were building their own fire escape. But I'm wrong to say that we were all asleep: a Marie Curie nurse was in the house, too. She took her time. She washed my mother, received the doctor to confirm the death, and waited until the Underground started running again before she, as I imagine it, quietly unlatched the door and stepped into the street.

In the morning, while we waited for the undertakers, my father sat at her bedside and ate a bowl of cereal. I walked past the room and only saw the scene sideways, but I remember smiling at the sound of the spoon. It was so perfectly him, and, for the last time, so perfectly them. Under different circumstances, my mum would have loved the bathos of the whole thing. 'It's all nowt' was one of her favourite lines, borrowed from Alan Bennett's memoir and used to undercut the gravity with which life is often taken. It strikes me now that she passed her time in a state of delight at the sense that, because it's all nowt, there is the space and levity for it to be 'all everything'.

But I don't try to rebuild the image in memory as a complete tableau because I know it would tell me too much. Whenever it threatens to resolve itself, like a game-show grid, I force it to tell me too little. I concentrate, as one might grasp a talisman, on what I can't see with either precision or accuracy: the cereal in the bowl. I wish I knew which fucking brand it was, I think. This can feel like a sacred detail, even though to know for sure would risk finishing the scene. I *want* to know exactly as much as I don't, so I stare with blinkers into the mouth of the ceramic blur. For a million game-show pounds, I would say Shreddies. I begin to fret that I can't remember, as if I've lost something important. Then I tell myself that this out-of-focus bowl of cereal is like bereavement itself. It is the breach in your everyday clarity that refuses to close over, the tear in the wider pattern of life. The tear that is part of the pattern.

EPILOGUE

Unoriginal Features

In May 2014, I arrived on the London flat-hunting scene during a buying frenzy. On weekends, the residential streets near the borough's various train stations teemed with hunters (except in 'The Village', which had already 'gone'). Thirty-something couples roamed with barely disguised contempt for one another, trading tight-lipped smiles as they squeezed out of one packed bedroom and into an equally packed hallway. I was among them with my motley crew of surviving loved ones, envious of those with imperious mothers, who narrowed their eyes at their daughters and gave almost imperceptible shakes of the head.

In the scrum of these open houses we wriggled our forearms free to grope at original features. It seemed possible, despite geopolitical unrest and climate change, to build a life around a defunct fireplace. If there weren't oversized pine cones already in the grate, there would be soon. Or candles – don't forget candles! Or the hopeful lie: you could open them up! We looked wistfully over a stranger's shoulder and into the road, imagining the soot-stained chimney sweep who would soon come whistling up the path. We convinced ourselves that crumbling sash windows wouldn't be cold and that plastic ones would be worth the energy savings and eco-righteousness.

In the London of my time, I could be someone's child or a mortgage-holder, but not both. In the midst of a disgraceful housing crisis, even this dilemma was a privilege. Once in the new flat, I began the work of assembling a post-parental world. After an adult life lived in temporary accommodation, I had fun buying bedside tables from markets, stocking up on towels and pillows, climbing a rung on the duck-down ladder. I walked to the flat carrying shopping bags with a blasphemous spring in my step.

Old things, a few inherited pieces, also came through the front door: a veteran card table, whose top swivels and folds, became my writing desk. Two of the large chimney pots from the roof of the hotel, which had been to Canada and back again, were walked into the small back garden. A clay vase my mother had made long ago as part of her degree went up on a high shelf. With both hands I turned it by its base to find its best aspect, like working a combination lock, as if I were trying to open something.

I didn't put up any pictures of my parents, and have yet to do so. There is only the ghost of a mural of them, which I'm always planning. But even though I'm quite a good draughtsman, I'm too afraid that I'll get their faces wrong, and that I'll be left with two uncanny impostors in the hall. My siblings and I all got some of my mother's talent for drawing, just as we inherited both parents' atrocious singing voices. One of my memorable school music reports once said: 'Sings with obvious pleasure.' In attempting to answer the classic existential question of 'Who am I?', you realise that many of your features are unoriginal.

But in those first months we had a great time, my partner and I, slinging sheets over things and taping around sockets, moving about a bald room at eleven at night with paint brushes, Billie Holliday singing with obvious genius from the laptop on the floor. Is this reality? Are we there yet? Alongside this contentment, and intruding on it now and then, was the idea that this was all part of a montage in a commercial for a department store, or life insurance. 'Whatever stage you're at, we have you covered!' Cue the flirtatious flick of the paint brush, the couch carried up the garden path, then cut to us in middle age with stuck-on crowsfeet and talcum-powder temples, waving some young scamp off to university. Then onwards still, stage after stage, until we're two dandelion clocks cuddled on a park bench, shot from behind. It was hard to get through a single coat, despite the companionable slurps of the roller and soothing podcast chatter, without at least one fantasy of a fast-forward, two-minute life, the pair of us dropping to dust beside a pot of Vanilla Mist Number 4.

Is this the stuff of our mortal reality, this fabric riven with self-conscious fantasies, superimposed with snapshots and clichés? Is there nothing else more real, more solid? We're certainly prone to think that the reality we perceive is obscuring a greater kind of reality, that there is something on the other side of life that would be the true life. For the Christian mystic and philosopher Simone Weil, we approach this reality by paying it attention. In a letter to a friend, Weil wrote that attention was 'the rarest and purest form of generosity.' It is our attention that makes it impossible to ignore the existence of other people, their individual sovereignty. It allows us to see who other people *are*. This kind of attention, for Weil, was a form of prayer: 'With time we are altered,' she writes elsewhere, 'and, if as we change we keep our gaze directed towards the same thing, in the end illusions are scattered and the real becomes visible.' While this a divine process for Weil, the ethics of this concept are easy to secularise. Today we are paying our altering realities much attention, turning fundamental, sacred ideas in our hands and considering how they are made, as well as assessing their value. In some cases, we're smashing these old ideas to the ground.

The concept of modern attention as it relates to our realities is, however, a complicated one. We fear for children's dwindling concentrations while at the same time we inhabit an 'Attention Economy', in which attention is a valuable crop to be harvested. The architecture of our online lives is designed to arrest our gaze, through videos loading automatically from one to the next, 'push' notifications that draw us back to social media platforms, or through the simple, addictive property of variable rewards: the shifting tallies of other people's responses. The business model of native advertising, which is a digital paradigm, commodifies our attentiveness. But besides the coaxing and massaging of our own attentions, we are also the *focus* of insistent attention, on the part of businesses and other agents who wish to know all about us, to gather the information of our lives. There is almost a novelist's curiosity at work here: what did you have for breakfast, how did you wash your hair, where do you like to go for your holidays? This kind of interest in daily minutiae is cultivated in creative writing classes around the world. In his essay 'The Art of Fiction', Henry James imagined that he would urge a novice writer to 'try to be one of the people on whom nothing is lost!' And yet isn't this what we fear when we worry for our privacies – that somehow nothing is being lost?

'Who am I?' is therefore not only a question for the philosophers. One major goal of this scrutiny is to give us a unique, well-defined face, by which we can be easily recognised. Like Sylvia Plath's broken Colossus, our treasured data is scattered across both physical and virtual landscapes, which are steadily merging into a commercial supercontinent. We now leave fragments of our consumer whims and desires wherever we go, and the challenge for advertisers and others is to assemble these pieces together into a single, coherent form. How can they tell, for instance, that the person who browses both on their laptop and their mobile is the same prospect or target? Our use of various apps and social media platforms produces a trove of discrete information, and so the project is one of integration.

For those who know us only from our data, we tend to manifest thoughtlessly online under a series of pseudonyms. Who is the real us? Antonio García Martínez, in his book, *Chaos Monkeys: Inside the Silicon Valley Money Machine*, explains the problem in terms of naming. We have a physical address associated with our name, and each of our different devices has a unique ID stored in those blandly titled cookies, via which our past preferences inform future targeting.

> The biggest thing going on in marketing right now, what is generating tens of billions of dollars in investment and endless scheming inside the bowels of Facebook, Google, Amazon and Apple, is how to tie these different sets of names together. That's it.

The prize, then, is the completion of a data colossus for each one of us, the mega-me, the perfect representation. Forget the tired cliché of the Selfie Generation. A different kind of portrait is the true image of these times, and is being slowly built at the speed of our lives. This quiet, obscene sculpting of the countless shards of our personal information seeks to render us as coherently as possible.

Of course, this isn't the kind of attention that Simone Weil had in mind. The condition of her generous attention was that it was 'a looking and not an attachment'. These interested parties that pay us this covert attention are highly attached to us. They want to find out the real you and me, in order to better influence our decisions, both commercial and political. In so doing, we become in one sense less real, since our behaviour is being insidiously contoured from outside. This, at least, is an ongoing and deepening anxiety. As I finish this book, the Cambridge Analytica scandal is in its early stages, the crux of which is the question of how our political positions have been manipulated by our exposure to a distorted view of reality, made bespoke to our biases. Where then does the real me end, and my influences begin? The old desire to find a true reality on the other side of things is thus taking a new shape, as we seek to map and regulate the transcendent algorithms that direct our attentions.

One large measure of freedom is the choices we have in our own unreality. What fantasies are we permitted to cultivate for ourselves, and which are forced upon us from outside? We no longer expect always to be original, perhaps, but at least we want to know the provenance of our often unconscious imitations, to understand the different faces that occupy our own. Some evenings, I close down the living room, picking up dropped papers and plumping up the cushions – ordinary enough pottering, when I remember to do it. Except that when I'm finished, I find myself standing and looking back into the darkened room, as I'd often seen my mother doing elsewhere, one hand still on the light switch. I can feel her face overlaid onto my face, an expression of satisfaction, but something else, too: a kind of abstracted interest that the shadow-room should be there at all. I'm sure everyone feels versions of these hauntings, even by those who are still alive. I like being suddenly possessed by them, my two old friends. They can hack me any time. Now and then, during flares of danger or indignation, my features find the shape of my mother's retracted, stoic mouth and hardened gaze. My father's habit of slightly fretful murmuring sometimes twitches my upper lip. Or else I can sense his benign, monkish smile settling over my own. It is his Canadian summer driving face, when he would have one big paw on the wheel, and silver mirages pooled endlessly ahead of us. In such moments of merged features I might ask them, in that silent language I have learnt in these years: Where are you? Where have you been?

NOTES

Introduction: Augmented Reality

xiii 'the only authentic . . .', Mavis Gallant, 'Voices Lost in Snow', in *The Collected Stories of Mavis Gallant* (Toronto: McClelland & Stewart, 1997).

xiv 'fiction is outperforming . . .', Guillaume Chaslot interview in the *Guardian*, 2nd February 2018; 'Falsehoods diffused significantly . . .', Soroush Vosoughi et al., 'The spread of true and false news online', in *Science*, Vol. 359, Issue 6380, 9th March 2018.

xv 'a coward in . . .', Friedrich Nietzsche, *The Twilight of the Idols*, trans. Duncan Large (Oxford: Oxford University Press, 1998 [1888]).

xvi 'How the Real . . .', ibid.

xvii 'best guess'; 'prediction engine'; 'The world we . . .', see Anil Seth, 'Your brain hallucinates your conscious reality', TED Talk, April 2017.

xix 'One example he . . .', see Donald Hoffman interview with Amanda Gefter, 'The Case Against Reality', *The Atlantic*, 25th April 2016.

xx   'perceptions will be . . .'; 'the ultimate nature . . .', ibid.

xxi   'A truth ceases . . .'; 'That would be . . .', transcript of the trial of Oscar
      Wilde, in *The Broadview Anthology of British Literature Volume 5: The
      Victorian Era*, ed. Joseph Black et al. (Peterborough: Broadview Press,
      2012).

xxii 'Who's to blame . . .', headline of article by Aditya Chakrabortty,
      Guardian, 17th October 2017; 'The having cake . . .', headline of article
      by Jeremy Warner, *Telegraph*, 9th February 2018.

xxiv 'Since the 1980s . . .', see, for example, Youssef El-Gingihy, *How
      to Dismantle the NHS in 10 Easy Steps* (Alresford: Zero Books,
      2015), Jayne Dowle, 'When will NHS Cuts End? Jeremy Hunt is
      dismantling our health service by stealth', *Yorkshire Post*, 4th
      December 2017, Simon Tilford, 'Brexit poses a bigger threat . . .',
      Independent, 25th March 2018; 'is dismantling the . . .', Malcolm
      Nance interview with 'AM Joy', MSNBC, 18th December 2017;
      'dismantling democracy', David Cay Johnston interview with
      Michael Krasny, KQED News, 14th February 2018; 'the long project
      . . .', see Jude Blanchette, quoted in Tom Phillips's article 'Xi
      Jinping to cement his power with plan to scrap two-term limit',
      Guardian, 25th February 2018.

xxv   'help expose and . . .', Sirry Alang, 'How to dismantle racism and
      prevent police brutality', *USA Today*, 12th May 2017; 'does little to
      . . .', see Sarah Sophie Flicker, 'Why the "Me Too" Moment is Just
      the Start of a Necessary Cultural Shift', *W Magazine*, 22nd November
      2017; '"prevailing mythology" that . . .', Janelle Zara, '"There's a
      lot of grief to process": how the #MeToo movement gripped Art
      Basel Miami Beach', *Guardian*, 13th December 2017; 'The master's
      tools . . .', Audre Lorde, *Sister Outsider* (Trumansberg: Crossing
      Press, 1984).

xxvii '(picnic, lightning)', Vladimir Nabokov, *Lolita* (London: Penguin,
      1995 [1955]).

Bedtime Stories

5   'yellow cream and . . .', J. R. R. Tolkien, *The Lord of the Rings* (London: HarperCollins, 1995 [1968]); 'your part of . . .', Kenneth Grahame, *The Wind in the Willows* (London: Puffin, 2015 [1908]); 'wonderful tales', C. S. Lewis, *The Lion, the Witch and the Wardrobe* (London: Lions, 1988 [1950]).

6   'Here is Edward . . .', A. A. Milne, *Winnie-the-Pooh* (London: Puffin, 1992 [1926]).

8   'The universe is . . .', Muriel Rukeyser, 'The Speed of Darkness', in *The Collected Poems of Muriel Rukeyser*, ed. Janet E. Kaufman and Anne F. Herzog (Pittsburgh: University of Pittsburgh Press, 2005); 'human mind is . . .', Jonathan Haidt, *The Righteous Mind* (London: Allen Lane, 2012).

9   'we are all . . .', Iris Murdoch, *Existentialists and Mystics* (London: Penguin, 1997); 'stories that are . . .', Paul Zak, 'How Stories Change the Brain', *Greater Good Magazine*, 17th December 2013.

10   'storytelling acts . . .', Daniel Smith et al., 'Cooperation and the evolution of hunter-gatherer storytelling', *Nature Communications*, No. 1853, 5th December 2017.

11   'cultivate a life . . .', Jennifer Aaker lecture for Haas School of Business, University of California Berkeley, published March 2017.

12   'If recent trends . . .', Arielle Pardes, 'Snapchat Stories Can Now Live Outside the App', *Wired*, 23rd January 2018.

13   'pandemic', 'Are Digital Distractions The World's Latest Pandemice', *reMarkable*, 6th February 2017.

14   'live in this . . .', A. S. Byatt interview with Ruth Joos at the International Passa Porta Festival of Literature, 24th March 2013.

15   'An experiment performed . . .', see Carsten K. W. De Dreu et al., 'Oxytocin promotes human ethnocentrism', *PNAS*, 108 (4), 25th January 2011; 'It should be . . .', see Xiaolei Xu et al., 'Oxytocin biases men but not women to restore social connections with

individuals who socially exclude them', *Scientific Reports*, No. 40589, 12 January 2017.

16 'the really frightening . . .', George Orwell, column in *Tribune*, 4th February 1944; 'doesn't matter', Chris Cuomo interview with Bernie Sanders, *Cuomo Prime Time*, CNN, 11th January 2018.

17 'built into the . . .', see Lily Rothman, 'Margaret Atwood on Serial Fiction and the Future of the Book', www.entertainment.time.com, 8th October 2012.

18 'were like dreams . . .', Margaret Atwood, *The Handmaid's Tale* (London: Jonathan Cape, 1986).

19 'They cannot see . . .', 'Trompe l'Oeil', *Westworld*, dir. Frederick E. O. Toye, Warner Bros. Television, 13th November 2016; 'Stories are hardwired . . .', Jeanette Winterson interview at the Sydney Writers' Festival, 'Riding in Cars With Writers', Sydney Writers' Festival YouTube Channel, published 23rd June 2016.

20 'Have you ever . . .', 'The Original', *Westworld*, dir. Jonathan Nolan, 2nd October 2016.

21 'the settled tiller . . .', Walter Benjamin, 'The Storyteller: Reflections on the Works of Nikolai Leskov', in *Illuminations*, ed. Hannah Arendt, trans. Harry Zohn (New York, NY: Schocken, 1968); 'taking Delight in . . .', Richard Steele, 'Alexander Selkirk', *The Englishman*, 1713.

22 'If I think . . .', John Berger in conversation with Susan Sontag, 'To Tell a Story . . .', dir. Mike Lloyd, Brook Productions, Channel 4, 9th February 1983.

24 'fantasy of impermeability', Wendy Brown, *Walled States, Waning Sovereignty* (New York, NY: Zone, 2010); 'If you are . . .', from Theresa May's Conservative Party Conference Speech, 5th October 2016.

25 'I want us . . .', Theresa May speech, 'The government's negotiating objectives for exiting the EU', 17th January 2017: https://www.gov.uk/government/speeches/the-governments-negotiating-objectives-for-

exiting-the-eu-pm-speech; 'I'm proud of . . .', see Carmen Fishwick and Sarah Marsh, 'Delight, regret, despair: how voters feel as article 50 is triggered', *Guardian*, 29th March 2017; 'can only destroy . . .', *London Can Take It!*, dir. Harry Watt and Humphrey Jennings, GPO Film Unit, 1940; 'Heroic mythology fused . . .', Angus Calder, *The Myth of the Blitz* (London: Pimlico, 1991).

26 'This is the . . .', Andrew Neil speech on *This Week*, BBC, 23rd March 2017; 'join hands with . . .', see 'Oswald Mosley – 1931, Speech in Manchester', History YouTube Channel, published 14th May 2011.

27 'They are so . . .', see Thomas More, *Utopia*, in *Three Early Modern Utopias: Utopia, New Atlantis and The Isle of Pines* (Oxford: Oxford World Classics, 2008 [1516]).

29 'Europeans, you must . . .', Jean-Paul Sartre's introduction to Frantz Fanon, *The Wretched of the Earth*, trans. Constance Farrington (London: Penguin, 2001 [1961]); 'trying to include . . .', Iain Sinclair, *The Last London* (London: Oneworld, 2017).

30 'Once upon a . . .', see 'Toni Morrison – Nobel Lecture', 7th December 1993, www.nobelprize.org.

33 'an underlying assumption . . .', Janet Malcolm, 'Dora', in *The Purloined Clinic: Selected Writings* (New York, NY: Alfred A. Knopf, 1992).

34 'We tell ourselves . . .', Joan Didion, *White Album* (New York, NY: Farrar, Straus and Giroux, 1979).

The End of Things

40 'I had no . . .', Stephanie Beacham, *Many Lives* (Carlsbad, CA: Hay House, 2011).

41 'There was the . . .', Virginia Woolf, 'A Sketch of the Past', in *Moments of Being* (London: Pimlico, 2002 [1939]).

43 'is trebly accursed . . .', Edward Heron-Allen, quoted in Crispin Paine, *Religious Objects in Museums: Private Lives and Public Duties* (London: Bloomsbury, 2013).

44 'each item within . . .', Zygmunt Bauman, *Modernity and Ambivalence* (Cambridge: Polity, 1991).

45 'holding it firmly . . .', Marie Kondo, *Spark Joy: An Illustrated Guide to the Japanese Art of Tidying* (London: Vermilion, 2016).

47 'What am I . . .', Virginia Woolf, *Jacob's Room* (Oxford: Oxford University Press, 2008 [1922]).

48 'seemed to fit', Muriel Spark, *Territorial Rights* (London: Virago, 2014 [1979]); 'A sigh of . . .', Gustave Flaubert, *Madame Bovary*, trans. Geoffrey Wall (London: Penguin, 2003 [1857]).

49 'in that quiet . . .', Alan Hollinghurst, *The Line of Beauty* (London: Picador, 2004).

50 'All at once . . .', Alain Robbe-Grillet, 'A Future for the Novel', in *For a New Novel: Essays on Fiction*, trans. Richard Howard (Evanston, IL: Northwestern University Press, 1989 [1963]).

51 'There was an . . .', John Banville, *The Sea* (London: Picador, 2005).

52 'the sun shone . . .', W. H. Auden, 'Musée des Beaux Arts', in *Another Time* (London: Faber and Faber, 1940).

53 'Furniture's knowing all . . .', Elizabeth Bowen, *The Death of the Heart* (London: Vintage, 2012 [1938]).

54 'are tools that . . .', David Rose, *Enchanted Objects: Innovation, Design, and the Future of Technology* (New York, NY: Scribner, 2014).

56 'What do you . . .', *Gosford Park*, written by Julian Fellowes and directed by Robert Altman, USA Films, 2001.

58 'Take a good . . .', 'Hodge the Cat', written by Catherine Hiller and animated by Nicholas Parsons, *Talking Statues London*; 'Finally they get . . .', see Ella Hickson testimonial: http://www.talkingstatues-london.co.uk/peterpan.php.

59 'The recent philosophical . . .', 'When a house . . .', 'The world is . . .', Graham Harman, *Guerrilla Metaphysics: Phenomenology and the Carpentry of Things* (Chicago, IL: Open Court, 2005); 'look for the . . .', 'forever withdraw from . . .', Graham Harman in conversation with Lucy Kimbell, see 'The Object Strikes Back: An Interview with Graham Harman', *Design and Culture* 5(1), 2013.

61 'Well, the fumes . . .', Tweet by J. K. Rowling (@jk_rowling) on 31st January 2017, www.twitter.com.

62 'disclosed to us . . .', Jean-Paul Sartre, *Being and Nothingness*, trans. Hazel E. Barnes (New York, NY: Washington Square Press, 1956 [1943]).

63 'monstrous masses', Jean-Paul Sartre, *Nausea*, trans. Robert Baldick (London: Penguin, 2000 [1938]).

65 'a disorientating experience . . .', entry for 'Tralfamidorification' by Jenny Odell et al., www.bureauoflinguisticalreality.com; 'miracle and insanity', Ben Lerner, *10:04* (New York, NY: Farrar, Straus and Giroux, 2014).

66 'all bigger on . . .', Timothy Morton, 'Art in the Age of Asymmetry', *Evental Aesthetics*, 1(1), 2012.

67 'Is this horrible . . .', Edward Heron-Allen, writing as Christopher Blayre, 'The Purple Sapphire', in *The Purple Sapphire and Other Posthumous Papers* (London: Philip Allan, 1921); 'a historical question', Martin Heidegger, *What is a Thing?*, trans. W. B. Barton, Jr. and Vera Deutsch (Chicago, IL: Henry Regnery, 1967).

Optical Disillusions

72 '[T]he mechanism of . . .', Henri Bergson, *Creative Evolution*, trans. Arthur Mitchell (Mineola, NY: Dover Publications, 1998 [1907]).

74 'It has only . . .', Oliver Sacks, 'In the River of Consciousness', *The New York Review of Books*, 15th January 2004.

75 'When unconscious processing . . .', Michael H. Herzog et al., 'Time Slices: What is the Duration of a Percept?', *PLoS Biology*, 14(6), 12th April 2016.

76 'Research published in . . .', see 'The Millennial Influence: How Their Love of Mobile Shapes Commerce', Osterman Research, November 2016; 'very important', see '#Millennials the next #MobileDisruptors', Zogby Analytics, September 2015.

77 'mobile photo gear', David Pierce, 'Become an Instagram Influencer with this Mobile Photo Gear', *Wired*, 13th May 2017.

84 'The camera introduces . . .', Walter Benjamin, 'The Work of Art in the Age of Mechanical Reproduction', *Illuminations*.

87 'This is the . . .', *Frame By Frame*, directed by Alexandria Bombach and Mo Scarpelli, CoPilot Pictures, 2015.

88 'no matter what . . .', Diamond Reynolds interview on *The View*, ABC, 11th July 2016; 'However lightning-like it . . .', Roland Barthes, *Camera Lucida*, trans. Richard Howard (New York, NY: Hill and Wang, 2010 [1980]).

91 'When acclaiming our . . .', *The Cameraman*, directed by Edward Sedgwick, Metro-Goldwyn-Mayer, 1928.

92 'Be cool', 'The One with the Prom Video', *Friends*, dir. James Burrows, Warner Bros, 1st February 1996.

93 'There's a lot . . .', Don DeLillo, *Mao II* (New York, NY: Penguin, 1991); 'pictures he took . . .', Alice Munro, *The Lives of Girls and Women* (Whitby, ON: McGraw-Hill Ryerson, 1971).

94 'Of the notes . . .', Luigi Pirandello, *Shoot!*, trans. C.K. Scott Moncrieff (Chicago, IL: University of Chicago Press, 2005 [1915]).

95 '"friendly" as a . . .', *Tootsie*, dir. Sydney Pollack, Columbia Pictures, 1982; 'a man who . . .', Roger Ebert, review in the *Chicago Sun-Times*, 17th October 1997.

96 'Better call an . . .', *Medium Cool*, dir. Haskell Wexler, H & J, 1969.

98 'But newer research . . .', see Lena Cowen Orlin, *Locating Privacy in Tudor London* (Oxford: Oxford University Press, 2008).

101 'Declining levels of ...', 'Executive Summary: The future of government communication', WPP, see www.wpp.com/govtpractice/leaders-report; 'Growing social distrust ...', 'Partnering Against Corruption Initiative (PACI)', World Economic Forum, see www.weforum.org.

102 'a nation's well-being...', Francis Fukuyama, *Trust: The Social Virtues and the Creation of Prosperity* (New York, NY: Free Press, 1995).

103 'Fake video and ...', Henry J. Farrell and Rick Perlstein, 'Our Hackable Political Future', *New York Times*, 4th February 2018.

106 'wants to give...', Michael H. Herzog, quoted in Nik Papageorgiou, 'How the brain produces consciousness in "time slices"', *EPFL News*, Ecole Polytechnique Fédérale de Lausanne, April 2016; 'ball of clichés ...', Jenny Diski, 'A Diagnosis', *The London Review of Books*, 11th September 2014.

Backstage Pass

111 'Obscenity is always...', Ludwig Marcuse, *Obscene: The History of an Indignation*, trans. Karen Gershon (London: Macgibbon & Kee, 1965).

113 'The horror movie...', the commentary on *Unfriended* first appeared in my essay 'Death by Skype' for the *Financial Times*, 1st May 2015. Thanks to John Sunyer for commissioning and editing this piece.

114 'either apologizing, or ...', Tom Rachman, 'Leakzilla', in *Basket of Deplorables* (Hastings-on-Hudson, NY: Riverrun, 2017).

117 'The archetypal choice...', a version of this description of the 'selfie' expression first appeared in my essay 'A Sentimental Portrait', *Emotional Supply Chains* (London: Zabludowicz Collection, 2015). Thanks to Paul Luckraft and Maitreyi Maheshwari for commissioning the piece.

119 'You're just going...', Episode 4, *Simply Nigella*, dir. Mike Matthews, Fremantle Media, 2015; 'I know it's ...', Instagram post by Nigella Lawson (@nigellalawson) on 25th July 2015

120 'a public health crisis . . .', from the draft of 'Republican Platform 2016'; 'public health hazard . . .', see Drafting Attorney RuthAnne Frost, 'S.C.R. 9 Concurrent Resolution on the Public Health Crisis', State of Utah, 29th March 2016.

122 'some told me . . .', Maggie Jones, 'What Teenagers Are Learning From Online Porn', *The New York Times*, 7th February 2018.

124 'one of the . . .', see Anjali Midha's Twitter blog, 'Study: Live-Tweeting lifts Tweet volume, builds a social audience for your show', 18th September 2014.

125 'What an episode! . . .', Tweet by Ross Kemp (@RossKemp) on 17th May 2016, www.twitter.com.

126 'So long as . . .', see 'Ken Clarke Ridicules Tory Candidates', www.skynews.com; 'not appropriate', see 'Boris Johnson recites Kipling poem in Myanmar temple', *Guardian News* YouTube Channel, published 30th September 2017.

127 'New York is . . .', Katie Couric interview for *Crazy About Tiffany's*, dir. Matthew Miele, Quixotic Endeavors, 2016.

128 'an obscene amount . . .', see 'George Clooney on Why He's Not Like the Koch Brothers', *NBC News* YouTube Channel, published 18th April 2016.

131 'All right, I'll . . .', I was informed here by the work of Ian C. Storey and Arlene Allan: *A Guide to Ancient Greek Drama* (Oxford: Blackwell Publishing, 2005); 'plays on the . . .', David Wiles, *Greek Theatre Performance* (Cambridge: Cambridge University Press, 2000).

133 'says what he . . .', see *The New York Times*/CBS Poll, 4th–8th December 2015; 'never turn around . . .', see 'Watch Ben Carson endorse Donald Trump full news conference', *PBS NewsHour* YouTube Channel, 11th March 2016.

135 'Anyone who knows . . .', see 'Donald Trump apologises for controversial video remarks', *Fox News* YouTube Channel, 7th October 2016; 'everyone can draw . . .', see 'Watch Live: The 2nd Presidential Debate', *CBS News* YouTube Channel, 9th October 2016.

136 'If, for example . . .', Herbert Marcuse, *An Essay on Liberation* (Boston, MA: Beacon, 1969).

137 'I had to . . .', *The Last Unicorn*, dir. Jules Bass and Arthur Rankin, Jr, Rankin/Bass Productions, 1982.

138 'pornography of information . . .', Jean Baudrillard, *Revenge of the Crystal: Selected Writings on the Modern Object and its Destiny, 1968– 1983*, ed. and trans. Paul Foss and Julian Pefanis (London: Pluto Press, 1999).

Romance Languages

144 'play a central . . .', George Lakoff and Mark Johnson, *Metaphors We Live By* (Chicago, IL: Chicago University Press, 1980); 'Metaphor creates a . . .', Wallace Stevens, 'Adagia', in *Collected Poetry and Prose*, ed. Joan Richardson and Frank Kermode (New York, NY: Library of America, 1997).

147 'very specific allergies . . .', Lorde interview with the *Guardian*, 17th June 2017.

148 'the breakdown of morality . . .', Two tweets by Mary Beard (@ wmarybeard) on 16th February 2018, www.twitter.com; 'Western aid workers . . .', Priyamvada Gopal, 'Response to Mary Beard', medium.com, 18th February 2018.

149 'I am growing . . .', Norman MacCaig, 'No Choice', in *The Poems of Norman MacCaig*, ed. Ewen McCaig (Edinburgh: Polygon, 2005).

150 'If there's *any* . . .', Norman MacCaig interview with *Off the Page*, dir. Erina Rayner, Scottish Television, 1990; 'Toad', *The Poems of Norman MacCaig*.

152 'I thought every . . .', Sylvia Plath, 'Daddy', in *Collected Poems*, ed. Ted Hughes (London: Faber and Faber, 1974); 'mega-fantasy', Jacqueline Rose interview with Justin Clemens, see 'Jacqueline Rose on Zionism, Freud, Sylvia Plath and more', *London Review of Books*

YouTube Channel, published 9th April 2015. All subsequent Rose quotations are taken from this source.

153 'it is demented . . .', Hilary Mantel, 'Black is Not Jewish', *Literary Review*, 1st February 1997.

158 The section on 'Bathos' is a revised and updated excerpt from an essay first published on www.newyorker.com: see 'The Big and Small of Bad Internet News', 31st December 2016. My thanks to Anthony Lydgate for commissioning and editing the original.

160 'the Martin Luther . . .', see Derek Hawkins, 'CNN's Jeffrey Lord called Trump the MLK of health care. He then had a very long day', *The Washington Post*, 14th April 2017; 'Nigel Farage, one . . .', Nigel Farage interview with Alex Kane, *Lisburn's 98FM*, July 2013.

161 'And all the time . . .', see 'Children interrupt BBC News interview', *BBC News* YouTube Channel, published 10th March 2017.

167 'You're celebrating her . . .', see Christian Red, 'Chris Evert tells News that Margaret Court Arena shouldn't be renamed', *New York Daily News*, 2nd February 2018; 'When your name . . .', Lindsay Davenport interview, see 'Tennis players on Margaret Court controversy', *AP Archive* YouTube Channel, published 10th June 2017; 'for one reason . . .', Martina Navratilova, 'An open letter from Martina Navratilova to Margaret Court Arena', *The Sydney Morning Herald*, 2nd June 2017.

168 'lust of the flesh', see Greg Baum, '"The devil's after our kids": Margaret Court's second serve', *The Sydney Morning Herald*, 1st June 2017 ; 'Do you think . . .', Olivia Sudjic, *Sympathy* (New York, NY: Houghton Mifflin Harcourt, 2017).

170 'relate to the . . .', 'Factsheet on the "Right to be Forgotten" ruling (C-131/12)', European Commission; 'He is troubled . . .', Roland Barthes, *Roland Barthes*, trans. Richard Howard (New York, NY: Hill and Wang, 2010 [1975]).

171 'I shall never . . .', Sylvia Plath, 'The Colossus', in *Collected Poems*.

Fellow-Feeling

176 'were a part . . .', Jorge Luis Borges, 'The Argentine Writer and Tradition' (1951), in *Labyrinths: Selected Stories and Other Writings*, ed. Donald A. Yates and James E. Irby (London: Penguin Classics, 2000).

177 'I always think . . .', see David Marchese, 'In Conversation: Sarah Silverman', Vulture.com, 10th October 2017; 'I want to . . .', see Claire Fallon, 'Zadie Smith Thinks We Should "Retain The Right To Be Wrong"', www.huffingtonpost.co.uk, 19th September 2017.

178 'All [these essays] . . .', Zadie Smith, *Feel Free* (London: Hamish Hamilton, 2018).

179 'thankfully do not . . .', Zadie Smith, 'Revenge of the Real', *Guardian*, 21st November 2009; 'ideological inconsistency is . . .', Zadie Smith, *Changing My Mind* (London: Hamish Hamilton, 2009).

181 'Blushing is the . . .', Charles Darwin, *The Expression of the Emotions in Man and Animals* (Oxford: Oxford University Press, 1998 [1872]).

182 'a blush is . . .', George Eliot, *Daniel Deronda* (London: Penguin Classics, 1995 [1876]).

183 'the novel task . . .', Lotem Peled and Roi Reichart, 'Sarcasm SIGN: Interpreting Sarcasm with Sentiment Based Monolingual Machine Translation', eprint arXiv:1704.06836, April 2017.

184 'There are countless . . .', for a valuation forecast of emotional data, see www.marketsandmarkets.com, 'Emotion Detection and Recognition Market by Technology . . .', December 2016.

185 'glue', see 'The Future of Digital – The Segment of One', *D&AD* YouTube Channel, published 29th August 2014; 'emotional stimuli', John B. Watson, quoted in Duane P. Schultz and Sydney Ellen Schultz, *A History of Modern Psychology* (Boston, MA: Cengage Learning, 2016).

186 'Technology is the . . .', 'The Wheel', *Mad Men*, dir. Matthew Weiner, Lionsgate Television, 18th October 2007; 'Emotion is the . . .', see Sean Hargrave, CMO.com, '"Emotion Is The New Currency Of Experience," Adobe's VP of Strategy Tells Summit Participants', 22nd March 2017.

187 'He must keep . . .', George P. Rowell, *The Men Who Advertise* (New York, NY: George P. Rowell & Co., 1870); 'all the things . . .', Marcus Mustafa, quoted in Jamie Carter, 'How mining human emotions could become the next big thing in tech', www.techradar.com, 20th April 2015; 'You can look . . .', see Mitra Sorrells, 'How Jaguar Is Using Technology to Visualise the Mood at Wimbledon', www.bizbash.com, 7th July 2015.

188 'We are now . . .', a version of these arguments first appeared in 'A Sentimental Portrait'; 'It's a big . . .', Rafael Nadal interview with TennisTV, August 2017.

191 'a comedy of . . .', this section has been adapted from my 'Openings' column for the *Financial Times*, 'As robots feel empathy, we get new emojis', 23rd October 2015. Thanks to John Sunyer for commissioning and editing the piece.

192 'I want to . . .', see 'Interview with the Life-Like Hot Robot Named Sophia', *CNBC* YouTube Channel, published 25th October 2017; 'What they really . . .', from Mark Zuckerberg's live-streamed talk during a Facebook 'Town Hall' meeting, 15th September 2015.

194 'simple', Pepper interview with Joanna Stern and Geoffrey A. Fowler, *WSJDLive2015*; 'It was like . . .', O. Henry, 'The Gift of the Magi' (1905), in *100 Selected Stories* (Ware: Wordsworth Editions, 1995).

199 'scanned the headlines . . .', Patrick Hamilton, *Hangover Square* (Penguin Books: London, 2001 [1941]).

200 'It's sometimes difficult . . . .', Gérard Biard, quoted in Mukul Devichand, 'How the world was changed by the slogan "Je Suis Charlie"', www.bbc.co.uk, 3rd January 2016.

201 '"shattered" and "pierced"', Andrew O'Hagan, 'A City of Prose', *London Review of Books*, 4th August 2005.

203 'a time which . . .', Doris Lessing, *A Small Personal Voice: Essays, Reviews, Interviews*, ed. Paul Schlueter (London: Flamingo, 1994).

205 'The Body's Truth', a bioreactive installation by Lightwave, see www.lightwave.io; 'Where's the maze?', Tweet by Tim Dowling (@IAmTimDowling) on 18th October 2017, www.twitter.com.

Final Fantasies

210 'punished', see 'YouTube punishes Logan Paul over Japan suicide video', BBC News, 11th January 2018; 'misguided by shock', Tweet by Logan Paul (@LoganPaul) on 2nd January 2018, www.twitter.com.

211 'that banal, unique . . .', Julian Barnes, *Levels of Life* (London: Vintage, 2013); 'There has long . . .', these ideas on the artistic rendering of death first appeared in my essay 'Virtual Mortality', *Financial Times*, 5th May 2016. Thanks to Horatia Harrod for commissioning and editing the piece; 'I excused myself . . .', John Niven, 'A brother in trouble: dealing with suicide', *Observer*, 18th August 2013.

213 'an allegorical symbol . . .', see Heiner Gillmeister, *Tennis: A Cultural History* (Sheffield: Equinox Publishing, 1998).

219 'He argues that . . .', see Slavoj Žižek, *Jacques Lacan: Society, politics, ideology* (London: Routledge, 2003).

221 'Let's talk sex!', Instagram post by Dr Mike Varshavski (@doctor.mike) on 21st December 2017, www.instagram.com.

222 'Christabel sits in . . .', Instagram post by Christabel (@BellyWellyJelly) on 17th November 2017, www.instagram.com.

223 'My Instagram is about sharing . . .', Xenia Tchoumi, quoted in 'Expanding access to the branded content tool on Instagram', www.business.instagram.com, 7th November 2017.

232 'a time for . . .', Charles Dickens, *A Christmas Carol and Other Christmas Books*, ed. Robert Douglas-Fairhurst (Oxford: Oxford World's Classics, 2006).

234 'One study, conducted . . .', see the study's researchers Rikke Duus and Mike Cooray, 'Research reveals the dark side of wearable fitness trackers', 'The Conversation', CNN.com, 1st September 2016.

235 'Our interactions define . . .', Joseph Cevetello, 'The Elite Glucometer', in *Evocative Objects*, ed. Sherry Turkle (Cambridge, MA: MIT Press, 2007).

237 'Only 803 omelettes? . . .', Jean-Paul Sartre, *The Reprieve*, trans. Eric Sutton (London: Penguin Modern Classics, 2001 [1945]).

Epilogue: Unoriginal Features

246 'With time we . . .', Simone Weil, *Gravity and Grace*, trans. Emma Crawford and Mario von der Ruhr (London: Routledge, 2002 [1947]).

247 'The biggest thing . . .', Antonio García Martinez, *Chaos Monkeys: Inside the Silicon Valley Money Machine* (London: Ebury, 2017), quoted in John Lanchester, 'You Are the Product', *London Review of Books*, 17th August 2017.

ACKNOWLEDGEMENTS

Immense thanks are due to Tom Avery, for his editorial guidance, imagination, and for keeping things real. Many thanks to Anna Argenio and Kate McQuaid, and everyone at William Heinemann. Tom Mayer at W.W. Norton has been a wonderful champion of this book, and of my writing in general, in the United States. Thanks for early, crucial advice about memoir.

The book owes much of its life to the talent and insight of my agent Tracy Bohan in London, as well as Jacqueline Ko in New York. Thanks also to the team at The Wylie Agency. And many thanks to all my clever students, who send me news from the future.

I would also like to thank Shahidha Bari, Dorothy Butchard, Melissa Clarke, Peng Cheng, Sue Curtis, Ludovica Gioscia, Horatia Harrod, Tom Lederer, Anthony Lydgate, Anne-Marie Scott, Jerome Scott, Vanessa Scott, Craig Smith, John Sunyer, Pete Trainor.

Deep gratitude to Rob Lederer for his stern but wise editing, and for whom this has been no picnic! And of course to my parents, David and Stella Scott, for all their rarest and purest forms of generosity.